# Using Poetry in the Classroom

## Engaging Students in Learning

Ross M. Burkhardt

Published in partnership with
National Middle School Association

Rowman & Littlefield Education
Lanham, Maryland • Toronto • Oxford
2006

Published in partnership with
National Middle School Association

Published in the United States of America
by Rowman & Littlefield Education
A Division of Rowman & Littlefield Publishers, Inc.
A wholly owned subsidary of The Rowman & Littlefield Publishing Group, Inc.
4501 Forbes Boulevard, Suite 200, Lanham, Maryland 20706
www.rowmaneducation.com

PO Box 317
Oxford
OX2 9RU, UK

British Library Cataloguing in Publication Information Available

**Library of Congress Cataloging-in-Publication Data**

Burkhardt, Ross M.
  Using poetry in the classroom : engaging students in learning / Ross M. Burkhardt.
      p. cm.
  "Published in partnership with National Middle School Association."
  Includes bibliographical references and index.
  ISBN-13: 978-1-57886-341-9 (hardcover : alk. paper)
  ISBN-13: 978-1-57886-339-6 (pbk. : alk. paper)
  ISBN-10: 1-57886-341-4 (hardcover : alk. paper)
  ISBN-10: 1-57886-339-2 (pbk. : alk. paper)
  1. Poetry—Study and teaching (Middle school)—United States. 2. Creative writing
(Middle school)—United States. 3. Oral interpretation of poetry. I. Title.

  LB1631.B7748 2006
  808.1'071'2—dc22

                                                                    2005023055

⊗™ The paper used in this publication meets the minimum requirements of
American National Standard for Information Sciences—Permanence of
Paper for Printed Library Materials, ANSI/NISO Z39.48-1992.

Manufactured in the United States of America.

For my mother, Lucille Hogan Burkhardt,
who taught me to *appreciate* poetry.

For my students,
who taught me *how to teach* poetry.

And for Jeanne,
who *is* poetry.

**The First Day**

It's the first day.
In they come—
Some pausing hesitantly
At the door,
Wondering and waiting;
Others boldly asserting
Their presence
As they stride to seats.

Heads swivel,
Eyes contact the classroom:
Posters and pictures,
Multi-colored images
Meet curious glances.
Saving seats for friends,
Adjusting clean-cover notebooks
Filled with clean ruled sheets,
They sit, expectantly,
In crisp clothing.

For some, the boredom of August
Gone at last.
For some, the restraints of structure
Unwillingly accepted.
For most, an unexplored world awaiting.
New seats permit new perspectives,
New possibilities, new patterns.

The student asks:
"What does he expect of me?
What is this room all about?
Who is this teacher?"
The teacher asks:
"Who are these people?
What are they all about?
What do they expect of me?"

A simultaneously shared journey
Through days and months ahead
Beckons. But for now,
All is new and trembling
Because
It's the first day.

—RMB

Composed in 1980, *The First Day* enabled me to introduce myself
as a poet to my students every year.

# Contents

# Foreword

Teachers! You will find here the answers to your questions about poetry in the classroom. Having taught teachers in a graduate course, Poetry for Children, for 20-plus years, I know you have questions and I even know what they might be. *Why teach poetry? What do I need to know to teach poetry effectively? What resources are available to help me? How do I begin? How do I develop a comprehensive curriculum? How do I motivate children to write poetry and how do I coach them to ensure that they grow as writers? How do I evaluate their work?*

Ross Burkhardt provides in this book substantive answers to these and other questions pertinent to poetry in the elementary, middle school, and high school classroom. Over two decades, he reflected on his own teaching of poetry to middle school students. "As I taught," he writes in the Introduction, "I kept returning to the question: how can I weave together the various aspects of poetry into a comprehensive program that simultaneously pays homage to the canon, develops academic skills, and engages students in worthwhile curricular activities?" Everything Ross has to say about his comprehensive program for middle school you will find adaptable to the needs of both younger and older students.

The subtitle of *Using Poetry in the Classroom* is "Engaging Students in Learning" and, as promised, the book provides a blueprint for helping students to think creatively about poetry, to read, listen, and interpret poetry, to memorize and recite poetry, and to write, revise, and publish their own poetry. But this unique take on poetry in the classroom does much more.

One teacher's love for poetry is communicated with a passion that can't fail to inspire. "I was not an English major," Ross tells us. "But as a child I listened to my mother recite poems by heart, and when I was in college

I became enamored of the poetry of Robert Frost." Enamor means "to fill with love, to charm, to captivate." In page after page, Ross shares his fondness for poetry and how it developed. He read poetry, listened to it, worked at writing it, and gradually honed his skills. Reading his poems, hearing his unassuming voice describing his teaching and learning experiences, any one of us might believe that it is possible to become a teacher-poet. Desire is a great motivator.

*Using Poetry in the Classroom* speaks directly to readers, teacher to teacher. Ross's style is conversational and supportive, a mentor's voice. He has thought of everything in providing a comprehensive resource for the poetry teacher and student. Parts I and III, "Before Class" and "Beyond the Classroom," frame Part II, "In the Classroom." In Part I, the author sets the stage, asking and answering the question, "Why Poetry?" and declaring himself as a teacher-poet. In Part II, supporting his discussion with detailed strategies and plentiful examples, he structures a curriculum through chapters titled "Memorizing and Reciting," "Composing and Publishing," "Discussing and Interpreting," and "The Process of Student Poetry." Part III, "Beyond the Classroom," offers inspiration through descriptions of personal experiences with powerful words and models of successful teaching. A reflective book fittingly ends with the chapter, "Reflections from the Classroom."

An impressive feature in a book rich with impressive features is the recurrent sound of students' voices. We read their e-mails about their days in Ross's class, we listen in on their comments about poetry in the classroom, we marvel at their many extraordinary ventures in poetic composition. We hear their stories, actually their teacher's celebration of their achievements and accomplishments, as well as their own insightful reflections on encounters with powerful words.

Years after she was a student in his class, Aurelie Shapiro e-mails:

> I always had this notion that writing poems wasn't something you could learn, that you were born with it. But I couldn't have been more wrong . . . I recall the results of the continual draft process quite well, where I would start with something so-so and surprise myself after many revisions that I actually had a poem.

The philosophy that guides Ross's teaching is exemplified in the classroom practice he describes. "When I hear the term, 'a teacher of writing,'" he says, "I imagine an individual who teaches writing by actually writing with his or her students, not unlike the basketball coach who shoots hoops with the team or the music teacher who plays with the school band." In 1983, he began with his eighth-grade class a tradition of a poem a week, poems written by him that chronicled the class's activities. He describes how he shared his writing with the student writers, first to last draft. A young poet told him, "When you write poems, Mr. B., it helps me with mine. In yours, you change your words around, and I try that, and it makes my poems go smoother. I get ideas from your writing."

This teacher delights in celebrating his students' creative work. As one of many examples, he quotes what he calls a "wonderfully whimsical four-line poem" by eighth grader David Glass:

> Eye dew knot sea Y their R to l's inn "spell"
> it sowans the sayem two mi
>
> sew if U ken reed thiss than its pruff
> thet eye shud have one thuh speling B

Ross Burkhardt will answer your questions and calm whatever fears you may have about your ability to teach poetry or to become a poet. Eve Merriam once said that we need to take poetry down from its pedestal. Ross does that. He brings it within everyone's reach. Using as examples his own experiences and those of his students, he assures us that poetry is accessible. Any one of us can find in the abundance of poetry poems to enjoy. We all, once we stifle our sense of awe before the great poets, can safely take a turn at composing verses of our own. Ross provides the knowledge we need to share in the delight and satisfaction he has enjoyed as a teacher-poet. Echoing Robert Frost, he beckons to us, "You come too."

Glenna Sloan
Queens College of the City University of New York
Flushing, New York

# Acknowledgments

I could not have written *Using Poetry in the Classroom* without the cooperation of many people, and to all of them I am deeply indebted.

First of all, I thank the students who entered my classroom from 1965 to 1997. To those students at Shoreham-Wading River Middle School who permitted me to use their poems and their reflections on past poetry experiences, sincere thanks. You entrusted me with your words, and I hope that I have done justice to them. And to the many other students whose poems do not appear in this book simply for lack of space, please know that I value our shared history. You inspired many of the *Poems For All Occasions*.

I am particularly grateful to former students Andrea Dicks James, Alyson Montgomery Perry, and Dawne Donohue Smith for allowing me to describe their writing process in such detail.

Many other individuals contributed to this book in ways large and small, and so I thank the following:

All of the teachers who opened their classrooms and lessons to me—in particular, Katie Budde, Robert Burkhardt, Debbie Cooke, Annie Darden, Diane Fallace, Jaynellen Behre-Jenkins, Susan Jones, Janice Smith, Flora Tyler, and Kernie Zimmerman.

The students of Katie Budde, Debbie Cooke, Susan Jones, and Janice Smith—for allowing me to include their poems in Chapter 9.

Tony Horan, Dartmouth '61—who read one of his poems in Alpha Theta one evening in 1961 and, without realizing it, changed my life. Also, Bill Foss, Dartmouth '62, a classmate and good friend—for recommending Jay Parini's *Frost: A Life*, and for sending me essays about poetry, poems, and poets.

Richard Sterling and Sondra Perl—who in a 1980 National Writing Project summer institute at Shoreham-Wading River Central School District awakened me to the ideas about writing that ultimately led to this book.

Charlie Aubuchon, a language arts teacher in California—for recommending Jean Little's poem, "After English Class," and for encouraging reactions to early chapter drafts.

Esther Fusco, a colleague at Shoreham-Wading River Middle School—for her assistance with Author's Week information and for her support throughout my teaching career.

In Albuquerque, my friend Linnea Hendrickson, an elementary school librarian and expert in children's literature—for introducing me to Sharon Creech's delightful book, *Love That Dog*, for inviting Rhymin' Ross to perform at her school, and for organizing our poetry presentation at the 2003 Children's Literature Association conference in El Paso where I met Glenna Sloan.

Another Albuquerque friend, Dr. Howard Bryant, professor emeritus of physics and astronomy at the University of New Mexico—for loaning me his copy of *The Apple and the Spectroscope*.

Ron Murray, a gifted middle school teacher in Albuquerque—for allowing me to include his poem, "Midlevel Minds."

Here in Las Cruces, Donald A. Esker, a teacher of writing at a Milwaukee technical college, now retired—to whom I owe a debt of gratitude for his insightful comments during fruitful afternoon conversations, for the loan of several excellent books about poetry, and for critical response to the early manuscript.

Eileen Taulbee, a friend and fellow language arts teacher, also retired—whose critique of the text resulted in a much improved and more coherent manuscript.

The Institute of Historical Survey Foundation in Las Cruces, and especially Dr. Evan Davies and Anne Morgan—for their unwavering support as I combed through my papers in search of student poetry.

Ken Binkley, a fellow Rotarian and good friend—who provided timely technical assistance when I most needed it.

Eleonor Hellman, a good friend here in the Land of Enchantment—for sending me a copy of *America's Favorite Poems* (Pinsky & Dietz) and sharing her own epiphany about poetry, and her husband Bruce Blossman, a fellow Peace Corps Volunteer in Tunisia—for e-mailing a steady stream of quotations about poetry, special poems, and Burma Shave jingles.

Dr. Glenna M. Sloan, professor of teacher education, literacy, and children's literature at Queens College, the City University of New York—for promptly composing the foreword on a very tight timeline.

Tom Koerner, vice president and editorial director at Rowman & Littlefield Education—for believing in this book, and National Middle School Association—for co-publishing this book with Rowman & Littlefield.

Finally, I thank my wife and librarian, Jeanne—for her careful research and editing, for her work on the index, and for cheering me on and being my muse. I could not have completed *Using Poetry in the Classroom* without her love and support, and for that, I am profoundly grateful.

# Introduction

**Poems**

Ideas and ideals
illuminating life and
all of its lessons.

—RMB

I love teaching poetry. I like playing with language, creating rhymes, and luxuriating in the lines of a familiar poem, wrapping its words around me as I contemplate a poet's intent. I get a kick out of reciting A. A. Milne's "Disobedience," which I learned from my mother, and I feel invigorated when I read the poetry of Robert Frost. Most of all I like to write poems for any and all occasions.

This book is my testament to how much I enjoyed teaching poetry to young adolescents. I loved writing poems and memorizing verses with them as well as listening to them when they offered novel interpretations of a particular poem. I worked hard, thumbing through my Penguin paperback rhyming dictionary to find interesting rhymes (June moon / croon tune / swoon soon / honeymoon / prune goon / impugn baboon / picayune pantaloon) to share with students. My penchant for rhymed couplets and attraction to alliteration affected my students, who also came to share my passion for poetry.

Poetry elevates and amuses us, explains our behavior, and tickles our fancies. We encounter poetry at weddings and funerals because certain verses speak concisely to the occasion, illuminating life's lessons in brief patterns of words and lines. Yet in May 2003, seven months after Ruth Lilly donated $100 million dollars to the magazine *Poetry*, writer Bruce

Wexler wrote a "My Turn" column for *Newsweek* bemoaning the status of poetry in America. Wexler's title summarized his main point: "Poetry Is Dead. Does Anybody Really Care?"

My response: No, it isn't. And yes, I do. So do many others, and not just educators.

Yes, teaching students to appreciate poetry can be challenging, but that has always been the case, as Donald Stauffer noted more than four decades ago in his essay, "Poetry and the Easy Life" (Drew & Connor, 1961):

> Understanding great poetry is a strenuous achievement that demands the full exercise of our minds. Teachers should not pretend that the reading of poetry is a comfortable and innocently indolent pastime; nor should readers and amateurs think of a poem as something you can drink in, in an off moment, as you would drink a chocolate milk shake. Lovers of poetry should give at least as much energy and undivided attention to their passion as, say, stamp collectors and ski jumpers give to theirs. (p. 298)

Yet the pleasures of poetry are many, as Eve Merriam (1962) asserted in *What Can a Poem Do?*:

> A poem can make you aware of language so that even in prose you can enjoy using words more because you know what tricks they can do and what they cannot do . . . You may not "get" all of a poem the first time you read it, because the words and the built-in music are so concentrated. Don't let it worry you; just go on to the end and then go back and read it again. (pp. 3–4)

## POETRY IN THE CLASSROOM

Poetry has an important place in the curriculum, and this book describes such a place, a classroom where its presence throughout the school year became a significant part of each student's academic experience.

In language arts, teachers promote reading, writing, and critical thinking as they teach vocabulary, debate, research, and essay structure. Short stories, plays, and novels receive significant attention, yet poetry often gets short shrift. Why? Some English/language arts instructors are uncomfortable teaching the poetic canon because they, themselves, do not appreciate poetry. They feel awkward when composing verse, and so they have difficulty teaching students to craft poems.

As a rookie teacher, I shared those concerns; I was not an English major. But as a child I listened to my mother recite poems by heart, and when I was in college I became enamored of the poetry of Robert Frost. These experiences served me well later in my teaching career.

Based on two decades of teaching poetry, *Using Poetry in the Classroom* focuses on the development of student skills as it celebrates the teaching of poetry. Poetic "interludes" between chapters feature specific activities for teaching poetry. Authentic adolescent voices resonate throughout the book as former students reflect on their experiences years earlier. Their perspectives offer telling testimony to the staying power of certain lessons. My emphasis, however, is on *how* to teach poetry rather than *which* poems to include in the curriculum.

## A COMPREHENSIVE APPROACH

As I taught, I kept returning to the question: how can I weave together the various aspects of poetry into a comprehensive program that simultaneously pays homage to the canon, develops academic skills, and engages students in worthwhile curricular activities?

I began by leafing through anthologies, looking for poems that resonated with me. Some that I found were serious, others humorous, and still others overflowing with insights into life. Along the way, a colleague's suggestion, an idea advanced in a journal, a memorable conference presentation, and thoughtful reflection about what worked and what didn't helped me to cobble together an approach to poetry that engaged middle school students. I came to see that poetry, when taught rigorously and consistently, develops many language arts skills.

My approach to poetry in the classroom included having students memorize and recite both teacher-assigned and self-selected poems; compose and publish verse; read, discuss, and interpret poetry; and listen as poems were read aloud. All students in my heterogeneously grouped classroom, ranging from special needs to beyond gifted, participated successfully in these activities. I soon realized that to nurture a classroom community of poets, a two-week unit would not suffice; students need more than ten class periods of poetry if they are to feel at ease with Erato. So, along with their study of prose texts, my students grappled with poetry in 40-minute English classes throughout the school year. In the process I became "the teacher as poet," sharing my unpolished drafts, reciting poems from memory, and celebrating students and school events with occasional light verse and, when the situation called for it, more serious pieces.

This approach succeeded; my pupils enjoyed poetry, and they improved their language arts skills. I discovered that when we celebrated poetry from September to June, the experiences became self-reinforcing. Pupils were able to compose poems with greater skill because they constantly read and interpreted them. They developed their memorization skills because they listened to classmates recite a variety of verse. By circulating early drafts of my own poems, I revealed my own struggles and, in the process, provided powerful coaching. And it was the slow accumulation of such poetic encounters, and their reinforcing effect on students, that made the difference.

## HOW TO READ THIS BOOK

The ideas presented in *Using Poetry in the Classroom* are intended to supplement a yearlong curriculum by interspersing poetry into the larger language arts mix.

Chapter 1 responds to the question, "Why teach poetry?"

Chapter 2 introduces the idea of the teacher as poet.

Chapters 3, 4, and 5 constitute the heart of the book. Each chapter explores a major aspect of teaching poetry—memorizing and reciting, composing and publishing, and discussing and interpreting.

Chapter 6 focuses on the experiences of three students, each of whom delved deeply into poetry.

Chapter 7 explains how, beginning on Day One, to set in motion the interconnected strands of memorizing, composing, and interpreting poetry.

Chapter 8 suggests some uses of poetry beyond the language arts classroom and further explores the notion of the teacher as poet.

Chapter 9 describes successful poetry teachers at work across America. These include my twin brother, Robert, in Colorado and my daughter, Katie Budde, in California.

Chapter 10 offers my personal reflections along with those of former students.

Essentially, *Using Poetry in the Classroom* is a response to two questions: What can we expect of our students? What are they capable of achieving when immersed in a comprehensive approach to poetry?

I believe that the strategies presented here are valid wherever you teach, at whatever level. However, what worked for me in a suburban, middle-class school district on Long Island in the 1980s and 1990s might not work for all teachers in exactly the same way. Therefore, I encourage you to rework these ideas, honoring your style of teaching, the nature of the students in your classes, and the realities of the community in which you teach.

Learning to teach poetry well and in a comprehensive manner takes time. Almost two decades passed before I felt that I had most of it in place; even then I had moments of doubt. So, start slowly. Test out an idea and learn from your students' responses to it. If something works, think about how to embellish it next year. If something doesn't work, think about why it didn't and how to fix it.

To be sure, the way you relate to kids will affect the way you infuse poetry in your curriculum. Along with listening to students, reflecting on actual classroom practice may be the best path to improvement. In teaching, we grow on the job every day.

*Using Poetry in the Classroom* is designed to be read from beginning to end, but if you are particularly interested in one specific aspect of teaching poetry, begin with that chapter.

May you and your students enjoy poetry in the classroom.

*Part I*

# BEFORE CLASS

# Chapter One

# Why Poetry?

*This chapter argues that poetry deserves a central place in the language arts classroom and that students develop academic skills and opportunities for self-expression through exposure to the many aspects of poetry.*

> Reader: "Why poetry?" Me: "Why not?"
> Poems should always be part of the plot.
> Verses can heighten most any occasion.
> Include them as part of your class persuasion.
>
> —RMB

Young adolescents, caught up in myriad changes in their bodies, minds, and, often, their behavior, are a sea of contradictions. They demand incremental degrees of freedom yet count on the familiarity and safety of imposed structure. They test limits, challenge authority, and conform to peer norms while, ironically, striving to be different.

In *What Every Middle School Teacher Should Know*, Trudy Knowles and Dave F. Brown (2000) put it this way:

> [E]very student is simultaneously at-risk and gifted. The causes of individual differences are not as important as the responsibility for teachers to assure that every student has opportunities to succeed at learning—daily. (p. 120)

Poetry enables students "to succeed at learning—daily." As young adolescents cope with the inexorable physical and emotional phenomena of puberty, they are particularly sensitive to poetry. I would argue that each middle school student is a poem unfolding, word by word, line by line, verse by verse.

Exposing students to poetry enhances their academic skills, including reading, writing, and critical thinking. Teachers who intersperse poetry throughout the school year, rather than limiting it to a two-week unit in April, serve students in the development of those essential skills.

But what is poetry? Why teach it? Why have students memorize, recite, compose, and publish verse? Why discuss and interpret poems? *Using Poetry in the Classroom* responds to these questions.

## WHAT IS POETRY?

What is poetry? Defining it is like trying to touch a rainbow.

In *The Nature of Poetry*, Donald A. Stauffer (1946) questioned the value of a definition when he wrote:

> Like life, poetry exists in so many forms and on so many levels that it triumphantly defies description. . . . Surely there is good reason to avoid a definition of poetry. The clearer and more concise the definition is, the more poems it leaves out. (p. 11)

Stauffer then suggested that "a poem is an individual imaginative experience recorded as faithfully as possible by an individual poet" (p. 17). He also cited "Wordsworth's dictum that the words of a great poem appear to be inevitable, and Coleridge's deceivingly simple statement that prose is composed of good words in good order, poetry of the best words in the best order" (p. 55)

John Barrington Wain, speaking on BBC radio on January 13, 1976, offered this delightful analogy: "Poetry is to prose as dancing is to walking."

Elizabeth Drew and George Connor (1961), in *Discovering Modern Poetry*, a collection of essays by poets about poetry, asserted that:

> The basic nature and function of poetry remains the same in all ages: it is to recreate the living truth of individual human experience through the medium of patterned language. Like the other arts, poetry brings form and order out of the confusion and discord of the living of life. (p. 2)

In that same book, Robert Frost, in his essay "The Constant Symbol," held that poetry "is metaphor, saying one thing and meaning another, saying one thing in terms of another" (Drew & Conner, 1961, p. 317).

E. B. White (Drew & Conner, 1961) spoke to poetry's brief intensity:

A true poem contains the seed of wonder; but a bad poem, egg-fashion, stinks. I think there is no such thing as a long poem. If it is long it isn't a poem; it is something else. . . . Poetry is intensity, and nothing is intense for long. (p. 295)

As is famously said about art, we know poetry when we see it. Yet, a persistent appeal of poetry is its inherent elusiveness.

## WHY POETRY?

Why poetry? Because poetry addresses the human condition, describing our dreams, desires, and dispositions. Poetry speaks to our "nobler nature"—an appropriate poem, recited with conviction in the proper setting, stirs the soul. Poetry raises fundamental questions about the nature of being and helps us to comprehend who we are and what we have experienced. Over the centuries, the voices of poets have augmented our collective under-standing of life in all its complexities, challenges, and charm. Young ado-lescents value those voices.

Glenna Sloan, in *Give Them Poetry!* (2003) speaks about the positive effect of poetry on children who are learning to read and write. She laments the fact that few teachers use it effectively in their classrooms, noting:

Many know little about poetry beyond what they learned in high school, knowledge that often results in the mistaken belief that poetry is an esoteric genre, full of mysterious metaphors that only certain elite minds can fathom. Some simply don't take it seriously, believing that in comparison to prose, it strains to communicate through artifice and artiness. (p. 1)

I remember feeling frustrated and inadequate when discussing poems in high school, and I appreciated few of the verses presented to me. A class-mate would offer an interpretation, and occasionally I would think, *Yes, I can see that*. But more often than not, I didn't. My opinions were tenta-tive and half-formed, and I was unsure of their value, so I rarely shared them in class. I chafed at teachers' admonitions that a certain poem had a specific meaning, particularly when my interpretation was some distance from the purported "truth" of it. When the teacher explained what the poem *really* meant, I thought, *No, that's not how I see it, and who says that's what it means, anyway?* I did not come to poetry easily, and I readily empathize with Jack.

Jack, the reluctant protagonist in Sharon Creech's enchanting book, *Love That Dog*, reacts in his journal in a not unfamiliar adolescent fashion to a William Carlos Williams poem introduced by Miss Stretchberry early in the school year:

> **September 27**
>
> I don't understand
> the poem about
> the red wheelbarrow
> and the white chickens
> and why so much
> depends upon
> them.
>
> If that is a poem
> about the red wheelbarrow
> and the white chickens
> then any words
> can be a poem.
> You've just got to
> make
> short
> lines.
>
> (Creech, 2001, p. 3)

Young adolescents easily memorize intricate rap chants, invent endless verses to songs on the bus returning from a field trip, learn complex lyrics from a current pop idol's latest compact disc overnight, and can recite almost every word of dialogue from the musical *Grease*. Asking them to memorize poems is not asking too much.

During my teaching career, I learned that when I shared my own enthusiasm for poetry with students, when I wrote verse regularly with and for them, and when I respected their evolving interpretations as we discussed particular poems, student attitudes toward poetry waxed positive. They appreciated certain verses for their timely, on-target messages. They discovered that composing poems for themselves, their families, and their friends was an enjoyable enterprise. And they memorized and recited poems with increasing skill.

## WHY TEACH POETRY?

Why teach poetry in your classroom? When students read, recite, interpret and compose poetry regularly during the year, they:

- engage in creative and critical thinking
- enhance their language acquisition
- develop their written expression
- polish their publish speaking skills
- learn tools of the genre (imagery, alliteration, dissonance, rhyme, rhythm, meter, onomatopoeia, etc.)
- become familiar with American literary traditions as well as those of other cultures

While these language arts objectives may be addressed through short stories, novels, essays, and drama, they also are easily accessed via verse. Poetry is a perfect tool for language skill development because of its imagery, brevity, vocabulary, and variety. The reluctant writer, unwilling to risk failure when challenged by a lengthy composition, may find drafting a short poem a less imposing task. The gifted student may find the business of word choice a stimulating undertaking—trying to say the most with the least number of words. And the student who rebels against structure may appreciate the latitude allowed by free verse.

## POETRY IN THE CLASSROOM

Poetry came alive in my classroom, permeating all other aspects of language arts, all year long. Posters spotlighting familiar verses festooned the walls; the classroom door was covered with poems that I composed to celebrate students and school events; sign-up sheets from poetry recitation days hung from the ceiling; poetry anthologies spilled out of the bookcase.

Rarely did a day pass without some reference to a poem or a poet. In this inviting setting, students became comfortable with poetry as a powerful form of spoken and written expression.

My students also read plays, wrote essays, and engaged in other language arts activities, many of which were featured in my book *Writing for Real: Strategies for Engaging Adolescent Writers* (2003).

## WHY READ POETRY?

In language arts classes, students read texts—novels, short stories, and plays. Poems, whether facile or complex, are simply other texts to be deciphered, decoded, deconstructed, and enjoyed. But why read poetry?

- to appreciate the creative use of language
- to study the ideas and images generated by a poet
- to understand poetry as a form of literature
- to comprehend a particular time period, or culture, or setting, or social phenomenon, or human experience as described by a poet

Poetry can be read silently or aloud; have students do both. When they read poems silently, students acquire glimmerings of understanding regarding author intent. When they hear the same poem read aloud by a classmate or teacher, they notice tone of voice, an emphasis on certain lines, the stress on certain words, and they gain auditory insight into the poem's message.

Of course, not all books are immediately accessible. The novels of Tolstoy, *Finnegan's Wake*, and Faulkner's tales of Yoknapatawpha County are not *oeuvres* intended for sixth graders. Nor were the poetic cantos of Ezra Pound composed for eighth graders. All poems contain words and concepts assembled intentionally by the author, yet not all poetry is the same. Just as music ranges from Mozart to Eminem, there is also a range of poetry from Shel Silverstein to T. S. Eliot. As with books, not all poems are engaging, interesting, or appropriate for all students. Know your students, be aware of your community's customs and traditions, read scads of poetry, then choose your examples wisely.

## WHY INTERPRET POETRY?

Reading is an essential skill, and the ability to decode text is a major goal at all levels of education. Poems have their own protocols, formulas, patterns, rhythms, and structures. As deliberate products of thoughtful beings, poems are embedded with ideas. At times, the message is readily apparent. Some poems, however, demand more of the reader; they require reflection, rereading, reconsideration.

When you invite students to interpret a poem, you are asking them to:

- grapple with both an author's intent and the author's intentional ambiguity
- think about the meanings of words
- share their interpretations with others
- consider other viewpoints as peers voice their own reactions
- refine their understanding of the world as informed by the poem's perspective
- recognize that, inherently, poems are thoughts, emotions, experiences, and events recaptured in words

When you ask students to interpret poems, allow them to develop their own ideas. They may not immediately grasp an author's purpose, but remember, they are developing learners. Be wary of forcing your own interpretations on pupils. A graduate student in children's literature at the University of New Mexico reflected on her early poetry experiences thus: "The teacher asks what a poem means, and then, after everyone gives their opinion, the teacher says what it is *really* about—and makes students feel stupid."

## WHY MEMORIZE POETRY?

In a December 29, 2002, *New York Times* opinion piece titled "A Lost Eloquence," Carol Muske-Dukes, a creative writing teacher at the University of Southern California, lamented the passing of "perhaps the last generation of Americans who learned poems and orations by rote in classes dedicated to the art of elocution."

My mother was a part of that generation; she learned pages of poetry by heart and could recite verses at the drop of a hat. But as the twentieth century advanced, classes in elocution waned.

Today's students are ripe for recitation. They know pop hits, chants, raps, choruses, holiday lyrics, camp songs, and commercial jingles. Since a poem can be simply a set of words and lines in a specific sequence, often with a unique rhythm, students are on familiar ground when they memorize poems. They can develop recitation skills, and so can you; in fact, students perform significantly better at recitations when the teacher also recites from memory and demonstrates appropriate delivery, expression, pace, and poise.

Why have students recite poems?

- A poem spoken or read aloud has a different quality to it than the poem read silently.
- Regular recitations develop elocution and public speaking skills.
- Those who are able to recite poetry advance the cause of literacy.
- Individuals who can recite a particular poem for an appropriate occasion enjoy a sense of accomplishment.
- Finally, to recite well, you have to understand the poem's intent, focusing both on *how* to recite the poem and on *why* you should recite it in that fashion. I also believe that through recitation, one's ability to interpret poems is enhanced. Conversely, the deeper one understands the text, the better the recitation will be.

Glenn, one of my eighth-grade students in 1979–1980, reflected on his poetry recitations 23 years later:

[P]oetry lessons in 8th grade put me in touch with writings that I most definitely would not have had an interest in. To this day, after all these years I am still able to impress others with my recital of *The Road Not Taken* and *The Fog*. These lessons also laid the ground work for memorization which was needed throughout my educational experience.

—Glenn Valentine
(E-mail communication, March 11, 2003)

There were, to be sure, some students who did not immediately appreciate the wisdom of memorizing verse. But in spite of their occasional objections, I persevered. I believed then and am even more convinced today that language arts teachers should ask students to commit poems to memory several times a year.

## WHY COMPOSE POETRY?

What inspires a poet? A sudden memory—an unexpected occurrence—a jarring juxtaposition—an insight into a prior experience—a passionate response to someone or something—a desire to arrest the fleeting tendrils of a subsiding emotion—any of these occurrences can trigger the muse.

When you ask students to compose verse, or when you compose verse yourself, you have multiple goals in mind:

- communicating an idea
- creating an image
- capturing a moment
- telling a story
- exploring a specific poetic form or rhyme scheme
- having fun with words and ideas
- connecting with a particular audience
- parodying an existing poem
- completing a homework assignment
- creating a gift of writing for someone special

Writing poetry is demanding activity. The tasks of idea formation, image development, word choice, line placement, and overall structure challenge the author simultaneously. However, an advantage when composing verse is that the end result is often shorter than a prose piece, which usually makes revision an easier task.

Playing with language is an important part of developing literacy. As Glenna Sloan (2003) observed, "Children who never feel delight and amazement at the wonderful things words can be made to do are unlikely to be keen about making the considerable effort it takes to read and write them" (p. 2).

Just as we can all be amateur musicians, or athletes, or chefs, we also can be poets, albeit of varying levels of skill. However, an awareness of individual differences (and a realistic appreciation of my own shortcomings) does not keep me from singing in the shower, or swimming in the Senior Olympics, or preparing Tunisian delicacies for friends, or composing a birthday ode for my nonagenarian mother-in-law.

Begin today—write a poem for a family member or a friend. Celebrate a special occasion in verse (rhymed or unrhymed), then share it with your audience. Keep at it, and save all drafts. As with most tasks, learning to compose poetry effectively takes time, practice, determination, and "on the job" training. One becomes a poet by writing poetry—it's that simple, and that complicated. The important thing is to get started—now.

## TOOLS FOR TEACHING POETRY

Teaching poetry in a comprehensive manner from 1979 to 1997 enabled me to develop several pedagogical practices that supported student learning and skill development. Reflective journal entries, teacher modeling, peer examples, drafting and revising, writing groups, publishing, and open-ended discussions were among the tools I used to teach poetry.

Students who write frequently in journals are forced to think. In their poetry entries, students can explore ideas, pose questions, explain understandings, and share insights on topics such as "How I composed my poem."

When I taught poetry composition, I always provided models, usually poems created by former students. I urged pupils to draft and revise their own pieces until they felt they had the words right. Additionally, I wrote along with students, sharing my own drafts and using these as examples of what I expected of them.

I also organized writing groups in which students read their poems aloud, posed questions to peers, received critical feedback, and gained a sense of audience while sharing their drafts. These groups, usually three or four pupils, changed several times during the year.

My students published their poetry throughout the year, and in most instances they were able to select which poems they wanted to publish. When students knew that their poetry was going public, I noticed that they consequently demonstrated increased interest in the conventions of mechanics and spelling.

Open-ended discussions encouraged many students to participate when we interpreted poems. Questions such as "What do you think?" and "Does anyone have a different perspective?" resulted in students sharing ideas more freely. I was careful not to tell a student that his or her interpretation was "wrong," and I held back my perspective on a poem until the end of the discussion, if at all.

## CLOSING THOUGHTS

Acquiring a sense of comfort with poetry does not necessarily come easily. It took me years before I believed that I could write poems, and years more before I felt comfortable sharing my verses with others. But I now call myself a poet. You can, too, and so can your students. Writing poetry is not as difficult an activity as some may imagine. We all have ideas that we want to communicate, and we are all capable of pushing nouns against verbs and incorporating adjectives and adverbs appropriately so that a message becomes memorable. Writing, and particularly the writing of poetry, is a discipline, yet as one writes more and more poems, the discipline becomes second nature.

My advice? Begin the school year with poetry on Day One, and make it a part of all the days that follow. This is an appropriate way to address the academic needs of students.

Why, then, poetry? Because poetry

- celebrates the human spirit
- speaks to specific occasions
- helps students understand imagery, allusion, metaphor, and the beauty of language
- transforms one's perspective on an idea by presenting it in a new way
- is often short, hence more accessible and more easily revised
- enables the artist within to emerge
- is part of our literary heritage

I believe that poetry engages students in thinking, in composing, and in comprehending their world and other, even larger worlds. They are better people for being immersed in verse. When presented properly, poems can be appreciated by all kinds of students for all kinds of reasons. Young adolescents in particular take to, revel in, and gain from a comprehensive exposure to the many dimensions of poetry. In short, they discover that poetry in the classroom can speak to them, and that they can answer back.

## POETIC INTERLUDE NO. 1: A POETIC LICENSE

You may discover that some students, when attempting to compose poems, profess that they don't know what to write. To ease their uncertainty, why not issue each student a Poetic License? Assure them that, just as the Scarecrow became smarter merely by receiving a diploma in *The Wizard of Oz*, your bestowal of such a license will unleash their poetic muse. Adapt the form below to your own students and setting:

---

Poetic License

This license hereby entitles the bearer, _____,

to create poetry whenever the Muse strikes!

Valid from _____ until _____

Signed: _____

Poet-in-Residence

---

# Chapter Two

# The Teacher as Poet

*This chapter explores the role of the teacher as poet, describing how original poetry can advance learning, chronicle school events, celebrate students, and nurture a classroom community of poets.*

"Mr. Burkhardt? Good to hear from you! Life isn't as fulfilling when someone isn't writing a poem about every little trivial event in my life."

—Mike Cast
(Eighth grader in 1991–1992; e-mail communication, March 10, 2003)

**Connecticut: The Fire Continues**
*(excerpt)*

Early Thursday morning, before we really awoke,
We loaded up the minibus, and Mr. Burkhardt spoke:
"Screens, projectors, slides, tapes, extension cords, and hurry
Because we've got to reach Port Jeff and drive aboard the ferry." . . .
Soon we reached East Ridge Middle School and set up for the show
In the huge cafeteria where 200 kids did go
To see our new production; Sal killed the lights and then
We showed the show, they cheered, and then we did it once again.
Lucinda changed the trays, Mike was running sound,
And Greg at some point dropped a tray of slides upon the ground.

—RMB

(Unpublished poem, October 18, 1991; Mike Cast
is referenced in the penultimate line)

On Memorial Day 1966, at the end of my first year of teaching ninth-grade social studies at Monroe-Woodbury High School in New York's Hudson Valley, I stood among a small crowd in front of the bandstand in Highland Mills, New York, listening to members of the American Legion speak about soldiers, sacrifice, and the stars and stripes. At one point, a petite sixth grader stepped forward. In a voice ringing with youthful conviction, Patty McInerny hushed the crowd as she delivered all 29 lines of Henry Holcomb Bennett's nineteenth-century tribute, "The Flag Goes By":

> Hats off!
> Along the street there comes
> A blare of bugles, a ruffle of drums,
> A flash of color beneath the sky:
>     Hats off!
> The flag is passing by!

As Patty recited, my spine tingled. The poem spoke to the event, a ceremony honoring our nation's dead at a time when the war in Vietnam was beginning to accelerate. Through Patty's 12-year-old voice, I could visualize a parade, hear the muffled tattoo of snare drums, see flags flying, and watch uniformed men and women marching in step. At that moment, the notion of poetry appropriate to an occasion came alive in my mind.

Looking back, I see this incident as one of several that nudged me toward becoming a teacher-poet.

## SCHOOL POETRY

I taught ninth-grade African/Asian Studies at Monroe-Woodbury High School for seven years, dabbling in poetry as part of my teaching but neither consistently nor effectively. When Patty McInerny became a ninth grader, she joined the cast of "Festique Afrique," a multimedia presentation my students and I created to celebrate African culture; students clad in authentic garb recited poems from Nigeria and Ghana and sang folk songs from Sierra Leone. During our study of Japan, I presented haiku poetry to Patty and her classmates to help them appreciate the culture of that insular nation. On a geography test, students were given excerpts from classic poems and asked to identify the climate zones they referenced; clues included the first eight lines of Robert Frost's "Stopping by Woods on a Snowy Evening" and the last five lines of Percy Bysshe Shelley's "Ozymandius."

Also in 1966, several Monroe-Woodbury High School students scandalized the community by smoking pot. Their actions inspired "Reflections on a Year of Light," the first poem I wrote expressly to and for students. The title now strikes me as pretentious, but the message remains heartfelt:

> They attempt to live their parts
> And end in breaking elder hearts
> In haste to taste and touch.
>
> They think theirs a proper path.
> They go and slowly grow too fast,
> Experiencing much.
>
> Do they remember others care
> Of who and what they are, and where
> And how they are alive?
>
> I will always go on caring,
> Wondering what next they're daring,
> Hoping they'll survive.
>
> —RMB
> (Unpublished poem, 1966)

I began teaching English and social studies at Shoreham-Wading River Middle School on Long Island in 1972. The following year I advanced with my seventh graders to eighth grade. Consequently, in the fall of 1973, I began the year with a classroom of kids I already knew well. As I got to know my students even better, I composed "School is a Time Machine." And, in spite of my nervousness, I shared it with them:

> School is a time machine
> taking me back
> through your eyes
> to a younger age . . .

taking me ahead
to grown (former) students
who see what I saw.
I remember:
the rush of love
as I watch you
holding hands in hallways . . .
the frustration of constraint
as I watch your eyes glaze over
under my gaze . . .
You put me in touch
with who I was
(who I still am?)
rekindling a youth
half my age
uncertain, confused, seeking . . .
I re-learn many things
from you.

—RMB
(Unpublished poem, 1973)


## POETRY IN PUBLIC

In 1978, an event triggered memories of Patty McInerny's recitation of "The Flag Goes By" in 1966 and convinced me that students should learn to memorize and recite poems. In the spring of that year, Jane Wittlock, who became principal of Shoreham-Wading River Middle School when her predecessor, Dennis Littky, resigned, spoke at a testimonial dinner for Dennis about his six years of outstanding educational leadership. She praised the courage Dennis exhibited in taking difficult paths that he knew were right, and she underscored her point by reciting "The Road Not Taken." The packed gymnasium quieted as Jane's voice animated Robert Frost's classic lines, so appropriate for the occasion. Listening in the audience, I experienced pride that Jane was our new principal, delight that she quoted Frost for the occasion, and amazement that she dared to recite poetry. Jane's eloquence reinforced my belief that the ability to recite a poem in public, with conviction, is a skill worth developing.

## AUTHOR'S WEEK

Our middle school held an Author's Week each year in which prominent "young adult" writers such as Avi, M. E. Kerr, and the late Paula Danziger visited the school, giving students an encounter with real authors. Arnold Adoff, author of numerous poetry books, enchanted pupils with his "shattered shape" poems from *Eats*. I invited students to create their own poems using Adoff's as models, and poetry classes were never the same after that.

One year, Ron Overton, a poet from the Reader Writers Workshop in New York City, came into my classroom for five consecutive days and presented a different poetry lesson each day. I observed him work with students in my morning class, then I replicated his lessons for my students later in the day. Overton used William Carlos Williams' "The Red Wheelbarrow" and "The Great Figure," along with "list poems" by American and Brazilian poets. He would write a short poem on the chalkboard, ask students to copy it into their journals, and then inquire of students what they saw in the poem. For homework each evening, students had to compose two or three poems based on the example presented in class.

Overton's modeling worked, and soon I had his approach down pat, revising it each year to make it my own. Eventually, Overton's classroom presentations became the basis of a two-week poetry-writing unit.

## "THE FIRST DAY"

In the summer of 1980, I participated in a National Writing Project summer institute, a professional development experience of the first magnitude. Sondra Perl and Richard Sterling, at that time codirectors of the New York City Writing Project, were my writing teachers. During the institute, I learned how to teach writing by reading about writing, composing in various genres, examining my own writing process through reflective journal entries, communicating my struggles and successes with peers, responding in writing groups to compositions created by colleagues, and drafting and revising pieces until they were ready to be shared with a larger audience.

I also composed several pieces, among them "The First Day" (the frontispiece of this book), a free verse poem honoring that auspicious moment when students first enter a teacher's classroom. John Dewey said, "Begin where the student is." On the first day of school, students come in, look around, and sit down, visibly curious and excited about the prospects ahead. I attempted to capture that moment in verse.

I believed that my most important task as a teacher was to take students from where they were to as far along the path of literacy as I could. So, for the remainder of my teaching career, "The First Day" became the initial piece of business on Day One. I consciously introduced myself as a poet to my students as soon as they walked through the door.

I saved all seven drafts of "The First Day," laminated them into a scroll, and revealed my writing process to students early in the year. The drafts were visible evidence of my efforts at getting "the best words in the best order," and the scroll underscored my message: "Save all drafts."

### The First Day
*Draft 2, July 14, 1980, 6:30 P.M.*

It's the first day
~~And~~ In they come—
Some hesitantly pausing at the door,
Wondering and waiting,
Other boldly asserting their presence
As they stride to seats.

Heads swivel,
Eyes ~~explore~~ contact? the classroom:
Posters and pictures (multi-colored images)
Meet curious glances.
Saving seats for friends,
Adjusting clean-cover notebooks
Filled with clean ruled sheets,
They sit expectantly in crisp ~~clothes~~ clothing.

For some, the ~~boredom~~ boredom of ~~August~~ waiting
Gone at last.
For some, the restraints of structure
Unwillingly accepted.
For some, the excitement of beginning
Reawakening dormant senses.

For most, an unexplored world awaiting.
New seats ~~allow~~ permit new perspectives,
New possibilities, new patterns.

The student asks:
"What does he expect of me?"
"What is this room all about?"
"~~What~~ Who is this teacher?"
The teacher asks:
"Who are these people?"
"What are they all about?"
"What do they expect of me?"

~~In~~ A simultaneous ~~exploration~~ journey
~~They set off seeking~~
~~Understanding~~
~~The~~ Through days and months that follow
Explored together?
    ~~Provide~~ ~~Contain~~ Reveal answers as yet ~~unvoiced~~ ~~undreamed~~ unvoiced,
~~But for now,~~ For now, however,
All is new and questioning for
~~For it is~~ ~~Because~~ ~~For~~
It's the first day.

— RMB

During the next two years, my poetry production increased considerably. In the summer of 1983, I took a computer course, and the drudgery of revision became a thing of the past. Computers made the alteration of text a pleasure and desktop publishing a reality.

## THE WEEKLY POEM

The opening of school in September 1983 went very well. To celebrate it, I composed a poem titled "Day Three" and read it aloud on the third day of school. One student, having heard me recite "The First Day" two days earlier, inquired innocently, "Mr. B., do you write a new poem every week?" His unanticipated question, and my off-the-cuff response, changed my teaching forever.

"I sure do," I responded, rashly committing myself to 40 more poems between then and June. Thus the tradition, and the challenge, began.

Weekly poems were usually rendered in free verse or as a series of rhymed couplets, most of them forgettable doggerel that recycled the events of the week:

### Week Twelve—December 3, 1983
*(excerpts)*

Boys and girls, now it's time to delve
Into the week known officially as "Twelve."
Lots of interesting things we did do,
Some of them old, some of them new.
In English class on Monday last,
We learned word processing—fast, fast, fast!
Insert/delete, recall your file,
Erase, call directory, see kids smile
As President letters they edit and revise
And try PETs and CBMs on for size.
Shift/clear home, cursor, format error:
There's more than just a tinge of terror
When it comes time to save/memorize
And green print disappears before one's eyes.
. . .
Stay tuned to this station for another weekly verse.
If you think this was bad, the next one's even worse!

—RMB
(Unpublished poem, 1983)

After presenting a weekly poem, I distributed copies to interested students. I was never in doubt about the less-than-timeless quality of most of my poems, but students enjoyed them because the verses chronicled their middle school experiences in an amusing manner.

As I grew more comfortable teaching poetry, I began playing with the weekly poems, attempting new structures, incorporating outrageous rhymes, and inventing novel twists to maintain student interest and attention. Through these poems, students gained an understanding of the power of poetry to speak to specific occasions. My examples also encouraged them to explore new forms, create parodies of poems they had previously memorized, and gain comfort with poetry as an effective means of expression.

## "POEMS FOR ALL OCCASIONS"

Committed to the concept of a weekly poem, I concocted a teaching strategy that became a hallmark of my pedagogy. Early each school year, I informed students that I had, at home, a unique volume of verse titled *Poems For All Occasions*. Actually, the nonexistent book was an apocryphal anthology.

"Today is the third day of school," I announced in class. "Here's a poem that I found last night while leafing through an amazing book called *Poems For All Occasions*," I lied effortlessly. "What makes this book so amazing," I fibbed again, "is that inside its covers you can find a poem for just about any occasion. For example, this poem here," I said, waving a typed sheet at the class, "seems just right for today's lesson." And why not? The verse in question had been written the evening before, recounting classroom events still fresh in students' minds.

### The Third Day

It's the third day.
Here we are
beyond the beginning,
learning to listen,
struggling to speak,
following the instructions
because it works.

Making memories,
respecting the door,
defining distinctions,
perusing poetry,
seeing slides,
getting acquainted,
creating community,
forming the team.

Next week and next month
poetry memorizations,

timeline posters,
weaving the fabric
of learning and living
and opening doors.

Our simultaneously shared journey
through days and months ahead
continues on Monday
because
that's the fourth day.

—RMB
(From the apocryphal *Poems For All Occasions*, 1985)

Some students got the joke instantly; others eventually realized that I had written "The Third Day" the previous evening specifically to celebrate Day Three. *Poems For All Occasions* became a useful device that enabled me to play the role of teacher as poet regularly.

In January 1988, when we were studying the poetry of Robert Frost in English class and the Declaration of Independence in social studies, my students and I received an unexpected gift—two snow days in one week. The second school cancellation inspired the following, enabling me to reinforce student understanding of both Frost's original poem (which we had studied earlier) and the opening lines of the Declaration:

### Writing Another Poem on a Snowday Morning
*(with even further apologies to Robert Frost)*

Whose poem this is I think I know.
His home's in Wading River, though.
His mind went back to times antique
To recall woods so filled with snow.

Of course we wish and dream and seek
For snow days, and, in prayers, so speak,
Yet rarely get, dear ladies and gents,
Two snow days in a single week.

But when in the course of student events
It becomes necessary ('cause snow is so dense)
To honor this Snow God that you seek, well,
Closing the school just makes good sense.

All days are not created equal,
But in 1988's first full week, well,
We had a snowday, and then a sequel;
We had a snowday, and then a sequel.

—RMB

(From the apocryphal *Poems For All Occasions*, 1988)

## THE TEACHER AS POET

The teacher as poet is not unlike a track coach who, on the first day of practice, high jumps six feet, then says to his athletes, "Let me instruct you on how it's done." He gains their attention by modeling a skill; consequently, they are more receptive to his coaching. Similarly, I believed that if I could present myself as a poet, I would be more effective when teaching poetry.

Sharing the struggle with students as you slog though the composition process is crucially important. Kids want to see that you also are in the trenches with them. Show them your early drafts, and the messier the better. Explain your writing process to them. Let students know that only on rare occasions do poems achieve final form in the first draft.

When I composed verse, I recycled student experiences, teaching the lesson that everyday life can provide great writing material. Middle-school students, narcissistic as only young adolescents can be, loved hearing references to themselves, to classmates, or to something they had done; thus they were attentive listeners when I shared my verses.

Through the weekly poems, students came to view me as another poet in the classroom, albeit a leader in our community of writers. Whenever I gave a poetry writing assignment, I composed verse along with my students. They were influenced by my style, my forms, and my ideas, just as I was influenced by theirs. As I chronicled the events of each week, students were constantly exposed to rhythm and rhyme, two essential characteristics of my doggerel verse.

How did I go about composing poems? I was guided by this adage: "Throw mud at the wall and see what sticks." I wrote down words—a mix of nouns and verbs, conjunctions and prepositions, proper nouns and punctuation marks—not worrying about sequence, just jotting ideas as they occurred to me, making a list that I knew I would revise later.

When I "threw mud at the wall," I trusted the process—I knew that some ideas would congeal, take shape, and form a pattern, and that something would emerge from random thoughts. I did not have to plan out where the text was going; I was confident that it would go somewhere, and that I would have abundant opportunities to alter vocabulary, shift lines, delete phrases, resequence ideas, and tinker with the title. This became my process, one with which I grew quite comfortable.

The last few minutes of Friday's English classes became moments for presentations of poetry. On occasion, inspired by my example, students wrote their own weekly poems and read them aloud to celebrate class or school events.

One December, the day after students completed "Radicals and Tories" (a simulation game in which the fate of a nation was determined by the votes of representatives from the 13 colonies at a mock Continental Congress), an Abraham Lincoln reenactor visited the school, the eighth graders had a big social studies test, and the winter music concert was scheduled for that evening. Two students wrote a 24-line account of these events, much to the amusement of their classmates. They alternated reading the verses aloud:

### New Poem This Friday

I'm happy to say
That we have a new poem this Friday.
I'm sure you won't be upset
Because this is a poem you won't forget.

Vote Independence! Vote Loyalty!
Posters to influence Moderates to vote for you.
Well, that's all over now;
You're not a slave being ruled by King George the 3rd,
And you're independent and free, not a slave to some kind of *nerd*.
For all the Tories that think I'm being unfair,
I just want to tell you I don't really care.

The Winter Concert is tonight.
If your parents can't drive you,
You can walk, run, or even ride your bike.
There is no excuse for you not to go
Unless you want coal from the man who goes, "Ho, Ho, Ho!"

The big test was today;
Hope you knew what you were doing or you will not get an "A."
Did all that information make you bored?
Or did it have something to do with Lexington and Concord?

Radicals & Tories—that brings back a tear,
But what's really exciting is that Abe Lincoln's here.
I'm really sorry to have to end this poem,
I would have made it longer but we all have to go home.

—Damon Lee and Jeff Campisi
(Eighth graders in 1988–1989)

Then another eighth grader, Liz, a victorious Radical, responded with a rebuttal in behalf of her rebellious cause:

### A Radical Report

The battle was fought; the Radicals won;
Twelve out of thirteen colonies voted for freedom.
There was Paul, Suzi, Craig, Ayelet, and Erika, too.
It was an uphill fight, but the Radicals pulled through.
The Tories were strong but not strong enough;
The Radicals were better—the toughest of the tough!
If there was a war, we would win over England.
We have better leaders, and we're fighting for our own land.
A lot of things happened through the years—
A lot of bloodshed, a lot of tears.
There was Lexington, Concord, and Bunker Hill.
If there is a war, guess who will win—*We will*!!!
Now we are through with all of Parliament's tyranny.
Our children have better futures; *We are free*!

—Liz Viola
(Eighth grader in 1988–1989)

Aware of their intentions to offer commentary in verse, I was ready. I thumbed through *Poems For All Occasions* and, *mirable dictu*, found exactly the right poem with which to respond:

### A Brief Thank-You

I want to acknowledge Jeff, Damon and Liz
for adding their part to this weekly poem biz.

They put rhymes together so we could remember
events that occurred this week in December.
Let's also thank Abe who came here today;
Mr. President, we learned from what you had to say.
Colonial diaries are now memory
(along with your voting against Loyalty).
Tonight at the concert, sweet music create.
That's it. No more rhymes except one—y'all are *great*!

—RMB
(From the apocryphal *Poems For All Occasions*, 1988)

## IMPACT OF THE TEACHER AS POET

A teacher rarely knows which particular words, gestures, actions, or examples stay with students. But I believe that the impact of the teacher as poet on my students during the school year was profound:

- From Day One, I was seen as a poet by my students. This allowed me to speak about poetry with more authority and authenticity.
- Poetry in many forms was presented throughout the school year, not just for one week or two.
- Through poetry, students had their school experiences chronicled, enhanced, reinterpreted, and, at times, raised to the level of legend.
- Students were empowered by my example to attempt new forms of poetry, to write parodies of famous poems, and to share their work with others in a safe community of writers.

## "TEACHER AS POET" CONCERNS

When I hear the term, "a teacher of writing," I imagine an individual who teaches writing by actually writing with his or her students, not unlike the basketball coach who shoots hoops with the team, or the music teacher who plays with the school band, or the art teacher who shares sketches and paintings with pupils. When I became "the teacher as poet," I discovered that by sharing my writing, I encouraged students to become better writers by providing them with examples of how to communicate effectively through the written word.

A major concern I had was whether my constant sharing was a positive thing for students. After all, I was a mature writer, fluent in many modes, blessed (cursed?) with a disposition for doggerel, and equipped with mature language arts skills. I wondered, *Will they be intimidated?* A conversation with a student helped clarify matters. He said, "When you write poems, Mr. B., it helps me with mine. In yours, you change your words around, and I try that, and it makes my poems go smoother. I get ideas from your writing."

Becoming a member of the community of poets in a classroom is a consuming yet rewarding experience. I had due dates, but they helped me to understand the demands on students' time. When I confessed, "Yes, I had the same problem with my poem," students perceived me as a colleague, one who shared their writing challenges. Whether it was an inconclusive ending, an ambiguous title, an underdeveloped theme, an inconsistent sequence, a weak image, or a missing modifier, when students had problems with their writing, they knew that when they talked with me "poet to poet," they were conversing with someone who had similar concerns.

Even my less-developed poems had value for students. They saw that I did not produce a great piece of writing every time, and they learned that their teacher needed to go through multiple drafts to make the meaning clear.

More than anything, I loved recycling the events and personalities of the classroom, enshrining in verse those unexpected occasions that kids seem to remember far longer than the past participle of work ("wrought") or the date of the Gadsden Purchase (1853). As a parting gift the end of the year, I compiled all of the weekly poems into a booklet and gave each student a copy of my no-longer-apocryphal *Poems For All Occasions*.

## LESSONS LEARNED

Throughout my teaching career I struggled constantly with the question, "How do I translate belief into action?" I always looked for ways to improve the presence and place of poetry in the classroom. But I was never in doubt about one central belief: poetry and kids go together.

Among the poetic lessons I learned were:

- Expose your students to a variety of poets and poetry to enhance their understanding of the world.
- Share with students your own poems (both early drafts and polished pieces), thereby providing powerful examples.
- Whatever happens to students in school during the year—and middle school is a place of infinite drama—can be recreated, reinterpreted, and referenced in poems that transform both mundane routines and bizarre events into humorous and memorable experiences.
- Invite a real poet into your class to share her or his work.
- Provide students with both the opportunity and the encouragement to compose poetry throughout the year.
- Have students select and publish some of their poems in class anthologies.

These lessons informed my teaching. If they resonate with you and your core beliefs regarding students and learning, I urge you to put them into action in your classroom. If you have different ideas about the proper place of poetry in the classroom, what are they, and how do you translate those beliefs into action?

Of course, you do not have to write a poem every week, as I did, to be successful at teaching poetry. But you may discover that an occasional poem created expressly for students will have a positive impact on them. When students relive school experiences through your verses, and when they hear their names embedded in poems that you write especially for them, they learn that poetry can speak to the moment.

## QUESTIONS FOR CONSIDERATION

As you consider your previous experiences with poetry, here are some questions that might assist you in identifying lessons you have already learned:

- Which poems do you remember from when you were a student? Which ones have stayed with you, and why?

- Which anthologies of poetry do you own? How often do you leaf through them?
- Are there certain lines of poetry lodged in your memory? Why did those combinations of words capture your imagination?
- Which poems can you recite from memory? Of these, which ones are appropriate for your classroom?
- Which poets, living or dead, speak to you? What do you know about their lives? What information about them can you share with students?

## CLOSING THOUGHTS

Through poetry, I connected with students by creating an inviting classroom in which I was an integral member of the community of writers. The more poems I shared, the more convinced I became that my efforts had a positive impact on student attitudes regarding the power of poetry to celebrate any occasion. I used verse to advance a philosophy of education that placed kids at the center of learning. A weekly poem composed in January 1985 captured my thoughts about teaching:

### The Atmosphere in the Room

One of the goals I set for myself
is the atmosphere in the room.
I work to create an environment where
my students are free to bloom.

September comes, all crisp and cool.
Posters of the past abound.
Yet to arrive are the circumstances
through which the year is found.

I set the stage and place the props—
couches, tables, chairs—
and bid the students enter in
with warm yet questioning stares.

Then to the task before us all—
of purpose, play, and poems,
of learning lines and making maps
of sending letters home.

The fall continues slowly as
the students settle in
to live, to lunch, to listen, to lounge,
to grimace and to grin.

Up above and all around
new posters accumulate,
marking moments as they pass
to cheer and celebrate.

As wheels on ice that slowly turn,
then catch and move ahead
so, too, the students grasp the days,
and so the mood is spread.

How far you've come from fall, my friends,
how far from seventh grade.
Your presence makes a difference,
and life is no charade.

Now that the room is working,
do you sense what we can gain
if we all work together
to enhance and to maintain?

Process, love, acknowledgment,
travel, trust, and care;
people, places, poetry,
a heady atmosphere.

The stage is set, the players act,
the drama does unfold.
We've half a year of sharing left:
what will the future hold?

—RMB

(From the apocryphal *Poems For All Occasions,* 1985)

# POETIC INTERLUDE NO. 2: INVENT A LINE

Select three or four short poems. Type them up, but leave out a specific line—the first, or the second, or the third, and so on.
Ask students to invent a line of poetry to replace the missing one.
Do this activity in class so students cannot look up the actual line

Two examples:

A.
Lives of great men all remind us
We can make our lives sublime,
And, departing, leave behind us

_____

(Henry Wadsworth Longfellow,
    "A Psalm of Life," 1839)

and:

B.
"Faith" is a fine Invention
When Gentlemen can see—
But Microscopes are prudent

_____

(Emily Dickinson, c. 1860)

Also, distribute poems with missing words and ask students to suggest a "best" word to fill in the blank and explain why. After a class discussion, share the actual missing words, and explore with your students what the author might have intended by using those specific words.

Here are the missing lines from the poems above:

A. "Footprints on the sands of time."
B. "In an Emergency."

*Part II*

# IN THE CLASSROOM

# Chapter Three

# Memorizing and Reciting

*This chapter describes memorization activities and assessment criteria for student recitations. Recollections by former students underscore the value of developing the skill of memorization.*

The biggest lesson learned from this 8th grade program was that it made me become a better public speaker. I don't know if you remember, but I would always become embarrassed whenever I spoke in front of others. These lessons enabled me to overcome those feelings and become confident with my public speaking. I owe that great accomplishment to poetry in 8th grade.

—Glenn Valentine
(Eighth grader in 1979–1980; e-mail communication, March 11, 2003)

Learning lines and saying same to peers
Can be unnerving.
Poise and pace and accuracy are what
The task's deserving.

—RMB

## WHY RECITE POEMS?

The skills of memorization and public speaking can be addressed through poetry recitation, a public performance in which no one can hide. Poetry recitation is a task that requires preparation and practice. Students either know the poem or they don't. Initially, many young people are shy when speaking before peers. Yet for two decades in a heterogeneous classroom, every student was required to recite, and most of them improved markedly as the year advanced. In the days leading up to Recitation Day, I observed students helping peers, coaching each other, offering encouragement, and prompting one another on difficult words and hard-to-learn lines. What at first seemed to be an individual assignment actually honed students' ability to collaborate with their peers.

Dan Rothermel (1996), in *Starting Points*, offers 17 reasons for challenging students through memorization (see Poetic Interlude No. 3). Rothermel cites self-discipline, the development of planning and organizational skills, and the habits of inquiry and diligence, among others. He also observes that "[r]eciting well is very difficult to fake" (p. 50).

I believe that the two most important reasons for engaging students in such a task may be to help them gain an understanding of the poem being recited and, simultaneously, to acquire a sense of comfort when speaking in front of others.

## IN THE CLASSROOM, PART ONE

I called Susanne Frische's name. She stood, smiled, and stepped confidently to the microphone. Eight students had recited; the rest awaited their turn. A few, those nearer the end of the list, still hoped that some unanticipated *deus ex machina* might put off the task to the following day.

Susanne, an accomplished flautist and captain of the field hockey team, had done well on four previous poetry recitations. Today, for her fifth recitation, she was presenting Edgar Allan Poe's "Alone," a poem unfamiliar to me. She selected the Poe poem, she told me later, because it spoke to her. I had a copy in front of me with which to assess accuracy during her recitation.

Susanne looked her classmates in the eye, smiled once again, took a deep breath, and began reciting:

### Alone

From childhood's hour I have not been
As others were; I have not seen
As others saw; I could not bring
My passions from a common spring.

Instantly the room fell silent. Four lines into the twenty-two-line poem, Susanne had everyone's rapt attention. Her delivery was impeccable; each word, each phrase, each syllable rang with conviction. As Susanne recited, time was suspended. Everyone was caught up in her sincerity, her credibility—she became the poem.

> From the same source I have not taken
> My sorrow; I could not awaken
> My heart to joy at the same tone;
> And all I loved, I loved alone.

Susanne neither paused nor hesitated. Seamlessly, words and lines poured out of her. We watched in awe and listened with admiration. To me, the moment remains magical.

> Then—in my childhood, in the dawn
> Of a most stormy life—was drawn
> From every depth of good and ill
> The mystery which binds me still:
> From the torrent, or the fountain,
> From the red cliff of the mountain,
> From the sun that round me rolled
> In its autumn tint of gold,
> From the lightning in the sky
> As it passed me flying by,
> From the thunder and the storm,
> And the cloud that took the form
> (When the rest of Heaven was blue)
> Of a demon in my view.

> —Edgar Allan Poe

When Susanne finished, her classmates and I responded with thunderous applause. Instead of waiting until the end of class, I immediately stood up and announced that Susanne's performance was the best eighth-grade poetry recitation I ever heard. I awarded her an A+ on the spot—the first I had ever given. Even today, more than two decades later, Susanne's recitation shines brightly in memory. In her performance, I encountered the majesty that middle school students can bring to seemingly dry words on a page.

Susanne's outstanding presentation of Poe's "Alone" came about because she understood the message, internalized the words, and, as she recited, literally became the poem. But then, Susanne had selected this
poem on her own, spent a week committing the lines to memory, completed four recitations prior to this one, and watched as her peers attempted, with various degrees of accomplishment, to master verses of
their own. As a member of a community of learners engaged in skill development, Susanne rose to the occasion.

Years afterward, I asked Susanne, now a speech pathologist on Long Island and the mother of two girls, what she remembered about reciting
Poe's "Alone." In an e-mail in which she typed out the entire poem from
memory, Susanne responded:

> Within a couple of days of talking to you the whole poem came back to me and
> I found myself reciting it around the house. I did identify with the words of that
> Poe poem as a kid. My mom said I was born 21 . . . so by the time I was in 8th
> grade I was an old lady compared to some of my peers. I guess I felt it. I was
> never an English person. Math/science was my thing. I took calculus, cogni-
> tive science, some research classes . . . as electives in college, and I also took
> poetry because I learned to love it in your class. I, however, was never really
> confident in my abilities w/ English/Language Arts, and I took my college po-
> etry class Pass/Fail. I have always regretted it because I got an A. . . . Language
> is an amazing thing. It's what keeps us from being lonely, it helps people un-
> derstand who we are and what we want, its infinite combinations allow us to
> come up with novel ideas and share them with others. It's the most powerful
> tool a human being can have. I related to the Poe poem on an emotional level,
> and when that happens, the spoken words take on a life of their own. They are
> no longer just letters on a white page, they are part of the human experience.

—Susanne Frische
(Eighth grader in 1980–1981; e-mail communications,
March 14, 2003 and May 1, 2005)

## ASSERTIONS ABOUT MEMORIZING AND RECITING

Based on two decades' experience of asking middle school students to
memorize and recite poems, I formulated the following seven assertions
to guide my classroom practice. I believe that:

- All students can memorize, and asking them to do so is an appropriate request.
- Students who recite poems on a regular basis develop public speaking skills such as eye contact, poise, and enunciation, and these skills improve over time.
- When students are given choice of poems to memorize, they become more invested in the task and consequently perform better.
- Students are inspired by accomplished presenters, especially their peers.
- Students should be given opportunities to recite for audiences beyond the classroom.
- Teachers who memorize and recite along with their students provide powerful modeling.
- Volume + Variety = Fluency (the more poems a student recites, and the more different kinds of poems a student memorizes, the better at recitation the student becomes).

*Question*: If these are the beliefs, what are the appropriate, ensuing actions? What happens in a classroom when these assertions are present?


## DEADLINES: POEMS AND THE OLYMPICS

Holding up a colorful, handmade sign on Day Three of the school year, I asked the class, "Why is reciting a poem like competing in the Olympic Games?"

Silence. Then a hand.

"Because you have to perform in public?" suggested Allison.

"Good answer. Why else?" I waited. Students looked intently at the sign, which spelled out the word "POEMS" in capital letters. The Olympic symbol, a set of five interlocking rings, replaced the letter "o" in "POEMS."

"Because you have to do your best?" offered Nick.

"Another good answer," I replied. "Who else has a response?"

More silence, and then another hand.

"Because both are difficult to do?" said Max.

"Also a good answer, and each answer is absolutely correct. However," I continued, displaying the sign one more time, "there is another way in which reciting a poem is like competing in the Olympic Games."

Students studied the sign again.

"Allison," I asked, "who is your favorite Olympic athlete?" Allison mentioned a gymnastics superstar; several other girls nodded in vigorous assent.

"Great," I replied. "Now, suppose at the next Olympics, when her name is called to do the floor exercise, if she said to the judge, 'I'm almost ready but I need one more day to practice my routine,' what would the judge say back to her?"

In the ensuing discussion, most students agreed that, having had ample time to prepare, a gymnast needed to be ready when called.

"So, how is reciting a poem like being in the Olympics?" I asked again, holding up the sign one more time.

"I get it," said Nick.

"What did you get, Nick?" I asked. "Please explain it to the class." And he did.

I posted the "Poems/Olympics" sign on the classroom wall in a prominent location and referred to it at every subsequent recitation, often repeating Nick's explanation that "you have to be ready when your name is called." When students encounter an inflexible deadline, they learn to plan ahead, budget their time, and organize their lives: "I'd better get busy. I've only got five days to learn this."

## THE IMPORTANCE OF RITUALS

During the 20 years that I asked students to memorize and recite poems in my heterogeneously grouped classroom, all students succeeded at this task, although some took longer than others to master their fear of public speaking. Few consistently reached the combination of passion and excellence demonstrated by Susanne, but that was not my goal. My aim was to have poetry recitations become a familiar ritual to students.

Rituals are important; their significance cannot be overstated when working with young adolescents who take comfort in the familiarity, the repetitiveness, and the predictability of certain routines. Structure and consistency enhance learning. Deadlines motivate individuals and produce results.

When, over and over again, students sign up to recite a poem, or go to the library to find a poem to memorize, or confront the challenge of reciting in front of their peers, they develop a sense of competency as they learn from the experience: "Oh, yes, I've done this before. I know what to do."

## FIRST POETRY RECITATION

For the first poetry memorization, assigned on Day Two of the school year, I distributed a handout containing six poems: "The Road Not Taken" by Robert Frost, "Ozymandius" by Percy Bysshe Shelley, "I Tramp a Perpetual Journey" by Walt Whitman, "Opportunity" by Berton Braley, "Sea Fever" by John Masefield, and "The First Day." Students chose one poem to memorize and recite the following week. Giving students choice is important, since they gravitate toward poems that they understand, making the task seem easier. Also, I scheduled the recitation so that students had five school days plus a weekend to memorize their poems. I wanted students to have every advantage and to maximize their chances for success.

When selecting poems for students to memorize, I drew from the canon in order to expose pupils to classic poetry. I also recycled three poems from my opening day program. With two exceptions, each poem was 16 lines or more (not including the title). This particular set of six poems worked well for me and for my students. Other teachers would select different verses. I recommend that you offer a range of poems that speak to you, your students, and your community.

Poets have created all kinds of poems suitable for memorization and recitation. Here are a few examples:

- Pat Mora's "Immigrants" (composed in both English and Spanish) addresses the concerns of new citizens.
- Janet Wong's "Noise" describes the way she was teased by classmates in school.
- "We Real Cool" by Gwendolyn Brooks captures the attitudes of some young adolescents.
- "All I Can Think About" by April Halprin Wayland celebrates adolescent obsession with osculation.
- Gary Soto's "Saturday at the Canal" voices the longing that some teens have to leave home for better pastures.

- Naomi Shihab Nye's "Rain" connects youth and adulthood in disturbing ways.
- Louise Glück's "Memoir" resonates with eighth graders who seek greater meaning in their lives.

How do you find poems such as these? Look in your language arts textbook. Go to the library and start leafing through poetry anthologies. Talk with the librarian. Head for the poetry section of your local bookstore. Ask other language arts teachers for recommendations. Ask your parents, friends, siblings, and neighbors about their favorite poems. A wealth of poems suitable for recitation awaits.

My point here is that your focus should not be on which poems students will recite (although your selections do become relevant to students); rather, your attention should be on the process of helping students develop public speaking skills by requiring several poetry memorizations throughout the school year.

Instructions for the first recitation:

---

*English 8 - Team 8-1*          *NAME:* _____
*September 9*                   *R. Burkhardt*

      *Poetry Recitation No. 1—Due Thursday, September 15*

*Select one of the following six poems*—"I Tramp a Perpetual Journey," "Opportunity," "Ozymandius," "The Road Not Taken," "Sea Fever," or "The First Day"—*and be prepared to recite this poem from memory in class on Thursday, September 15.*

---

After distributing a handout with the complete text of the six poems, we read aloud and discussed each poem so that students became familiar with all of them. This enabled them to select the poem with which they were most comfortable. John Masefield's "Sea Fever," apparently the shortest at 12 lines (because of the way I typed it), was always popular with students. But appearances can be deceiving. Masefield used 180 words to describe his maritime mania, and so, by word count, his poem actually is the longest of the six.

Also, "Sea Fever" attracted many students because of its easy rhymes and wonderful description of something they knew well—the changing moods of the sea. (Our middle school was situated two miles from Long Island Sound, and students went to the beach all the time.) Year after year, I counted on many pupils to select "Sea Fever." And, year after year, many of them did. I was delighted; the teacher as poet had something up his sleeve.

## JOURNAL ENTRIES

In my language arts classes, every student kept an English journal in which he or she wrote a weekly entry related to classroom activities. These journal entries provided me with insights into how well students understood the lessons I taught.

As homework on the day that I distributed the six poems for Recitation No. 1, I also assigned a journal entry, "Memorizing My Poem," in which students were asked to respond to three questions:

a. What poem did you select to memorize, and why?
b. What strategies are you using to memorize it?
c. What else do you have to say?

One purpose was to have students reflect on the task of memorization. Another was to remind them of the task ahead—each had to choose a poem to memorize and then recite in class five days hence.

The following day I invited students to share excerpts from their journal entries. As they read aloud, other students listened attentively, reaffirmed that they were not alone in this common struggle to master 16 lines of verse. Also, by hearing numerous peer examples over time, students learned the parameters and possibilities of journal entry responses.

Jenny's unvarnished entry was typical:

a. I choose the poem Leaves of Grass written by Walt Whitman because I liked his choice of wording he picked to include in his writting.

   b. When I sit down to memorize or learn something in a short amount of time I'll divide it into small sections. In this case, memorizing a poem, I'm breaking the poem into small sections and repeating out loud 4 or 5 times untill I know it with out looking at the words. When I accomplish a section I'll continue the rest of the poem untill it's complete and reread it as a whole poem untill I feel I have memorized it enough.

—Jenny Furano
(Eighth grader in 1994–1995)

Ben shared the following:

a. After reading every poem you selected, I chose The Road Not Taken by Robert Frost to memorize and recite. When I read this poem I thought it was the best one. I liked it because first, it is very well written and second: I really liked how Frost used a metaphor of a simple path in the forest as a path in his life. "I took the one less traveled by, and that made all the difference," Frost wrote. I think it has to do with his life, meaning that he was unique in taking his own path in life, doing what he and only he wanted to do. In other words, not following everyone else but he wanted to be different. Anyway, I really enjoyed it.

   b. My strategies for memorizing this poem will be one sentence at a time, (or phrase), not line. I wouldn't memorize a line at a time because memorizing a part of a sentence is difficult for me. I'll do a stanza or two each night until I can read it. My strategy for reciting it is to try not to be nervous and just concentrate.

—Ben Kalb
(Eighth grader in 1994–1995)

Reading through the journal entries, I learned how students memorized their poems. I also encountered differing levels of interpretation present in the class. Several students provided incidental information when voluntarily responding to Question "c," which invited students to share whatever was on their minds.

In her journal, Jenny added:

c. I'm happy to be reading poetry this year and sharing it to the class. Most teachers may spend a few days teaching their class poetry, but being able to learn new poetry each day and sharing it to the class is very fun. It's a good way to be fermiller with all sorts of different forms of writting not just stories.

—Jenny Furano
(Eighth grader in 1994–1995)

Ben let me know that:

c. I learned two words—you can probably guess which ones they are—and used them in this EJ [entry]. *Stanza* and *metaphor*. I've come across many metaphors but I've never known what they were called so I asked my [older] sister. Oh, by the way, I really hate it when people say: "Look it up" (when you ask them what a word means).

— Ben Kalb
(Eighth grader in 1994–1995)

As a result of reading countless journal entries over the years, I gradually refined my teaching techniques for the better, using student feedback as coaching for my teaching.

## RECITATION LEAD-UP ACTIVITIES

Three days prior to the first recitation, I posted a sign-up sheet to remind students of the pending task. Some students wanted to get it over with early, others preferred reciting nearer to the end so as to have more time to practice, and still others attempted to postpone the inevitable by praying to the poetry muse that not all 24 recitations would be completed in one class period. I always signed up to recite first.

At the 2003 National Middle School Association conference, keynote speaker Dr. Jocelyn Elders stated, "You can't be what you can't see." I agree. So, two days before recitations, I presented two deliberately contrasting styles of poetic delivery. First, I recited "Sea Fever" flawlessly, looking each student in the eye, speaking with passion and conviction, and animating Masefield's measured cadences to the best of my ability— when you say the same poem year after year, you become very familiar with the lines. Composed in 1902, "Sea Fever" is a wonderful poem for students to memorize:

### Sea Fever

I must go down to the seas again,
    to the lonely sea and the sky,
And all I ask is a tall ship
    and a star to steer her by,

And the wheel's kick and the wind's song
　　and the white sail's shaking,
And a gray mist on the sea's face
　　and a gray dawn breaking.

I must go down to the seas again,
　　for the call of the running tide
Is a wild call and a clear call
　　that may not be denied;
And all I ask is a windy day
　　with the white clouds flying,
And the flung spray and the blown spume,
　　and the seagulls crying.

I must go down to the seas again,
　　to the vagrant gypsy life,
To the gull's way and the whale's way
　　where the wind's like a whetted knife;
And all I ask is a merry yarn
　　from a laughing fellow-rover,
And quiet sleep and a sweet dream
　　when the long trick's over.

—John Masefield

Then I offered a second rendition, this time mumbling the words hesitantly while staring blankly at the ceiling, swaying from side to side as if on the deck of a rolling ship, deliberately transposing words and lines (". . . and the sea's kick, and the wheel's face . . ."), pausing and pondering, muttering *I know it. I know it. What's the line? I know it. Let me think, . . .* all the while looking as if I were about to make a mad dash for the exit. My students' laughter told me that they got the point—there are appropriate and inappropriate ways to deliver lines of poetry.

Finally, I asked the class to reflect on my two presentations of "Sea Fever" and suggest performance assessment criteria for poetry recitations, which I listed on the chalkboard. Every year that I did this exercise, students came up with essentially the same items:

- *Accuracy* (Did the reciter say all the words in the correct sequence?)
- *Poise* (Did he or she exhibit confidence while reciting?)

- *Expression* (Did the speaker bring the lines to life and speak with appropriate passion?)
- *Pace* (Was the delivery measured and seamless?)
- *Volume* (Did the speaker use appropriate voice dynamics?)
- *Pronunciation* (Were the words pronounced correctly?)
- *Eye contact* (Did the speaker look the audience in the eye?)

We discussed each of the criteria, underscoring their significance and fleshing out nuances. I let students know that I would use a stopwatch to time their delivery; most 16-line poems can be recited effectively in 60 seconds or less. Students left class that day with a clear understanding of how their recitations would be evaluated. More important, they had ownership of the evaluation process because they participated in establishing the criteria.

The day before the first recitation I distributed an assessment form to each student (see figure 3.1), instructing them to complete the top section and to review the criteria one more time.

| Student _____ Period ____ Date _____ Mem. # _____ | |
|---|---|
| Title of poem _____ | |
| Author _____ | |
| **Recitation Criteria** | |
| *Accuracy* | |
| *Expression* | |
| *Eye Contact* | |
| *Poise* | |
| *Pace* | |
| *Volume* | |
| *Pronunciation* | |
| *Overall Presentation* | |
| *Other Comments* | |
| | Grade: _____ |

**Figure 3.1.   Poetry Recitation Assessment Form, Single Poem**

After collecting and organizing the forms for the following day, I informed students that everyone would begin with an A, and their grade would descend, depending on how distant from the agreed-upon criteria their recitation was. I also announced that if a student were absent on Recitation Day, he or she would be expected to recite the very next day.

## RECITATION DAY

On Recitation Day, kids came into class buzzing with excitement, and we got right to the task at hand. I always recited first, both to establish a serious tone in the classroom and to demonstrate appropriate presentation skills. Because students had already signed up, the order in which they were to recite was known to all.

Using a cassette tape recorder and a microphone mounted on an adjustable stand, I recorded each student's recitation. The microphone provided students with a point of focus while reciting and made the experience even more real for them. Recording also allowed me to review a student's performance for accuracy and, by comparing tapes from early in the fall with those recorded later in the year, to assess growth.

Early in the year, it was not unusual for a student to begin reciting, miss a word, and start again. If a student became stuck at a particular point in the poem, I offered a one- or two-word prompt; this enabled the student to regain composure and continue reciting. Following each recitation, the class acknowledged the reciter with polite applause.

For me, teaching was never about grades. I was required to give them, and I did so, but I was far more interested in students demonstrating growth, competence, improvement, responsibility, and mastery by performing real tasks such as reciting poems. Using check marks and plus signs as students performed, I scribbled brief comments on each assessment form, noting which criteria had been met and which hadn't. As a student delivered the last line of a poem, I entered a performance grade.

At the end of class, I offered general observations and coaching based on what I had seen, sometimes praising specific students for positive aspects of their performances. After class, I approached certain students privately, either to coach, console, or compliment them. If a responsible student completely messed up the recitation, I allowed him or her to recite the following day, but to be fair to the others, that student began with a grade of B.

## "C FEVER"

Invariably, the first recitations of the school year were not as polished as those that came later and, on the whole, were lacking in finesse. A few students might receive grades of B or B-minus, but the vast majority, who the previous spring had been earning As as seventh graders, were now, understandably, disappointed to receive a C or worse during the first week of eighth grade. And while I understood that for many students this was a first attempt at public speaking, I saw no reason to reward kids with inflated grades for substandard recitations. And they complained.

Inspired by their grumblings, I went home and, using John Masefield's "Sea Fever" as a model, composed a poem designed to let students know that I understood their concerns about their less than inspiring recitations. The next day, I began class by telling a whopping fib.

"Last night," I prevaricated, "I was looking through my copy of *Poems For All Occasions*, and wouldn't you know it—I found a poem that seems just right for today's class. It's called 'C Fever.' Let me share it with you."

I wrote the poem's title on the chalkboard, waited for the inevitable groans, then recited all three verses, acting them out dramatically and echoing some of the more egregious behaviors of the previous day: wobbly knees, blank stare, and breaking voice as I rocked back and forth.

**C Fever**
*(with sincere apologies to John Masefield)*

My grade goes down to the C's again, to the lowly C's and the D's,
And all I ask is memory, and an end to knocking knees.
And the first line of the first verse and my knees still shaking,
And the second line, and it's getting worse, and my voice now breaking.

My grade goes down to the C's again, for the call to recite a poem
Is a clear call and a fearful call that sets my mouth afoam;
And the clenched hand and the blank stare while I'm up here dying,
And the missed word and the blown line and the fear of crying.

My grade goes down to the C's again, where the grades are below C level,
To the fool's way and the mumbler's way—recitations are works of the Devil!
And all I ask is a straight face from a laughing poetry lover,
And a quiet room and polite applause when my long task's over.

—RMB

(From the apocryphal *Poems For All Occasions,* 1981)

"C Fever" invited students to chuckle at their own inadequacies; they instantly recognized themselves in a parody of the classic poem many had struggled with just 24 hours earlier. They also appreciated the fact that their teacher understood their distress. My exaggerated performance, and the resulting laughter, assuaged their academic distress.

## SECOND POETRY RECITATION

Recitation No. 2, scheduled one week after the first, consisted of a set of seven short poems, each four to eight lines. Students selected two or three poems and then recited a minimum total of 16 lines (not including title and author). Each poem had to be recited completely—I did not allow partial verses.

| *Recitation No. 2—Select 16+ lines* | | |
| --- | --- | --- |
| **Poem** | **Poet** | **Lines** |
| *Recollection* | Frances Cornford | 8 |
| *Fire and Ice* | Robert Frost | 8 |
| *Divinest Sense* | Emily Dickinson | 8 |
| *The Golf Links* | Sara N. Cleghorn | 4 |
| *Fog* | Carl Sandburg | 6 |
| *The Pasture* | Robert Frost | 8 |
| *Requiem* | Robert Louis Stevenson | 8 |

Some students who struggled with a "long" poem during the first memorization discovered that reciting two or three shorter poems seemed a much easier task. As before, we read aloud and discussed each poem in class. The sign-up sheet was again posted three days in advance. The day before recitations, each student filled out a slightly revised assessment form (see figure 3.2), and again we discussed the seven performance criteria.

| Student _____ Period ____ Date _____ Mem. # ____ | | | |
|---|---|---|---|
| Titles/authors of poems | | | |
| _____ | | | |
| _____ | | | |
| _____ | | | |
| _____ | | | |
| **Recitation Criteria** | **Poem 1** | **Poem 2** | **Poem 3** |
| *Accuracy* | | | |
| *Expression* | | | |
| *Eye Contact* | | | |
| *Poise* | | | |
| *Pace* | | | |
| *Volume* | | | |
| *Pronunciation* | | | |
| *Overall Presentation* | | | |
| *Other Comments* | | | |
| | | | Grade: _____ |

**Figure 3.2.    Poetry Recitation Assessment Form, Multiple Poems**

"Because you now are veterans," I informed students, "I will expect more of you on future recitations. The same caliber performance on Recitation No. 2 as on Recitation No. 1 will earn a lower grade." And in this way I continued to raise the bar all year long. Not surprisingly, I noticed steady improvement in public speaking skills as the students, now "veterans," grew more comfortable with the task of reciting poems in public.

## THIRD POETRY RECITATION

For the third poetry recitation of the year, scheduled two weeks after Recitation No. 2, students selected either one long poem (16+ lines), or 16+ lines from a set of five short poems. Most students based their choice on previous experience—were they more comfortable committing a longer poem to memory, or did they perform better reciting two or three shorter poems? In either case, all students memorized at least 16 lines of poetry.

| *Recitation No. 3—Short or Long?* | | |
|---|---|---|
| **Poem** | **Poet** | **Lines** |
| *Signatures* | Candace T. Stevenson | 16 |
| *I Hear America Singing* | Walt Whitman | 16 |
| | | |
| *Resumé* | Dorothy Parker | 4 |
| *Changing the Wheel* | Bertolt Brecht | 5 |
| *Old Men* | Ogden Nash | 6 |
| *Grass* | Carl Sandburg | 9 |
| *The Eagle* | Alfred, Lord Tennyson | 6 |

A follow-up journal assignment asked students to explain which they preferred—memorizing one long poem or several short poems. Their explanations underscored the importance of giving students choice when selecting poems to recite.

## FOURTH POETRY RECITATION AND BEYOND

For the fourth recitation of the year and those that followed, students had to find a poem on their own to memorize. They went to the school library and perused poetry anthologies in search of verse; they examined my classroom collection of poetry books, and they leafed through anthologies at home. I required only that the poem (or poems) be substantive (16+ lines) and worthwhile (a judgment call, but one that allowed me to reject choices such as "Twinkle, Twinkle, Little Star" or other, all too familiar, verses). Students had to provide a copy of their poem at least three days before the recitation. This requirement ensured that each student actually selected a poem to recite with sufficient time remaining in which to memorize it. I used my copy of the student's poem for prompting if he or she faltered while reciting. In all, we did ten recitations during the school year, one or two a month from September to March.

## CELEBRATING RECITATIONS THROUGH POETRY

One December when I had little else to do (a circumstance shared, I am sure, by many a language arts teacher), I reflected on what occurred in class that day during our fifth poetry recitation. Most students performed well. A few ambitious kids created a breakthrough by reciting, not classics from the canon, but rather their own original poems or verses authored by classmates.

That evening I furiously flipped through my well-worn copy of *Poems For All Occasions*, seeking just the right verse for the morrow. Lo and behold, I found such a poem and shared it in class the next day to honor my students' progress as reciters and to celebrate what five pioneer students had done (*they are cited in lines 3 and 4 of the second stanza*):

### Observations on Recitations

I watched my students share their poems
and marveled at their youthful poise,
with confidence reciting rhymes,
communicating sorrows, joys.

I heard my students say their poems:
Robert Frost, Shel Silverstein,
and Gallis, too, and Eldridge, France,
Forster, Blake, and one of mine.

I marveled as they read their poems,
at how expressively they spoke,
and with each calm delivery,
increasingly my pride awoke.

And when they finished saying poems
(Recitation 5 this year)
I realized they had achieved
the skill of speaking without fear.

Teachers plan, then dream and worry
how a lesson will unfold.
Friday afternoon our class
was poetry, alive and bold.

—RMB
(From the apocryphal *Poems For All Occasions,* 1983)

Students relished hearing their names in the weekly poems, and they appreciated the compliments embedded in the verses. Additionally, through such poems I portrayed the tasks of memorizing and reciting in a positive manner.

"Stopping By Woods On A Snowy Evening" became part of every school year; many students opted to memorize it. When Frank Kish stood up to recite Frost's classic one cold winter day, it became instantly clear to the rest of us that he was not at all prepared. His transpositions of words and lines rendered Frost's verse almost unrecognizable, inspiring the following tribute which I located, much to my delight, in my tattered copy of *Poems For All Occasions*. The next day I read it to the class, much to Frank's delight:

### Remembering Frank Kish After Recitation Tuesday

Whose house this is I know, I think.
His woods are in the village, inc.
He will not woods me seeing here
To snow his stopwatch filling drink.

My little farm must think it horse
To house without a stop, of course
Between the evening and the dark
The frozen wood lake of remorse.

He bells his some a harness give
To shake if there is ask or live.
The only other sweep's the view
Of frozen sounds and woods I driv-.

The dark is promise, lovely, too,
But I sleep deep to keep to you,
And miles before I go—I'm through,
And miles before I go—I'm through.

—RMB
(from the apocryphal *Poems For All Occasions,* 1987)

Eighteen years later, Frank cheerfully informed me:

I love the poem you wrote about me. I show it to everybody. I think it was one of your finest that year. Ha ha ha.

—Frank Kish
(E-mail communication, April 28, 2005)

## RECITATION STRATEGIES

The strategy of assigning one long poem for the first poetry recitation was intentional on my part. I knew that I was asking a lot of students at the beginning of the school year, but I wanted to set high expectations. Most struggled valiantly to master all seven assessment criteria simultaneously, and most fell somewhat short of the mark. When they did Recitation No. 2 and were given choice among several short poems, many students found it an easier task; it was their second experience reciting, and to many students, the shorter poems seemed less intimidating. The third memorization, in which students could recite either one long or several short poems, seemed easier still. By the time we reached the fourth recitation, most students were comfortable with the task. Because I structured recitations so that the task seemed progressively easier, and because I provided choice throughout, students were able to achieve success gradually and on their own terms.

As pupils learned how to memorize, as they became familiar with the recitation ritual and gradually relaxed, as they saw peers improve over time, and as they watched me recite, they gained more confidence with the most difficult aspect of the task—performing in front of peers. Also, by listening to other students recite a wide variety of verse, they were constantly exposed to a diverse range of poems and poets; this enhanced their appreciation for poetry.

Because students chose their own poems starting with Recitation No. 4, they recited a far greater range of poetry than I could have provided. They memorized the usual suspects from Shel Silverstein and Jack Prelutsky as well as reciting less familiar poems by poets such as Ogden Nash, Langston Hughes, Sara Teasdale, Henry Wadsworth Longfellow, Emily Dickinson, and A. A. Milne. David Ostrander chose Edgar Allan Poe's "El Dorado" and delighted in it. I would not have selected that 24-line verse for students to recite (its archaic opening, "Gaily bedight . . ." is not typically appreciated by young adolescents), but we all gained from David's choice.

## STUDENT PERSPECTIVES

Memories of recitations stayed with students for years afterwards, and their reflections are instructive. One eighth grader noted at the time, "I did not like to speak in front of people I know because I got embarrassed. However, after doing a few poetry recitations, I have the hang of it." Another commented, "I like being able to pick my own poem because I get to do something that I like."

Upon reflection, many students realized the important lessons they had learned. Twenty-three years later, Glenn remembered supporting his friends:

> All I can remember about class recital is that we all wanted to have our friends finish their poems without messing them up, we kind of urged each other on. There was also a sense of accomplishment when you were able to recite your poems without any mistakes and were able to deliver them in the proper tempo and feeling.
>
> —Glenn Valentine
> (E-mail communication, March 11, 2003)

Danny, one of Glenn's classmates, recalled sweaty palms as well as the life skills he acquired through recitations:

> Memorizing and reciting poetry was frightening and fun, nerve racking and exciting and a lot more. The first time you stand in front of your peers and are required to do something you might not like and may not be good at is quite a feeling. The way you handle that situation is what separates you from everyone else. My palms were sweaty, my mouth dry yet I was able to do it. I was able to do it!!! A teacher can do many things for their students, they can teach them how to read and write, how to add and subtract and how to apply physics and chemistry, but can they bridge the gap from classroom to everyday life? I believe this was one of the few times in my early education that a lesson made me better prepared for life outside the classroom . . . I still apply the techniques of dealing with the nervousness and excitement in my business dealings every day.
>
> —Danny Smith
> (E-mail communication, March 20, 2003)

Danny also spoke about the fears that he had to confront when reciting:

> The biggest fear for all students I would imagine was looking bad in front of their friends. I had already made myself look dopey in front of my best friend, so the classroom was less intimidating. The hardest part of reciting was getting the words to sound less like an assignment and more like I knew

what the poet was trying to say. I always felt as if the words were stiff and boring (coming from my mouth), or I was in a rush to get to the end. A strong knowledge of what the poet was trying to say would give the student the power to recite the poem with confidence.

—Danny Smith
(E-mail communication, March 20, 2003)

Recalling the torture of listening to unprepared students and the pleasure of appreciating well-rehearsed recitations, Danny also observed:

For the kids that gave no effort, it was like the drill at the dentist. I'd feel sorry for them and want to be a bit cruel as well (it's easy to want to make fun of others in 8th grade). I thought that they skated through an assignment while I had my dad busting my chops to get it right, so I was probably a little mad, too. For the kids that were exceptional, I was excited and a bit amazed. Not only did they have the memory to recite the correct words, but they had an understanding of the ideas of the poet, and the poise to make it sound wonderful.

—Danny Smith
(E-mail communication, March 20, 2003)

Eighteen years after he left eighth grade, Jay Urgese shared his thoughts about being asked to memorize and recite poems:

I remember getting up in front of the entire class and reciting poems by Robert Frost, concentrating and enunciating the words clearly and expressing the words in proper tone. That experience is something I hope every student has a chance to have and is something I will never forget. In the real world everybody, no matter what their lot in life, will have to speak in front of people.

—Jay Urgese
(E-mail communication, February 22, 2003)

Aurelie, an eighth grader in 1990–1991, enjoyed memorizing and reciting poems, and she reflected on that enjoyment 12 years later:

I enjoyed the poem recitations more than any other assignment because it was something I could do while on the bus, out with my friends, at the beach, whenever I had a free moment. I would carry my poem around in my pocket, and the memorization never required anything else. And it was always something to think about when I had the chance. And the thing is, those poems always stuck in my brain long after the recitation. I can still recite "My father's friend came once to tea. . . ." At the end of the year I had 20 or so poems under my belt, in my repertoire, if you will.

What was most valuable for me was the melodic enunciation. I remember the first time we had to recite (my poem was the one about going back to the sea again). Many students emphasized certain words in that same predictable singsong way. You told us how to convey it better orally, and that was something I tried so hard to do every time. And I still do that in presentations and such, or reading aloud. And I always think about all the poor people out there who never recited a poem in front of a class of their peers. It made me a better speaker, and a better performer.

—Aurelie Shapiro
(E-mail communication, March 27, 2003)

## GUIDELINES

The recitation strategies and activities suggested here represent my best efforts to put the seven assertions about poetry into practice. I also found the following guidelines helpful:

- Discuss and establish with your students specific assessment criteria for evaluating recitations, then use the criteria consistently.
- Post a sign-up sheet and invite students to pick their own time slots for recitations. This encourages personal responsibility; students make a commitment when they sign their names, and the act of signing up reminds each student of the pending task.
- Distribute an assessment form to each student the day before the recitation, both to signal kids about the task ahead and to have them handle the administrative responsibility of completing it.
- Remind students frequently about an upcoming recitation in the days preceding it. Middle school kids tend to forget things, and a poetry recitation might not be the most important item on their minds. Don't leave them unaware; do something in class every day as a red flag, a clear signal that they will soon be standing in front of the class, reciting a poem.
- Always recite first. Set a positive example for your students.

- Have students recite one after the other, without interruption. Complete all the recitations in one class period.
- After the first three recitations, have students select their own poems to recite. When students go to the school library in search of poems to recite, they learn that the library has more than just novels, newspapers, and magazines. They learn about the shelves of poetry anthologies and poetry books.

## SUGGESTIONS

Here are some activities that may enhance the recitation experience for students:

- *Duo or Dialogue*: Have pairs of students learn the same poem and recite it as a duo or dialogue (for this exercise, the poem needs to be substantially longer than 16 lines).
- *Repetition*: If you schedule 10 recitations during the year, you can allow students to repeat a poem recited earlier. This enables both student and teacher to see growth over time.
- *Reading From Text*: On the eight or ninth recitation, let students actually read a poem aloud from text, without having to memorize it. Tell them that since they will have the words in front of them, performance criteria of delivery, expression, and speaking ability count significantly more than accuracy.
- *Confronting Fear*: Read to your students Danny Smith's memory of his "biggest fear" (see pages 58–59) to let them know that they are not alone, that other students before them have coped with recitations, and that "a strong knowledge of what the poet [is] trying to say" can give students "the power to recite the poem with confidence."
- *Recording*: Tape record students as they recite. The tape allows you to assess accuracy at a later date. Also, you can measure a student's growth over time as his or her voice becomes more confident. Be advised, however, that kids often say the darndest things. Brynna Connolly, in a moment of complete forgetfulness, muttered a scatological epithet to herself, *sotto voce,* when she couldn't remember a line. We all heard it, and it's on tape.

- *Props and Gestures*: Encourage students to use appropriate gestures to accentuate words and lines of their poems and to employ props to enhance the visual appeal of their recitations. In late fall, Jeannie Vallely and Dawn Trettner co-recited Tom Hood's *November* and, as a visual aid, gathered dried oak leaves from the school parking lot earlier that morning and tossed them about the classroom as they recited.
- *Encouragement*: When students perform badly, and some will, reassure them that you know that they will improve with practice, and that one poor recitation is not the end of the world. After the very first recitation, read "C Fever" to your students (if you do, it is a good idea to familiarize them in advance with Masefield's original so they can more fully appreciate the parody).
- *One Poem for All*: Later in the year, have every student learn the same poem, one selected for its significance. For example, the message of Emma Lazarus's "The New Colossus" ("Give me your tired, your poor . . .") is a significant part of our American heritage, something with which every student should be familiar.

One year, after students memorized Lazarus's poem, I looked through my battered copy of *Poems For All Occasions* and discovered a brand new version, which I read aloud to the class:

### The New Reciters
*(with apologies to Emma Lazarus)*

Unlike the brazen students of years past
With bellowing voice bombarding halls with noise,
Here at our orange lockers now stand boys
And girls who say their poems a bit too fast,
Like unchained lightning. They are classed
As Team 8-I. They love computer toys
Like World Wide Web. Their wild eyes show joys
When hair-ridged heads appear 'neath sporting hats.
"Keep, Mr. B., your storied poems," they cry
With silly lips. "Give us your Sandburg, your Frost,
Your Jack Prelutsky, Shel Silverstein. We'll try.
The wretched refuse to hear, but at what cost?
Send these, the poemless, verses tossed, too shy—
I say my poem inside the classroom, lost."

—RMB
(From the apocryphal *Poems For All Occasions,* 1985)

## IN THE CLASSROOM, PART TWO

Public speaking does not necessarily come easily to young adolescents; they need multiple experiences with it before they achieve mastery. However, students do rise to the occasion brilliantly, providing both classmates and teachers with memorable examples of competence and courage. Following in Susanne's footsteps, four students—Katie, Érica, Andrea, and Nancy—delivered memorable recitations ranging from the alpha to the omega.

During the spring of 1996, two capable students, Érica Piteo and Katie Joos, put on such polished performances, complete with gestures, props, body language, and audience participation, that students in other classes demanded to see them in action. Katie moved animatedly about the classroom as she exuberantly recited all 44 lines of Shel Silverstein's "The Unicorn," grinning broadly each time she mentioned the "humpy bumpy camels."

When her turn came, Érica became a storyteller. Instead of standing in front of class as was our practice, she sat informally in a chair and recited a lengthy poem about a mother and her children. Érica invited classmates to clap rhythmically as she slapped her thighs to the beat of the poem; before long, the entire class was caught up in a joyous celebration of rhyme and rhythm. Both Érica and Katie earned standing ovations from their peers. Their performances were, in two words, sheer poetry.

In 1983, for her seventh poetry recitation, Andrea Dicks decided to memorize all 129 lines of Henry Wadsworth Longfellow's "Paul Revere's Ride"—a tour de force! I was initially skeptical, but Andrea, a diligent student, turned my skepticism into a challenge.

On Recitation Day, Andrea was ready. She began reciting the familiar lines, and we listened intently, wondering if she would actually make it to the end.

> Listen, my children, and you shall hear
> Of the midnight ride of Paul Revere,
> On the eighteenth of April, in Seventy-five;
> Hardly a man is now alive
> Who remembers that famous day and year.

As Andrea recited, her neck turned pink, then red, then crimson, the increasingly darker shades underscoring the stress her body was experiencing as she struggled to remember lines, maintain eye contact with the audience, retain her poise, and be expressive. But Andrea persevered, and we honored her accomplishment with wild applause.

Twenty years later, Andrea wrote to me of her "great lesson from that year":

> I will never forget you telling me that I could not memorize The Midnight Ride of Paul Revere. That was one of those frozen in time, "a-ha" moments in life when you discover your character. I knew with crystal clarity that no one will set limitations for me, no matter how well intentioned. I also remember the faces of those poor classmates suffering through verse 17. I'm surprised they didn't kill me! Thank you for having the patience to not stop me. [A teacher] who didn't understand what I was doing could have taken my actions as a waste of time or misplaced challenge. I always knew I had your support.
>
> —Andrea Dicks James
> (E-mail communication, February 25, 2003)

Also among the memorable recitations over the years were two by Nancy Bartow. One was her very first, the other her fourth. I don't recall the title of either poem that Nancy recited; yet her actions remain indelible in memory.

For the very first poetry recitation, Nancy signed up as presenter number twelve. An average student and quick with a smile, Nancy was a member of the chorus and the girls' soccer team. When I called out her name, she walked hesitantly to the front of the room, then edged cautiously to the microphone. Visibly uncomfortable, she stared at her shoes. Tresses of hair fell over her face, and her hands trembled slightly at her sides. Seconds passed. Nancy stood motionless, head bent. More seconds. Her classmates and I waited quietly, each of us silently willing her success. To no avail.

Twenty seconds. An eternity.

Someone coughed.

Thirty seconds.

Forty seconds.

Silence, still.

Finally, a single tear gathered at the corner of Nancy's left eye, trickled down her cheek, then dropped and splashed off the tip of her sneaker.

Wordlessly, Nancy turned slowly and returned to her seat. She had officially completed Poetry Recitation No. 1 without having uttered a single word. Her peers offered polite applause. I gave her a D− for effort.

Six weeks later when Nancy did Recitation No. 4, she began by establishing eye contact with the entire class, spoke with conviction, maintained her poise and eye contact with the audience, and made it to the end of the poem without any major errors. When she finished, the entire class rose as one and, remembering the anguish of her first effort, gave Nancy a sustained standing ovation. She grinned sheepishly from ear to ear. Nancy had, as a colleague so eloquently put it, engaged successfully in conquering self.

For the rest of the day, Nancy's classmates continued to congratulate her on a job well done, and deservedly so. I was as proud of one of my students that day as I ever was.

## CLOSING THOUGHTS

Why did poetry memorizations succeed as a learning activity for young adolescents?

Several reasons.

Poetry was omnipresent throughout the year. On Day One, I recited three poems to introduce students to the power of poetry and to the skills of memorization and recitation. One of these poems, "The First Day" (the frontispiece to this book), established me as a poet in their eyes, bringing both the poem and the moment alive through a description in verse of what they had just experienced as they came into class on the first day of school.

Second, on Recitation Days, I always recited first, intentionally modeling proper presentation skills and establishing a purposeful tone. Students became serious about reciting because they saw that I was serious about reciting. Eventually I became just another reciter in class, and I looked forward to presenting "The New Colossus," Henry Wadsworth Longfellow's "Excelsior," A. A. Milne's "Disobedience," and Lewis Carroll's "Jabberwocky" year after year.

Third, my playful poetic acknowledgments of the realities of reciting (e.g., "C Fever," "The New Reciters," "Remembering Frank Kish . . .") let students know that I understood and appreciated the challenge of the task. They appreciated my sensitivity as well as my sense of humor.

Also, students wanted to look good in front of their peers, so they struggled to learn lines and, in the process, impress classmates.

Choice, I believe, was one of the most significant success factors. Because students could decide which poems they would recite (particularly beginning with Recitation No. 4), they had control over their learning. Why do kids memorize popular songs so readily and, apparently, so easily? Because of the strong beat. Because peers are doing it. But mostly because they want to, because they have chosen to do so.

Measuring student growth over 10 recitations rather than seeing one effort as definitive also had a positive impact on achievement. Students knew that if they messed up on a particular recitation, they would have other opportunities.

Throughout, students were treated as individuals, their preferences for poetry were respected, and they had significant input into the process of selecting the poems they recited and the criteria by which they were evaluated.

Ultimately, students recognized that memorizing and reciting are authentic tasks, real life skills, useful in and for themselves, and they stepped up to the challenge when asked to do so. Can we ask more of our students?

## POETIC INTERLUDE NO. 3: ROTHERMEL'S
## REASONS FOR MEMORIZING AND RECITING

If your students ask you why they have to memorize poems, the following reasons may prove useful.

1. Preparing to recite promotes self-discipline and is a means of challenging oneself.
2. Students may be asked to memorize facts and formulas in school and in life. Quick recall saves time in most jobs. It requires an active, not passive mind.
3. Successfully reciting helps students develop self-confidence.
4. Reciting is an opportunity for students to become more comfortable in front of classmates.
5. Reciting is an opportunity to show determination.
6. Reciting develops a sense of community within the classroom since the students share the same challenge and experience.
7. Reciting and feeling what it is like to be in front of an audience develops empathy for others.
8. The memorizing selections are examples of good writing.
9. Reciting is an opportunity for students to change their reputation by showing classmates how well they can do with a challenging assignment.
10. Reciting allows students the chance to excel in a very visible way.
11. Memorizing requires the development of organizational and planning skills. Preparing to recite helps students learn to set goals and use their time well.
12. The memorizing selections can be used effectively to introduce a unit of study or a workshop.
13. The recitation day makes for an exciting school day. It gives the student an opportunity to be both dramatic and the center of attention.
14. Successful reciting requires adequate preparation. Reciting well is very difficult to fake.
15. The selections to recite teach vocabulary in context.
16. Preparing to recite provides an opportunity to collaborate with others in completing a task.
17. Preparing to recite is an opportunity to develop the habits of inquiry, diligence, and quality. (Rothermel, 1996, p. 50)

*Chapter Four*

# Composing and Publishing

*This chapter describes a variety of classroom activities through which students improve their written expression skills by composing and then publishing their own poems.*

[T]he object in writing poetry is to make all poems sound as different as possible from each other, and the resources for that of vowels, consonants, punctuation, syntax, words, sentences, meter are not enough. We need the help of context—meaning—subject matter.

—Robert Frost
(Drew & Connor, 1961, pp. 321–322)

Share ideas. Write a poem.
On the bus, in school, at home.
Capture thoughts. Draft. Revise.
Verse appears before your eyes.

—RMB

## WHY COMPOSE AND PUBLISH?

Why begin the school year by having students write poetry, and free verse in particular? Several reasons.

Poems composed by middle-school students tend toward brevity. In addition, free verse, which has very few rules, if any, makes the task of composing a poem both challenging and achievable. There are many decisions to be made, including topic, audience, opening line, and absence or presence of pattern; a short poem does not appear to have the same degree of difficulty as a 500-word essay; and finally, students don't have to concern themselves with the complications of meter and rhyme.

## IN THE CLASSROOM, PART ONE

On the fourth day of school, I distribute several student poems and invite volunteers to read aloud the first one, "Obsession." (I deliberately select what I consider to be the best of the free verse poems composed in previous years, casually passing them off as average; I deliberately do *not* introduce the term "free verse poetry" until well into the lesson.)

Jeremy raises his hand. I nod, and he begins to read:

an obsession
turns into romance?
only in the movies
but . . . maybe
she looks everyday . . . trying to find somebody new
but she can't
convince herself
to give him up
just yet
maybe sometime
she'll be able to look back
and smile
at the way
he ruled her life completely
but
not today
today she is still obsessed
with his
image
she can't
give
him
up
today

—Emmy Ludwig

Rachel gives a slightly different reading of the poem. The class acknowledges both Rachel and Jeremy with polite applause following their readings.

"Now, reread the poem silently," I instruct, "and ask yourself, *What's going on in this poem?* Feel free to make notes in the margins."

Students bend to the task. After a couple of minutes of silent industry, I inquire, "Okay, what's this poem about?"

"Love, Mr. B.," suggests Vanessa. "It's about a girl hung up on a guy."

"'Love,'" I repeat, writing the word on the chalkboard. "Great. Anything else?"

"Hey, did Emmy actually write this?" Luisa asks. "I sat next to her on the bus a couple of times last year. She's a pretty good poet."

"I'm glad you like the poem, Luisa," I reply. "What do you get out of it?"

"Like Vanessa said, it's about this guy and a girl. It seems honest to me. I guess Emmy went through something like this."

"Thank you, Luisa," I respond. "Anybody else? What else do you notice?"

I wait as they reread the poem. Their silence is not unexpected. It is early in the school year and students are still adjusting both to my style of teaching and to one another.

Rich raises his hand. I nod to him.

"Well, maybe it's just a typing error," Rich volunteers, "but the ninth line is not centered the way the others are. It's a little bit off, more to the right."

"Good observation, Rich," I respond. "And do you think it's a mistake, or is it intentional?"

"Well, I'm not sure, but it kind of emphasizes those two words—'just yet'—like she's not really sure, and she might give him up some day but she's not ready to give him up now."

"Very interesting," I comment. "Thanks, Rich. Does anyone else notice anything?"

During the next five minutes, other students offer a variety of observations about and reactions to Emmy's poem. We move on to two readings of the second poem, followed by more discussion. We then read aloud and discuss two more poems.

"Good job, kids," I say. "Now, what do you notice about all of these poems? What common elements do they share? How are they alike?" I ask the question three ways in order to engage more students. They begin suggesting similarities among all four poems, and I make a list on the chalkboard as students note common elements (e.g., no rhyme, brevity).

"Now, I'm going to introduce a new term that describes these four poems," I say. "These are called 'free verse poems.' Anyone care to venture why?"

A brief moment of wait time while they think. Then Juan raises his hand. "Because they don't rhyme—they're free," he volunteers.

"Exactly, Juan," I reply. "When you write a free verse poem, there are very few rules to follow—no rhymes, no same number of beats to the line (we call that meter)—and the verses, if you divide up your poem that way, can be of different line lengths."

After a bit more discussion, I assign two free verse poems as homework and instruct students to save all drafts. I also suggest that they use the poems we discussed in class as examples.


## ASSERTIONS ABOUT COMPOSING AND PUBLISHING

In his preface to *Writing Poetry* (1992), Shelley Tucker states:

> I believe that everyone can compose good poetry and benefit from writing it. Poetry writing is not dependent upon age or academic accomplishment, so . . . children with low test scores are as successful writing poems as people with stronger academic skills. Poetry writing instead relies on a writer's feelings, history, and perceptions, so every person has the background needed to write poems. Because poetry draws on the senses and the senses give deep access to memories and feelings, poetry writing is relevant and interesting. Poetry has fewer rules than prose, so people feel confident when they write. (p. *iii*)

Tucker's convictions resonate with me. Over the years as I considered the task of teaching students to compose and then publish their poetry, I developed a set of assertions that informed my classroom practice. I believe that:

- Every student is a poet and has ideas she or he wants to communicate in verse.

- Student poets are inspired by models, particularly those created by classmates.
- Student poets consider audience, purpose, topic, and form when they compose.
- Student poets are more invested in composing when they select their own topics.
- Composing poetry is a recursive process: invent, rehearse, draft, revise, edit, and publish.
- Student poets discover their voice when they read their poems aloud to peers.
- Student poets should publish regularly for audiences beyond the teacher.
- When students prepare poems for publication, they become more invested in learning the conventions of the English language.
- Teachers who share their own poetry with students, both early drafts and polished verses, provide powerful coaching.
- Volume + Variety = Poetic Fluency. Simply put, the more poems that students compose, and the more different forms of poetry that they master, the more fluent as poets they become.

These assertions may be useful as you ask students to draft, revise, and publish their poetry, and if they are, please adopt them. If you take issue with any of them, revise them accordingly.

## IN THE CLASSROOM, PART TWO

As students come into school the next day, some are already buzzing about one friend's efforts.

"Ask Mike to read his," three different pupils urge. "They're really good." On the bus to school that morning, Mike shared his poems with a buddy, and word spread fast. Clearly, the peer grapevine is alive and well.

To set a good example and to show students my writing process, I go first, passing around three messy drafts of a free verse poem composed the night before. Students practice their listening skills as I read aloud:

> I sit
> pen in hand

waiting
      waiting for my muse
            to strike

Silence . . .

Blank page . . .

No words emerge
      (am I dry?)

The poem resists
      taking shape
each word becomes
      a struggle

Yet, somehow,
slowly they accumulate
and descend
      down the page
      idea following idea

My eyes scan
words already written
seeking threads to tie

      random

          thoughts
together

And in reviewing
what I've written
I notice
the poem
is almost complete.

But somehow
a vague dissatisfaction
remains

And I wonder
what does it mean
who cares
so what

End of
free verse poem

—RMB
(Unpublished poem, n.d.)

Several students murmur agreement with the thrust of the poem. Then Mike, the subject of much buzzing before class, volunteers to read. His poem resonates with foreboding:

### The Shark

I stood there on the ocean floor,
this great creature looming above.
He moved with a beat,
with an elegance that could match all dancers.
Then it stirred,
the reason he is feared.
I did not notice it,
but I had intruded,
intruded on his largest secret,
the one he hides from us.
His eyes went from a crystal ball,
to a bonfire of hate and evil.
I had been detected,
and it was the shark who wondered deeply,
not pausing or resting his eyes.
At all time he viewed me
and I realized for the first time.
His eyes were a reflection,
of future and of doom.
And the fear I saw in them,
was none but my own.

—Mike Cast

Charley, who lives for hoops, reads aloud an experientially based poem:

### Playing Basketball

Shooting the ball
passing the ball

dribbling the ball
running up the court
fouling your opponent
losing the ball
missing a shot
making a shot
hustling after the ball
fighting for the ball
congratulating your teammate
getting a bad call
sweating
and getting tired.

—Charlie Wirth

Frank draws laughter as he references his own history of frequent scrapes with authority:

### Getting In Trouble

I hate getting in trouble
especially when you
get in trouble in school
if your parents would
just find out on the spot
I would not hate it as
much I would not like
it but it would not be
as bad.

—Frank Kish

Danielle shares a poignant perspective:

### Christmas Morning

I run downstairs to see
a room filled with presents.
I scream, "Wake up, it's Christmas, everyone!":
We tear open presents
and have a jolly feast.
Only one thing isn't there:
My mom.

> If I had one wish
> it would be
> to see my family together
> on Christmas morning.
>
> —Danielle Susskraut

As student after student shares, some of the usually reluctant pupils become caught up in the moment and volunteer to read their poems. Because I asked students to compose two poems yet invited them to read only one aloud, they can choose which poem they want to reveal, and so they feel more comfortable about contributing. At the end of class I assign homework: students are to revise one of their free verse poems.

The next day we read aloud even more poems as students share revised drafts.

In the weeks that follow, students compose interior monologues and personal essays. We then create a class anthology to which each student submits two pieces of writing. Many choose to submit their poems. This anthology is the first of many publications created during the school year. When students realize that their writing is going public, they become more invested in grammar and mechanics. They revise their poems even further, working intently at mastering the conventions of spelling, punctuation, sentence structure, and capitalization because they want their poems to look good to others.

## REVISION

Middle school students want their voices to be heard. They want to express their emotions, and poetry enables them to do so. That is one reason why I assigned free verse poetry as the first creative writing task of the year. To set a good example, I composed and revised poems along with my students.

Revision, an essential step in writing, is easier to accomplish with a short poem than with a longer prose piece such as a first- or third-person narrative, a newspaper article, or a persuasive essay, all of which my students composed later in the year. When students seek just the right word, or design a purposeful line break, or craft an inviting title, or adopt a central image as the basis of their poem, they are engaged in critical thinking and decision making.

As they revised, I insisted that students "save all drafts," and I set up a classroom file for their writing. Students were instructed to staple the newest version of a piece of writing, numbered and dated, on top of a growing sheaf of earlier drafts. This paper trail enabled me to trace the development of ideas in a particular piece of writing, minimizing the possibility of plagiarism. Also, because students saved all of their drafts, they discovered that words excised prematurely from draft two could be retrieved and inserted appropriately into draft five, and that a change in the sequence of lines or stanzas in an early draft could be undone or restored in a later draft.

In *The Apple and the Spectroscope*, T. R. Henn (1966), speaking of the poet William Butler Yeats, asserted:

> [E]ach one of us re-creates the poem for himself. Probably we re-make it to some extent on each successive reading. Part of the pleasurable excitement comes from the sense of re-creation, of making the poem for ourselves, which the poet felt at its fullest in the original act of creation. But this excitement and pleasure are closely related to our own development; that is why Yeats revised his early work so extensively to keep in tune with his own changing set of values. He put the whole matter succinctly:
>
> > The friends that have I do it wrong
> > Whenever I remake a song
> > Should know what issue is at stake:
> > It is myself that I remake. (p. 11)

Yeats understood the significance of revision. So did Anne Lamott (1995), who, in *Bird by Bird,* wrote that "[a]lmost all good writing begins with terrible first efforts" (p. 25), not exactly comforting words to an emerging adolescent. Lamott later added:

> You write a shitty first draft of it and you sound it out, and you leave in those lines that ring true and take out the rest. I wish there were an easier, softer way, a shortcut, but this is the nature of most good writing: that you find out things as you go along. Then you go back and rewrite. Remember: no one is reading your first drafts. (p. 71)

One reason for drafting and revising a piece of writing is to discover what you want to say. The National Writing Project and Carl Nagin (2003) observed:

> Many writers don't know their subject well until they've written a draft; few professional writers start with a topic sentence or outline; and most struggle through multiple drafts and acts of editing and revision. (p. 25)

I wrote many poems while serving in the Peace Corps in Tunisia. One free verse poem described Cap Bon, a windswept peninsula jutting northeast into the Mediterranean towards Sicily and the boot heel of Italy. When I completed it, I sent a copy to my older sister, who suggested that I change the word "crumpled," with its sense of limitation, to "gathered," which suggests potential:

> Cap Bon . . .
> Edges vertically
> As from a level forearm
> And wrist narrowing to fist
> ~~Crumpled~~ Gathered in dramatic being
> Soaring onward
> To heights above
> And stops— . . .
>
> —RMB
> (Unpublished poem, 1964)

My sister's advice made a difference. I learned about the power of revision and that, in a poem, every word counts.

*Lesson learned*: Let students know, over and over again, that their first drafts are not finished products, and that they will have ample opportunities to revise. Encourage students, as they compose, to make it messy so that they can make it right.


## "YOU DECIDE WHEN IT'S DONE"

Early in the school year, I said to my students about their writing, "You decide when it's done." I wanted them to understand that an author must take responsibility for his or her writing, and that they had the final say about their own writing. One poem might take four drafts to achieve clarity, while another might need fifteen.

One year when I asked students to revise their free verse poems as homework, Jason quoted my words back to me, saying that his poem was "done," two drafts were sufficient, and he wasn't going to revise it any further. Rather than resist his challenge, I asked Jason if I could look over his drafts and, if I had any, pose a few questions.

"Sure, but I'm not going to revise it. I like it the way it is," he responded.

"Fair enough, Jason," I replied.

That evening as I read through his 16-line poem about drag racing, I typed a letter containing extensive questions, suggestions, observations, and comments for Jason to consider. Among other things, I asked:

> What is it like for a driver sitting behind the wheel of a car as the lights flash down to green? What is going on with him, both physically (sweat, etc.) and mentally (is he running the race in his mind? Is he thinking of his wife or girlfriend or victory or breakfast or his cat? Is he thinking of crashing?) What is he thinking of? Do you want the reader to think about what the driver is thinking about?

One line of Jason's poem said, "The Pirellis spin." I commented:

> Is this a top fuel race? "Top fuel" is a technical term that you might want to use. When you use technical terms, they add to the authenticity of the poem. What if you were to make a list of terms related to drag racing and see if some of them could fit into this poem to give the reader a sense of your intimate knowledge of what is going on. Specific details help. The use of "Pirellis" is a perfect example—so much better than just saying "tires" because it shows that you know what kind of tires drag racers use, and it forces the reader to say, "What's a Pirelli?" Using that is great—can you use other terms that are "insider" terms and give more of a flavor of conditions around a racetrack? Are they racing on a curve or a straightaway? Should you say so? Is the track wet or dry? Did it rain earlier? Is it morning? Afternoon? Does it matter what time it is? . . .

> Does the driver shift only once? Twice? Three times during the race? How many times does he shift? Is there only one power shift?

Near the end of his poem, Jason used the line, "A few seconds more . . ."
I asked:

> "A few seconds more . . ."—how many seconds. Ten? Fifteen? Forty five?
> Poetry works best, I say, when the poet chooses words with real care to
> communicate the most he can with the least amount of words. What if you
> were precise? How many seconds, actually, have passed since the light
> turned green? How is the end of a race signaled? Is there a flag? Another
> light? Something else? Does the crowd react? Is there a crowd? Does the
> driver react? What color is the other car? Is it on his left or his right?

> —RMB

The next day I handed Jason a thick envelope. He sat at his desk and
read my letter quietly, saying not a word in class. Over the next few days,
however, he turned in several more drafts, increased the number of lines
from 16 to 40, and ultimately submitted his drag racing poem for the class
anthology. He also showed my letter to his friends, who quietly passed the
word that "Mr. B. is serious about poetry."

*Lesson learned*: When you ask students legitimate questions about their
writing, they listen, and often they respond positively.

## OPPORTUNITIES TO COMPOSE AND PUBLISH

My students had occasion to compose, revise, and publish verse many
times during the school year. These recurring occasions allowed students
to develop a level of comfort with poetry along with the sense that they
were, indeed, emerging poets. From the first writing activity of the year
(free verse poems in September) to the last (Memory Minutes in June), students crafted words into lines and lines into verses, revised their writing,
and published the results. My goal was to give them numerous opportunities to play with words, and I used any and every occasion to do so.

In October we published poems based on our outdoor education field
trip. In November, after reading *The Miracle Worker*, students summarized in verse what they had learned. In December we composed holiday
commemorations; a number of students chose to write poems. When students created Gifts of Writing for family and friends in February, poetry

became one mode of expression. In March each student created an individual poetry booklet. In social studies class students composed American History poems. During an interdisciplinary English/Science/Poetry unit, students communicated their knowledge of scientific information through poetry. When we had celebrations—the return of a teacher following surgery, the departure of a classmate—students composed "tribute poems." The culminating activity of the year, the individual magazine project, gave each student the opportunity to write on a self-selected theme, and they all chose to include poetry in their magazines.

And as students drafted and revised their verses, this teacher as poet was inspired to compose occasional verses of his own.

## PEEC POEMS

Three weeks into the school year, our team took a field trip to the Pocono Environmental Education Center (PEEC). For three days students performed kitchen duties, shared cabins with old and new friends, and took on the challenges of the Project Adventure ropes course, pond study, square dancing, and orienteering. To conclude the Thursday night Talent Show, the trip chaperones sang "The PEEC Rap" (I scribbled all nine verses while waiting for students to check in at orienteering locations):

It's September, and we're on the PEEC trip.
Enjoying the Talent Show—this group is really hip.
We've seen some good acts, but it's no time for a nap
'Cause your awesome advisors are doin' the PEEC Rap!

*Chorus:*
Do the PEEC Rap (4x)

Write in your journal, paddle a canoe
Orient your compass—keep North in view
Pond Study, Square Dance, Astronomy, too
PEEC is the best—you know it's true!

Well, this is the end of our little song
It wasn't too bad and it wasn't too long
Just one more thing before we're through
We love to do the PEEC Rap with you!

—RMB

Following the field trip, I asked students to reflect on their experiences in the woods and compose three pieces of writing about PEEC, two of which were reportorial. The third had to be a creative piece of writing in either poetic, interior monologue, or personal essay form that described some aspect of the trip.

Many students opted to reflect in verse. Matt used a simile to describe the neatly aligned rows of pines that he saw in the woods at PEEC:

### Walking

Walking to canoeing
A walk through the woods
Step by step
The trees!
They tower over us
In straight lines
Like soldiers marching
Row by row
Escorting us to the pond.

—Matt Clancy
(Eighth grader in 1995–1996)

Erin Cathey recalled the night hike, a popular activity:

### Night Hike

Darkness
Rocks, trees, grass
Stumbling
Falling
I can't see
Where I'm going
Animal noises
Bats and bugs
Disappearing heads
And candle light fun.
Walking through the woods
And stepping on rocks
The moon is out
And we're having fun.

—Erin Cathey
(Eighth grader in 1995–1996)

As I recuperated from the rigors of the trip, I browsed through my dog-eared copy of *Poems For All Occasions* and, I'm happy to report, found a poem that seemed perfect to share in class—a 30-stanza bonanza whose opening verses depicted the field trip as a building block for the school year ahead:

### A PEEC Experience

Our three day trip to PEEC now lives as team history
And clearly, you kids, it's no complicated mystery
How we created a sense of cooperative community
And in those days become a quasi-extended family.

I say that it was entirely by intentional design
That what you experienced at PEEC turned out so fine,
From McDonald's Wednesday morning where you did dine
To hiking among the Poconos maple and pine.

PEEC was meant to be a positive beginning
And to serve as a structural underpinning
To an 8th grade year both fun and winning
And filled with learning, growing and grinning.

The closing verses echoed a similar theme—that this three-day trip was meant to do more than expose students to pond study, astronomy, and orienteering:

PEEC captured the heart of the team this fall.
We went, we risked, we survived, one and all.
The challenges came one on another; we responded to the call,
And in the process of meeting them, had ourselves a ball.

PEEC enabled us to build a strong foundation;
The year ahead will be founded on trust and communication.
PEEC reinforced acknowledgment and appreciation,
Responsibility, risk, respect, commitment and participation.

Your advisors intended that PEEC occur this way,
That our trip would be more than just pizza and play;
Yes, PEEC is now past, our year is fully underway
And this, my students, is but the 14th day.

—RMB
(From the apocryphal *Poems For All Occasions,* September 1995)

By saying back in poetic form many of the highlights of the field trip, I helped to shape students' memories of this formative experience. As souvenirs of the trip, students received copies of both the PEEC Rap and "A PEEC Experience."

*Lesson learned*: Take students on outdoor education field trips, then have them write poems about their experiences.

## "THE MIRACLE WORKER" POEMS

In November my students read William Gibson's *The Miracle Worker*, the inspiring story of Annie Sullivan and the "miracle" she achieved working with Helen Keller. To assess their understanding of the play, I posed six questions and instructed students to respond to any three. I believed that no matter which three questions a student answered, I would get a good sense of what he or she learned from the play. One of the six questions asked students to engage in "Creative Writing" and offered three choices:

Select only one (1) of the three activities below—scene, poem, or interior monologue.

a) Create a new **scene** in the play involving at least two characters. Include dialogue and stage directions. This scene can take place during the time of the play or after Helen acquires the distinction language.

b) Write a **poem** of at least 16 lines that in some way relates to the play and/or the characters in it. Turn in all drafts.

c) Write an **interior monologue** from the point of view of one of the characters in the play. Include setting (who, where, when).

Typically, about 20 percent of my students chose poetry. I presented this option because it tapped their creative writing abilities, allowed greater choice when responding to the play, encouraged the creation of poetry, and built upon poetic activities of the previous months.

Vanessa placed herself in Helen's shoes:

**Trapped**

Trapped in darkness.
Trapped in silence.
Where do I turn?
What is this?

What does this do?
They don't understand.
They think they do, but they don't.
I want to learn.
I need to learn.
How can I tell them how I feel?
How do I make them understand?
I'm desperate for knowledge!
I want to know everything,
Everything in the entire world.
Why should I do this?
Leave me alone!
They'll never know.
They'll never know how I feel.
I'll never get through to them.

—Vanessa Rom
(Eighth grader in 1991–1992)

David recapped the entire play in his poem:

### The Miracle

The doll had no eyes and Helen cried.
Annie came with a beautiful doll.
The eyes opened and closed.
She tried to teach her to communicate.
Annie's fingers were always spelling.
Hoping the miracle would happen.

Breakfast turned out to be a fight.
Annie showed strength but so did Helen.
Kate and Keller didn't want to let go.
But Helen ate off her own plate
And she folded her napkin over and over again.
The first miracle happened.

They moved to the garden house by themselves.
Two weeks to perform a miracle.
The miracle was tough but so were they.
She learned to eat off her own plate.
Then time was up and back they went.

Unfortunately the miracle of language
Had not happened yet.

At supper Helen went back to her old ways.
But Kate surrenders her to Annie.
They fill the water pitcher over and over.
And now the miracle happens.
Helen says, "Wah-wah."
Now she can see "five thousand years back in a light of words."

—David Szymanski
(Eighth grader in 1991–1992)

My question: "Do these two very different poems indicate that Vanessa and David understood the play and its major themes?"

My response: "Absolutely!"

Inspired by the students' poems, I crafted my own tribute to the "miracle" and shared it in class:

### Thoughts on Helen and Annie

I know I would mind
were I deaf and blind,
but both? I'm not sure I could.

When Helen was born,
these gifts had been shorn;
she moved touching wall, flesh, wood.

Consider young Helen
and all of the yelling
the Kellers engaged in back then.

Annie's arrival
meant Helen's survival
became but a matter of when.

How *do* you get through
and open the view
of one who is trapped in a cage,

especially when she
is hiding the key
and flying right off in a rage?

Would I or would you
have known what to do
if linked to that obstinate creature?

I have to admire
the incessant fire
that Annie displayed as her "teacher."

She helped us to see
that disability
need not restrain as a tether.

A miracle, yes,
emerged from the stress
of teacher and student together.

—RMB

(From the apocryphal *Poems For All Occasions,* November 1991)

One nice thing about having written "Thoughts on Helen and Annie" was that I could use it in succeeding years and get a lot of mileage out of it. Which I did.

*Lesson learned*: Have students read plays and then communicate their learning through poetry.

## HOLIDAY POEMS

Poems were always an option when it came to the holidays. One December we created a booklet called "Commemorative Creations," and each student contributed a piece of writing. Students shared their commemorations on the last day of school before Christmas vacation. Half of the students selected poetry as their mode of expression. The introduction to the booklet, composed by a student, stated:

This booklet is the fourth one Team 8-1 has created this year . . . We decided to commemorate [the end of the year] by preparing pieces of writing that celebrated the beginning of our school year together and the end of the year. Everyone on the team wrote something and their writing is in this book. The pieces range from poems to personal essays to letters. These pieces mean

something to all of us, the students and teachers on Team 8-1, and we hope
it will mean something to you, to look back on, and remember the beginning of this school year. Read it now, remember it later.

Kathleen, a perceptive teen, asked:

### What Is Christmas?

Is it getting presents,
getting money,
getting cards?

Is it not having to get up early,
not having homework,
not having school?

Is it chaos in the stores,
chaos in the house,
chaos everywhere?

Or is it being with family,
being with friends,
being merry?

You decide.

—Kathleen Wynne
(Eighth grader in 1990–1991)

My contribution was a retrospective review of the first four months of
the school year. Here is an abridged version:

As my commemorative creation
to celebrate this festive occasion
I've written a retrospective poem
to send you off to hearth and home,
a set of verses that recall
and celebrate the end of fall:
our trips to PEEC, Vermont, Rye, Maine,
and sports—both victory and pain,
reporting, typing and revising,
selecting poems and memorizing,

Halloween and the Talent Show,
"and miles to sleep before I go,"
the busy hum of keyboards clicking
in the computer lab, as time was ticking
towards this day that marks the end
of a third of the year—these lines I've penned.
Students new to the team arrived,
students old took risks and thrived,
students left, and students shared,
and students acknowledged, and students cared.
We grew together as Team 8-I,
working, producing, having fun,
questioning, learning, and all the while
remembering to wear a smile.
So, teammates, Happy Holiday,
and at this merry Yuletide, may
our family blessings never cease
and may our lives be filled with Peace.

—RMB
(From the apocryphal *Poems For All Occasions,* December 1990)

Each Christmas, one of our team advisors, Nick Naccarato, loved it when we performed a special holiday presentation for the students on our team. Embedded with the name of every student in bold and modeled after the lyrics to a familiar poem, this annual ritual provided a model of parody and acknowledgment. After our dramatic reading, we distributed copies to one and all:

### A Visit from St. Nicholas Naccarato (and Others)
*(excerpts)*

'Twas five days before Christmas and all through the school,
No students were studying—it just wasn't cool.
**Advisors** were standing in front of the room
Reciting the lines of an old Christmas poom.

The children were dressed all in greens and in reds
While **Mathematics** of **minibus** danced in their heads.
**Viola** was hung by the chimney with care
In hopes that **Campisi** soon would be there.

When out in **Phys Ed** there arose such a clatter
We sprang to our **PEEC** to see what was the matter.
Away to **Shapiro** we flew like a sprinter,
**Wynne**, **Cepelak**, **Ludwig** and **Frank Kish**, **John Finter**.

Now **Carey**! now **Cathey**! now, **Urgese**, **Ferreira**!
On **David**! on, **Dani**! on, **Platz** and **Liz Barra**!
To the top of the **Hintze**, to **Furano**, **Gallucci**!
Now, **Donohue**, **Vallely**, **Jason Jendrewski**!

—RMB
(From the apocryphal *Poems For All Occasions,* n.d.)

*Lesson learned*: Use any and all holidays as occasions to create poems.

## POEMS ABOUT LOSS

Years ago I read a book whose title said it all: *The Geranium On The Windowsill Just Died But Teacher You Went Right On* by Albert Cullum (1971). Time is our most precious classroom resource, and as teachers we confront multiple demands on it daily. But when something out of the ordinary occurs, we serve students by taking notice, by paying attention, by acknowledging what happened.

When the space shuttle exploded, when the slaughter at Columbine horrified the nation, when the Twin Towers were attacked on 9/11, students and teachers across America composed poetic tributes as a way of dealing with their grief. Sometimes it is the death of a teacher, other times a student moving out of the district. But whenever a sad occasion occurs, and schools today need to be ready for such occasions, poetry is one way of helping students cope with their emotions of the moment.

Dan Greenberg, a popular student, unexpectedly moved away to New Jersey one January. I knew that Dan's abrupt departure would result in weeping and wailing from his many close friends, effectively rendering teaching on that day a fool's errand. To counteract this probability, I scheduled a farewell event for the last period of Dan's last day so that students could focus during morning classes and postpone expressions of sorrow until it was time to officially say goodbye. I invited students to prepare plaudits and send Dan on his way. Chrissy Cardinali, one of Dan's many admirers, took her farewell tribute through 15 drafts before being satisfied that it said what she wanted to say to him:

When being together for so many years,
a friendship grows that's very sincere.
It's happy at times, and sometimes there's sorrow.
In good times you laugh with no thought of tomorrow.
Then the friend whom you care for has something to share;
he says he is moving; you just stand and stare,
not really knowing quite what to say,
cause you feel the hurt and it won't go away.
He sees you hurt; he knows you care.
How do you tell him? It's so unfair
to lose someone so close to you
and wave goodbye to the friendship that you both knew.
Why is he leaving? Is it something you've done?
The date grows closer and you've only just begun
to accept his departure and live day by day.
You can't hold him back—Let him go his own way.
Let him meet new people and have new friends
and develop new dreams that go on without end.
But the time has finally come when you have to say goodbye,
and you know that when you do, you'll only start to cry.
So you look at him to say goodbye my special friend.
But instead you turn to hide the tears cause you know this is the end.

—Chrissy Cardinali
(Eighth grader in 1983–1984)

My own salute to Dan's departure attempted to capture the wistful mood of students on our team as they coped with their emotions and the inevitability of his absence:

**Resonance**

Have you ever had the feeling
of time flowing by
and you aren't really sure
if hello means goodbye?

Have you ever known the pain
of losing a friend
and you find difficulty
in accepting the end?

Have you ever sensed the rush
of haste all around
and you barely feel your feet
skimming over the ground?

Have you ever been confused
by demands on your time
and you modify your pace
to the angle of the climb?

Have you ever asked yourself
what the melody means
and you dream rainbow thoughts
filled with monotone scenes?

Have you ever read a poem
where the meaning isn't clear
and you push it away
in a gesture of fear?

And if I can question
and touch who you are
can the distance between us
be very far.

—RMB

(From the apocryphal *Poems For All Occasions*, January 1984)

At our end-of-the-year team farewell ceremony in 1991, my teaching partner Cliff Lennon, clad in purple dress and garish hat, used Jenny Joseph's poem "Warning" in his Memory Minute. He brought down the house. A year later, Cliff, the varsity basketball coach, died suddenly of liver cancer, and poetry became part of his memorial service. The assistant principal read "On Teaching" from Kahlil Gibran's *The Prophet*. Two of Cliff's former students read poems, one original and one by Edgar A. Guest ("People Liked Him"). At the memorial, one of Cliff's former students, clad in a purple sweatshirt, recited "Warning" to end the service.

A year after Cliff's passing, I composed the following poem to celebrate his memory and to deal with the pain still in my heart:

### Passing Days

A dozen months have eased our pain
yet still we'd have him back again;
his smile and easy going ways
remain with us through passing days.

And in his class and on the road
and with his teams he lived a code:
give of yourself, participate,
affirm, enjoy, appreciate.

Time heals, they say, and though it's true
the memories we lived and knew
stay ever present, and we find
he lives in hearts he left behind.

—RMB
(Unpublished poem, January 27, 1993)

*Lesson learned*: When loss occurs, and it will, steer students and yourself to poetry. It helps.


## GIFTS OF WRITING

Each February I invited students to create special pieces of writing for important audiences. We called them "Gifts of Writing" and delivered them
on Valentine's Day. Most students chose to compose personal essays; occasionally, a student chose to create a poem as a gift of writing.

Chris Waldemar used this writing assignment to honor his father. He
penned five verses, one for each member of the family, and, at his dad's
mid-February birthday party that year, revealed his surprise—a small, illustrated booklet of poems titled "Waldemar Family Poems." He even
composed a verse for the family dog:

### Pepsi

The people lover
And licker

She inches her way
Into the living room to see
If she could lick me
But Dad would tell her
To leave the room
Or else she'll come to
Her *doom*!!!!!!!!!!

—Chris Waldemar
(Eighth grader in 1982–1983)

Impressed by the industry my students exhibited when they composed gifts of writing for family members and friends, I searched
through my somewhat shabby copy of *Poems For All Occasions* to see
if I could find a fitting tribute to honor their efforts. And, interestingly
enough, I did:

### The Gift of Writing

Don't engage in thrift
when nouns and verbs you send.
Writing is a gift—
be lavish with your friend.

Keep your goal in mind,
what you intend to say.
Be intent and find
the words, the will, the way.

This task intimidates
when lines don't come with ease.
Details illuminate;
be specific, please.

And when the gift's received,
fashioned by your hand,
can it be perceived
as anything but grand?

—RMB
(From the apocryphal *Poems For All Occasions*, February 1988)

*Lesson learned*: Writing is a gift—make it a poem.

## PHILADELPHIA FIELD TRIP

Following a social studies simulation of the Second Continental Congress
in which eighth graders portrayed Tories, Radicals, and Moderates and de-
bated Loyalty or Independence, we took our students to Philadelphia to
see the Liberty Bell, walk through Independence Hall, explore the
Franklin Institute, and visit Valley Forge. Upon returning to school, each
student composed a piece of writing about some aspect of the trip. Nine
students out of 45 chose poetry as their mode of expression.

For the inevitable trip anthology, I composed two list poems, "Pre-
Trip" and "Post-Trip," both of which used the name of the City of Brotherly Love as a structural device:

> **Pre-Trip**
>
> **P**lanning a visit
> **H**istoric sites
> **I**ndependence Hall
> **L**ists of roommates
> **A**mount needed: $13
> **D**etails, details, details
> **E**xcitement
> **L**eave Wed. 8:45 a.m.
> **P**ermission forms
> **H**ead out
> **I**n minibuses
> **A**way!
>
> —RMB

Pat Blake used the same structural device for a rhyming poem. His
mention of Dan refers to the student who moved to New Jersey in January but who joined us for the three-day trip to the City of Brotherly Love:

> **PHILADELPHIA    rbea**
>
> **P**hilly get ready because here we come!
> **H**ere is where we shall stay for three days of fun.
> **I**n the Budget Lodge is where we got set.
> **T**hen at the Liberty Bell is where Dan we met.
> **A**t McDonald's and Burger King is where we all ate.
> **D**own the Rocky steps, the ice fight (that was great).

Everyone got a talk about the night before (that was no fun)
Looking at Ben Franklin Court (it sure seemed like one).
Places to go—to the mall or the movie.
Hunger then came, to Roy's we went and that was real groovy.
In the Budget Lodge we had a 10:00 curfew from the ice we seized.
And I have some news—we weren't all pleased.

right now I am sorry, but I have run out of letters
but after that, it didn't get much better.
except for the Franklin Institute which wasn't that bad
and then it was time to leave Philly and Dan, which was sad.

—Pat Blake
(Eighth grader in 1983–1984)

Josh celebrated one of America's most enduring symbols:

### The Liberty Bell
*(an in-depth history)*

There it is
The Liberty Bell,
It's real beat up
(It's been through hell)

But still it's part
Of our history
It's an American symbol
Like Chef Boyer Dee

It was made before our country
A long time ago
Created by a company called
Pass and Stow.

They rang the bell
Over Independence Hall.
It rang so many times
They discovered a small

crack on the bell
that needed repair,
Too bad that technology
just wasn't there.

In the 1800's
the bell went on tour,
but the crack got larger.
It don't travel no more.

The bell's still around;
you can see it today.
Just go to it's home
in Philadelphia!

—Josh Silverstein
(Eighth grader in 1983–1984)

Peggy loved shopping at the mall on Market Street, where a pair of striped pink pants caught her fancy. She captured that moment in a poem laced with now-obscure frames of reference but which, at the time, convulsed Peggy and her friends:

### The Gallery

Pink and Grey Stripes,
too big, what a relief

Pizza and Diet Coke
beside an old lady

A dog named "Chow Chow"
Empty glass cages

Ugly army coat
gorgeous brown eyes

—Peggy Vallely
(Eighth grader in 1983–1984)

My closing list poem referenced many of the trip highlights:

### Post-Trip

Philadelphia memories:
How do you open a door with these keys?
Ice fight
Liberty Bell
A race up the "Rocky" steps

**D**an
Exploring the Gallery
Log huts at Valley Forge
Pink pants at the mall
Having dinner at Roy Rogers
Institute (Franklin)
And then back home!

—RMB

*Lesson learned*: Field trips to places of historic and cultural significance provide students with experiences and memories that can be celebrated and recycled as poems.


## PARODY

Creating a parody of a classic poem is a great fun, and the weekly poems
allowed me to model this notion for students. I recycled Robert Frost's
"Stopping by Woods on a Snowy Evening" regularly (see "Stopping by
Frank Kish . . ." in Chapter 2) because students were familiar with Frost's
meter, end couplet, and AABA rhyme scheme. "C Fever" (see Chapter 3)
also encouraged students to take on familiar poems.

In 1989, Charlie Wirth, who lived for basketball, paid homage to the
New York Knicks, a sidelined Larry Bird, and "The New Colossus" in his
end of the year magazine with this knockoff:

**The New Spirit**
*(A Slam Dunk to Emma Lazarus)*

Not like the amazing spirit of Celtic Pride
When hitting three with 2 seconds left
But opening our door for any newcomers.
With Larry on the bench, whose injury
Is the imprisoned spirit, and being in
The last place team not helping at all. Now the Knickerbockers
Whose team beacon hands glow world-wide
Attendance. "Keep, hitting three, with your range," they cry
With a loud mouth. "Give us your support,
Your undivided attention. We promise to make it

To the play-offs, this year at least. Send anyone, a team,
So we can kick their butt.
We put on the lights at Madison Square Garden."

—Charlie Wirth
(Eighth grader in 1988–1989)

In the Foreword to his magazine, Charlie observed, "Poems . . . even though they are small pieces of writing, took a lot of time and a lot of thought to write. So don't get fooled by saying a poem takes less time than a story."

Josh Silverstein, a self-professed chocoholic, referenced his friend Greg Whitledge while borrowing from Frost. Josh's writing group played a major role in helping him craft this poem:

### Stopping By Greg and It's Chocolate I'm Eating

Whose Mounds this is I think I know.
His locker's in the 3rd wing, though.
He will not see me stopping here,
So I can eat it really slow.

I tremble and I shake with fear.
If he finds out he'll kick my rear.
Between the wrapper and coconut flake
The darkest chocolate I have right here.

I look around for safety sake
To make sure he doesn't catch me by mistake.
I see a kid—he's half asleep.
His name's Greg Whitledge. What a flake!

The chocolate's lovely, dark and deep;
This is one bar I'll have to keep.
And Whitledge there, still half-asleep,
And Whitledge there, still half-asleep.

—Josh Silverstein
(Eighth grader in 1983–1984)

*Lesson learned*: Introduce a classic poem, make sure your students are familiar with it, then create a parody of it to describe a familiar student experience.

## THE INDIVIDUAL POETRY BOOKLET PROJECT

In March students created individual poetry booklets, a project that brought together many aspects of our comprehensive approach to verse.

I began this activity without fanfare and seemingly out of the blue. One day in March, emulating teacher-poet Ron Overton's approach that I learned in the early eighties, I wrote William Carlos Williams' poem "The Red Wheelbarrow" on the chalkboard and asked students to copy it into their journals. They dutifully obliged, blithely unaware that they were about to undertake a two-week poetry writing activity during which they would compose more than 20 poems and select 10 for publication.

After two students read aloud "The Red Wheelbarrow," I asked the class what they noticed. Invariably a perceptive student mentioned Williams' 3-1 word pattern repeated in each pair of lines of each verse. I asked students to close their eyes, visualize the poem, then tell me what they saw as I read it aloud one more time. Students reported farmyards, barns, silos, fences, fields of crops, a farmhouse, and a porch, along with objects specifically cited in the poem. After remarking on the power of imagery in an apparently slender piece of writing, I suggested that this 16-word poem presented a "still photo," one without a lot of movement or action. For homework, I asked students to compose two "still photo" poems, to save all drafts, and to be prepared to share one of their poems in class the next day. Telling students in advance that I expected them to share their writing in class the following day made it more likely that they would be prepared to do so. It was not my intention to catch a student unawares.

## POETRY BOOKLET ACTIVITY, DAY TWO

The next day, Jessica, at first stymied by the task, revealed that she drew on that experience to create her "still photo":

### Writer's Block

The pencil sat
thoughtfully,

then picked itself
up,

placed it's point
gently

on the lined
paper

and wrote a
word . . .

The pencil sat
thoughtfully . . .

—Jessica Cepelak

Rachel revisited her childhood:

**The Hideout**

So much depends
upon

the bright pink
treehouse

covered with green
leaves

on top of
the tree

—Rachel Ferreira

Once students had shared their "still photo" poems and I collected them, I introduced a second William Carlos Williams poem—this time a slow-motion description of a cat stepping gingerly into a flower pot. Following two readings and a discussion of the poem, I assigned homework: compose two "slow motion" poems.

## POETRY BOOKLET ACTIVITY, DAY THREE

The next day I shared first, then invited students to read their slow-motion poems. Joe depicted a part of his morning ritual:

**The Brush**

As he picks
up the small
blue toothbrush

at the same time
the left arm
reaches for

the tooth paste
both arms meet
and the tooth paste

is on the
brush then
the right arm

begins to scrub
back and forth
until the teeth

are clean then
the brush is
run under water

and put
back into
its holder

—Joe Warren

Later that period, using still another William Carlos Williams poem, I introduced a form that I called the "fast action" poem. Students read William's "The Great Figure," resonant with "gong clangs," "wheels rumbling," and other sensory descriptors, and then composed two "fast action" poems as homework.

## POETRY BOOKLET ACTIVITY, DAY FOUR

Ben used his memories of Manhattan to compose the following, clearly inspired by WCW:

### Headlights

Underground
in the dark
city station
two eyes
staring me down
the blinding brightness
moving closer
with a bang
clang screech
the silver subway
speeds
through the endless
tunnel.

—Ben Kalb

After a number of students shared their poems, I wrote two Robert Frost couplets, "The Span of Time" and "The Secret Sits," on the chalkboard, and students copied these short verses into journals. We read each couplet aloud and discussed each of them. Students quickly noted the basic ingredients of a couplet:

- two lines
- end rhyme
- consistent meter in both lines

For homework that evening I invited students to compose two or three couplets and, of course, to save all drafts. They used the remaining minutes of class to get started.


## POETRY BOOKLET ACTIVITY, DAY FIVE

I began class the following day by reading one of my couplets:

### Couplet

A pair of lines and steady meter.
Ending rhyme. What could be sweeter?

—RMB

One edge of the Shoreham-Wading River school district is an eight-mile stretch of Long Island Sound. Courtney drew from her experience living near the beach to raise this question:

### Seashells

The seashells sit in a clear glass jar
How have they ever come so far.

—Courtney Brain

Later that class we moved from couplets to metaphor, in which an object or an action is compared to another. First we discussed Ezra Pound's "In A Station of the Metro." Then I asked students to compose two-line metaphors as homework. Many students struggled; abstract thinking does not come easily to concrete thinkers. Some, however, got it.

## POETRY BOOKLET ACTIVITY, DAY SIX

In class on Day Six of our poetry-writing activity, Mette waxed philosophical:

### Life

His life's candle became no more
than a blob of wax.

—Mette Arnmark

Chrissy, who was having a terrific eighth-grade year in spite of her friend Dan's departure, composed this metaphor:

### The Best

Being with friends,
A Championship game.

—Chrissy Cardinali

And Erik brought down the house with this two-liner:

### Starving Romantic Man

Your eyes are
two glistening hamburgers

—Erik Platz

Next I introduced the concept of the list poem, drawing upon Whitman's *Leaves of Grass*.

### I Hear America Singing

I hear America singing, the varied carols I hear,
Those of mechanics, each one singing his as it should be blithe and strong,
The carpenter singing his as he measures his plank or beam,
The mason singing his as he makes ready for work, or leaves off work,
The boatman singing what belongs to him in his boat, the deck-hand singing on
　　the steamboat deck,
The shoemaker singing as he sits on his bench, the hatter singing as he stands,
The wood-cutter's song, the ploughboy's on his way in the morning, or at noon
　　intermission or at sundown,
The delicious singing of the mother, or of the young wife at work, or of the girl
　　sewing or washing,
Each singing what belongs to him or her and to none else,
The day what belongs to the day—at night the party of young fellows, robust,
　　friendly,
Singing with open mouths their strong melodious songs.

—Walt Whitman

As was our practice, we read the model poem twice, discussed it, then analyzed its form. Only then did I introduce the term "list poem," allowing students to construct their own knowledge first. The homework: two list poems.

## POETRY BOOKLET ACTIVITY, DAY SEVEN

My list poem honored the topics about which students had recently composed their couplets, metaphors, and "fast action" poems:

> They write poems about trees
> and seashells and bees
> and candles and knights
> and hockey fights
> and shooting hoops
> and Boy Scout troops
> and dogs and cats
> and funny hats

and softball bleachers
and English teachers
and baseball gloves
and secret loves
and hidden sunsets
and household pets
and living schemes
and magic dreams
and friends they see
and memory . . .

—RMB

A. J. Kretschmer created a list poem inspired by Robert Hershon's "New York City Firemen":

### Baseball Players

I never met a baseball player I didn't like.
  Baseball players are something else
that we will never be.
  Baseball payers are dedicated at
what they do so well.
  Baseball players show their bats as
they stand up at the plate.
  Baseball players dress in their
uniforms almost every day.
  Baseball players wear their helmets
so they won't get killed someday.
  Baseball players stand up at
the plate staring down at each other.
  Baseball players don't stop
playing unless they break a leg.

—A. J. Kretschmer

Liz Barra crafted a back-and-forth list poem cataloging her desires and celebrating a special relationship:

### Wishes

I wish I was a cat
I wish you were a mouse

I wish I was lipstick
I wish you were lips
I wish I was a pen
I wish you were paper
I wish I was an envelope
I wish you were a stamp
I wish I was a flea
I wish you were a dog
I wish I was peas
I wish you were carrots
I wish I was a sock
I wish you were a shoe
I wish I was music
I wish you were ears

I wish we'll always be together

—Liz Barra

By this point, students had experimented with six different forms of poetry, yet they were still unaware that they were actually preparing a body of poems from which they would create individual poetry booklets.


## POETRY BOOKLET ACTIVITY, DAYS EIGHT AND NINE

I introduced two more forms: haiku and "shattered shape," based on the poetry of Arnold Adoff in his book *Eats* (1979). In class we read and discussed the examples, then constructed "rules" for composing a haiku or a "shattered shape" poem. As homework each evening, students drafted two or three poems in that particular form. I composed my own verses based on the models studied in class and, to break the ice as well as set a good example, read my drafts first on the following day. As homework for the ninth day of the poetry booklet project, students composed two more poems. I invited them to revisit any form we had studied previously or to write free verse if they wished.


## POETRY BOOKLET ACTIVITY, DAY TEN

Aurelie Shapiro, committed to the environment, used the ninth-day homework assignment to design an Arnold Adoff-inspired "shattered shape" poem:

**If Cows**

> If cows
> could fly
> and
> monkeys
> could jump rope

I would be happy

> and
> if chickens
> had lips
> and
> cats ate
> ice cream

Someone would be happy

> but
> if people
> were conscious
> and
> didn't destroy
> our environment

Everyone would be happy

— Aurelie Shapiro

At no time during this 10-day activity did I announce, "Poetry Unit!" Neither did I mention publishing an individual poetry booklet. I never said to students, "During the next nine days you are going to compose 22 poems using eight different poetic forms." I believed that would be counterproductive. Rather, very casually, I put a short poem on the chalkboard each day for students to copy in their journals, we discussed it in class, and I asked students to draft a couple of poems as homework, inspired by that day's model. The next day, after sharing my own efforts and inviting students to do the same, I collected the students' new drafts.

We repeated this activity nine days in a row, and each day students encountered a different poetic model. I did not make a big deal out of the many poems students were composing. Consequently, when I returned all of their drafts on the tenth day, students were amazed at how many

different poems they had created. Only then did I introduce the idea of
publishing an individual poetry booklet.

*Lesson learned*: Don't tell students everything all at once; they'll learn
what they need to know soon enough.

## PUBLISHING A POETRY BOOKLET

From the more than 20 poems they composed, students selected 10 to
publish in their individual poetry booklets. The challenge was to winnow
the drafts down to the best material. I required a "Foreword" to the booklet in which students explained three of their poems, and each student
composed an "About the Author."

I provided students with two 9" by 12" sheets of white construction paper for the front and back covers. Using lined composition paper, students
wrote one poem per page, then stapled everything together—an instant
poetry booklet. Many students added illustrations to enhance their poems.

Seth Lang, a self-described "mosher" (a form of teenage dancing), went
through a creative spurt and penned over 30 poems in February and
March. At the time, Seth was having a romance with lower-case letters,
and his poetry booklet reflects that infatuation.

Seth's Foreword set the tone:

in march of 1993 team 8-1 had 8 poetry assignments in which we wrote 21
poems.

   i enjoyed all of these assignments, and I will continue writing poetry. mr.
burkhardt has had a tremendous influence on my poetry writing. this book
contains ten of my favorite poems, 5 of which are from the assignment of
21 poems. the other 5 are a collection of various other poems that i wrote in
february–march of 1993.

—seth lang

A deep thinker, Seth lamented the despoliation of our planet:

**earth**
the splendor
of this planet,
uncomparable to

any other
slowly,
it gets destroyed
slowly,
it fades away
why.
why do we do this
to ourselves.—

— seth lang

Seth explained his poem "picture" in his Foreword: "this poem is about how some important objects go unnoticed and how one boy noticed what many others passed by." In "picture," Seth used five syllables in every line except the last:

**picture**

hanging on the wall
walked by many times,
unnoticed by most.
crooked it hangs, as
it is gazed upon,
by a small child
slowly the boy, he
reaches for the frame,
straightning the picture,
noticed by one.—

—seth lang

*Lesson learned*: Individual poetry booklets provide creative outlets for students and their muses.


## MORE POETIC PUBLISHING

Once students identified ten poems for their booklets, I asked them to select five of those to publish in our class anthology (more decisions, further winnowing). "Poeticalibration," which I accidentally stumbled across one evening while perusing my tattered copy of *Poems For All Occasions*, celebrated what we had done:

Aligning words
    and images
and metaphors
    and rhyme
this time
    in measured meter
so that visions
    and messages
calibrated to achieve
    poetic introspection
appear unexpectedly
    in that unseen space
between the lines
    and in our minds:
poetry!

—RMB

(From the apocryphal *Poems For All Occasions,* March 1993)

Next, I asked students to submit their three best poems to the editors of *Contemplations*, our school literary magazine. Every March the *Contemplations* advisor rejoiced when I handed her nearly 150 polished poems for consideration. And, over the years, many of my students' poems were published in *Contemplations*, much to their delight.

As a final activity, each student took one poem and created a poster showing several drafts of it along with an explanation of the composing process the author went through, highlighting the ways that certain lines changed over successive drafts. These poetry posters were displayed in the school corridors

*Lesson learned*: Once students have composed a set of poems, they can publish selected verses in a class anthology, then submit their favorites to the school literary magazine.

## A WORD ABOUT PROCESSING

In 1983 I did word processing for the very first time on a Commodore CBM, which back then was considered state of the art. I was inspired to compose the following:

**Word Processing Pleasures**

The CMB enables me
to write with electronic ease,
revising and inserting and
deleting as I please.

—RMB

Today I would update that first line to read "My iMac now enables me, . . ." but otherwise the impact of computers on writing remains the same: immense. Students can type their poems exactly as they want them to appear, change fonts and enter revisions easily, spell-check the text, and alter the alignment from left-justified to centered with the click of a mouse. Thanks to the power of computers, desktop publishing in schools has become easier and more attractive with each passing year.

*Lesson learned*: Encourage students to compose right on the computer screen and to take advantage of the tools that the software provides.

## "WHY IS IT, TEACHER?"

Sometimes, poems are but the tips of icebergs that hint at circumstances we can only imagine. Jean Waltz composed a poem for the script of a multi-media production, *School Is . . .*:

**Why Is It, Teacher?**

Why is it, teacher,
When I do something that makes me feel proud,
It is not acceptable to you, Teacher?
And my ideas that I think are great
Are silly stupid things to you, Teacher?

Why am I a failure in your class?
Why do you make me hate myself
And think I'm not acceptable to all things in life?

—Jean Waltz
(Eighth grader in 1980–1981)

Years later I asked Jean, now a single mom working as an art teacher in Vermont, if there had been a particular teacher or incident in school that prompted her questions:

JW—I really think this was one of those typical cries for help. I am also sure the word "teacher" could have been replaced by many others: friend, father, etc.

*RB—Now that you are a teacher, how do you see this poem?*

JW—Well, I see the poem for what it is: a struggled summary from a kid with very low self-esteem. I had very little success academically. At least that is how I felt. I knew how it felt to do well in the arts, and I have many fond and proud memories from those interactions. I have no memories of getting that kind of fulfillment in any of my academic classes. This is in part why I wanted to be a teacher to kids who are in a situation where either their previous school didn't work for them or they didn't work for it. If one of our students had written this it would be communicated to the staff so we could be sensitive to the student's needs.

*RB—You wrote this poem for a team multi-media production. Would you have written this poem on your own, anyway, or did doing the production help you focus your ideas?*

JW—Without a doubt the direction of any assignment influenced me. I know that I had a hard time finding appropriate ways to communicate and ended up using ALL venues to express myself. In other words, yes, this [poem] would have not been [written] if not for the assignment, but I had so many other "rejection related" works it's hard to tell if the negative tone was influenced by the assignment.

*RB—What else can you tell me about this poem?*

JW—It makes me really sad. I still wonder if I was getting what I needed in school. I definitely admired all of my teachers at SWR but had such a difficult time. When I went to college I had to constantly get tutoring to learn the basics. I ended up doing really well with one on one guidance. I think back in middle school I was so plagued by social failure and my parents' alcoholism and abuse that I barely functioned. I often went to school in clothes I had slept in. How I learned anything at all is amazing. So there I was, an unsophisticated learner, struggling for affirmation from people who valued academics. I should have been taken out of my home. When I did move out in 11th grade I ended up living with a teacher.

—Jean Waltz
(E-mail communication, March 20, 2003)

*Lesson learned*: Students use writing opportunities to deal with personal issues.

## THE THEME MAGAZINE PROJECT

As a culminating activity each spring, I asked each of my students to select a different theme, create several pieces of writing based on that theme, and assemble them into a magazine. This exit project encouraged eighth graders to draw upon everything they had been taught previously about writing. Individual poetry booklets, completed just a month earlier, served as an excellent warm-up for this more ambitious writing project.

Although poetry was not a requirement, students published poems in each of more than 700 magazines published in my classroom from 1981 to 1996. Students created first- and third-person narratives, interior monologues, personal essays, letters, editorials, journal entries, and interviews. And everyone wrote verse.

Why did so many students voluntarily turn to poetry to express themselves? Because they had been exposed to it from Day One. Because they had already written poems using many different forms. Because they had seen and heard poetry used appropriately on many occasions for all sorts of purposes—to celebrate, to mourn, to comment, to commemorate, to inform, to exaggerate, to amuse, to honor, and to satirize. Because their teacher did, every week. And because they had become comfortable with poetry.

One requirement for the magazine was a "Foreword" in which students explained why they chose their theme and commented on three pieces of writing. This forced students to think about what they had written and what they wanted to say about it to the reader.

Pat Blake's theme was "People." In his Foreword he explained, "I chose this title because I think that no matter what you write, it is usually about people." He continued:

Another piece of writing that you can find in this magazine that I truly think that everybody can understand is called "Grandma." This piece of writing is a poem. It is brief, but through this piece of writing I can see many elderly people. It is a special piece of writing and I think you will enjoy it.

### Grandma

She sits.
Stands.
Sits again.
Here it comes.
But do we listen?
She thinks we do.
Wrong is all she is.

—Pat Blake
(Eighth grader in 1983–1984)

In her Foreword, Jennifer Chan, a crackerjack student with a warm disposition, hinted at something unexpected ahead:

My theme is animals. I picked this theme because it seemed like an easy topic to write about, but mainly I wrote it because I like animals. The animals I wrote about aren't domestic animals like your good ol' cat and dog. I just didn't want to write about that. I wanted to write about something that I thought would be more interesting.

She did not disappoint:

### The Snake

The snake
   slithers
s  l  o  w  l  y .  .  .  .
    d
    o
    w
    n

the dry and dusty
                    road
from
side        to        side.

Then it turns its head
s l o w l y  again
to face the hot black tire
                    of an
                              approaching
                                        car.

*S q u a s h* !
The dust slowly settles
            over the
                    road and
                              soon the
                                        day
                                        is
                                                  over!

—Jennifer Chan
(Eighth grader in 1984–1985)

Rich Jones selected "Thoughts About Summer" as his magazine title because "it's my favorite time of year." He offered a brief apology in the Foreword to his magazine, in which five of the seven pieces were poems:

Even though our magazines are supposed to use several types of writing in them, mine consists mainly of poems. It has poems in it that are long, short, sad, happy, dramatic, and even comical such as "It's Summer Time in Oklahoma." That particular poem, was a lot like a poem that the famous poet, Shel Silverstein, might write. I couldn't say that mine was as good . . . but it was on the same idea as one of his.

—Rich Jones
(Eighth grader in 1983–1984)

Rich's tribute to Shel Silverstein employed irony:

### It's Summer Time in Oklahoma

It's summer time in Oklahoma
time to hit the beaches

surfing, sailing, and scuba diving!        .
cried the boy who was eating peaches
Let's take a trip to Oklahoma
he cried to Mom
The sun's just right
so let's leave tonight
and get there by tomorrow noon!
The boy flashed an ad into her face
showing a picture of the place
"Oklahoma" it read
"A white sanded beach near every surf shop"
that's all it took
a skip, jump, and a hop
for that little boy to cook
up his plot
to get to the place
that it's hot
Oklahoma!

—Rich Jones

One of Rich's poems concluded with a stunning image in the third verse:

### A Blue Summer Bike

A boy is swimming
out in the sea
he is happy
he is free

He's now on a bike
rolling through the air
like a beam of light
while the people stare

They just can't believe
the wet Summer boy
cutting through time
on the blue Summer toy.

—Rich Jones

David Glass's theme was "Communication," for which he composed this wonderfully whimsical four-line, untitled poem:

> Eye dew knot sea Y their R to I's inn "spell"
> it sowans the sayem two mi
>
> sew if U ken reed thiss than its pruff
> thet eye shud have one thuh speling B

> —David Glass
> (Eighth grader in 1983–1984)

Kim Derwitsch selected "Images" as her theme. In one poem, she looked ahead to the following year when she would enter ninth grade, and she depicted the image evoked in her mind by this pending, often anxiety-provoking transition:

### High School

> The thoughts buzzing around in our head,
> Some of us wishing we'd rather be dead.
> The ordeal of being lost in the hall,
> And the cowering ninth graders feeling too small.
> What about the classroom—what would you do
> If the teacher has a question and calls on you?
> If you get it wrong, people'll snicker,
> But don't get upset, or start to bicker.
> Some of us will worry about good grades in school,
> While others'll try not to be the class fool.
> There are personal problems involved with the sensitive one,
> They can't handle the situation, so they escape and run.
> These are just a few of our problems that will arise,
> They're all very important, no matter their size.

> —Kim Derwitsch
> (Eighth grader in 1983–1984)

An accomplished tennis player, Aaron Behrens drew on that experience as he explored his theme, "Striving." In his Foreword Aaron wrote:

One of the first pieces that came to my head was a poem about me standing out on the tennis court and striving for the top. The poem started out with one draft, then it led to three more drafts before I was finally satisfied with the quality. I ended up doing this with all my writing pieces. I put essays, poems and even an interview in my booklet. I think writing the poems were the most enjoyable to write of all the pieces.

—Aaron Behrens
(Eighth grader in 1983–1984)

One of Aaron's poems reflected his authentic ambition to excel:

### Striving for the Top

As I stand
out on the light green tennis court
outlined
with white lines
to verify the doubles
from the singles
and from the ball
being in or out,
I hit the ball
cross court
with a topspin motion
from the breaking of dawn
till the sun sets.
I find that
to make it to the top
you must strive
for the impossible,
for it's only
you
who can make yourself
strive.
You determine
your fate
or victory.

—Aaron Behrens

In his Foreword, Jeremy Kropp wrote:

I chose "Changing in Motion" as my theme because I feel that every experience, important or not, has something in it that you can learn from. Every piece that I have written is original (although some of them are parodies of pieces already written).

—Jeremy Kropp
(Eighth grader in 1983–1984)

Inspired by *Resonance*, my tribute to Dan, the student who moved to New Jersey (see Chapter 2), Jeremy composed the following:

### Regretfulness
*(with respects to Mr. Burkhardt)*

Have you ever had the feeling
  of wondering what to do
    as you try to organize things,
      but you haven't got a clue?

Have you ever known the pain
  of having a lump in your throat?
    and you realize the tears you create
      are enough to make a moat?

Have you ever sensed the rush
  of people's screams flow by your face
    and you think to yourself,
      what am I doing in this place?

Have you ever been confused
  by something coming up so soon
    and you wished you'd planned ahead
      but now must face your doom?

Have you ever wondered why
  something wasn't right for you
    but you did it anyway
      because your parents asked you to?

Have you ever asked yourself
  which one mattered more
    as you try to decide
      while looking down at the floor?

Have you ever read a poem
  that was tough to understand
    but you did it anyway
      just to lend a hand?

And if I can question
    the meaning of what your reading
    can the moment it takes to read this
    be considered "fleeting"?

—Jeremy Kropp

Ever the teacher as poet, I created my own individual magazine, both to model the activity for students and to understand more fully the dimensions of the task. One year it was "RossRitings," another year, "Classroom" (my Foreword thanked "Keith Bach and Mike Forster, with whom I spent time in a writing group, for their contributions to this magazine"). A third year I created "Milestones" and, in the Foreword, acknowledged "Dan Cast for his inspiration for my poem, 'Lists'—Dan's poem, 'Parts,' was clearly the source of my poem."

My classroom was festooned with over a thousand posters, pictures, quotations, and bumper stickers. I put a new one up every day as a challenge to students and their powers of observation. A poem in my magazine "Classroom" described the posters, at one point acknowledging a student who contributed a paper bag puppet to that year's array. Here are excerpts:

### Poster Poem

Roots, Woodstock, pie in the face
(postcards and posters all over the place)

Snoopy, Big Apple, Liberty Bell
(a range of stories these posters tell)

Reagan, Nixon, JFK
(who spotted the new poster first today?)

Donald Duck, Mickey Mouse, also Darth Vader
(they all catch your eye sooner or later)

Peanuts, Beatles, more than one Muppet
(Pat Blake contributed a paper bag puppet)

Popcorn and candy and car bumper sticker
(each week the visual thicket gets thicker)

Rocky, the Coneheads, and Fonzie are there
(kids like to drift off, dream, and stare)

"Ask not what your country . . ."—part of a speech
(regularly I cite them when I teach)

Pickle Family Circus, Man on the Moon
(everything comes down—bare walls in June)

—RMB

*Lesson learned*: The magazine became an exit project for students, one through which they could demonstrate all that they had learned about writing, publishing, and poetry. Preparing a magazine along with my students helped me to understand their challenges and to talk with them as a participating member of the classroom community of writers.

Why did I do so much publishing with students? To give them real reasons for real writing. To enable them to enhance their self-esteem by seeing their words in print. And to put students in situations from which they could not escape without thinking, drafting, revising, editing, and working cooperatively in writing groups.

I did desktop publishing in the classroom because there were so few guaranteed outlets available to students. My students did not enter national poetry contests because they felt that the odds were against them. But every student's writing could appear in the class anthology.

If funding for publication is an issue, I suggest that you ask the PTA for assistance; they are always looking for good causes, and the publishing of student writing is the best cause there is. If you cannot afford to print multiple copies of a publication, create a single class copy—each student will know that his or her poem is enshrined in its pages, and they will take greater care when preparing their writing. Sometimes the school district website is a place for posting student poetry. But in whatever ways you can, publish your students' writing.

In *Bird by Bird*, Anne Lamott (1995) writes, "I understood immediately the thrill of seeing oneself in print. It provides some sort of primal verification: you are in print; therefore you exist" (p. xiv). Simply put, we need to publish student poetry to let them know that they exist.

## A TEACHER'S MISTAKE

Julie Vallely was an accomplished poet long before she arrived in eighth grade. As a sixth grader, Julie's poem "Nature" was selected as the closing piece for *Contemplations*, our middle school literary magazine. She had a poem published in *Contemplations* again when she was in seventh grade. Clearly, I did not teach Julie to write poetry. At best, I made it safe for her to continue to express herself in verse, and I provided occasions for her to do so.

Midway through eighth grade Julie wrote an extraordinary poem titled "I." Because I thought so highly of the poem, I urged her to submit it to *Contemplations*, but she declined. I submitted it anyway, without Julie's knowledge or permission, because I thought she was being unreasonably modest. And, once again, the student editors of *Contemplations* awarded Julie's poem a place of honor as the very last piece of writing in the booklet.

**I**

I used to
hear your voice,
speaking from your head
and ask,
why not from your heart?

I used to
see your face
in black and white
and ask,
why not rainbows?

Now I understand . . . .
your voice is music
I just didn't hear the melodies.

Your face is a prism
I just couldn't see past
the sharp edges.

—Julie Vallely
(Eighth grader in 1980–1981)

When Julie saw her poem in print, she became upset and incensed. She told me off in no uncertain terms. "Who gave you permission to submit my poem?" she demanded. I immediately apologized for my mistake.

When Julie, now a researcher for a hedge fund in New York City, looked back at this incident, she recalled the distressing emotions that it provoked:

To this day I find it unnerving to think about that poem. I was and still am profoundly uncomfortable about how needy and vulnerable it makes me feel. When I saw it published, I felt completely and utterly exposed. The experience was devastating. The anger and humiliation I felt then had nothing to do with what I thought of the poem itself. I wasn't embarrassed by the writing, but I was definitely embarrassed about the emotions behind it. I knew that it was well crafted—perhaps *too* crafted, actually. I remember being pleased with the formal structure I'd made it fit, though even then I was vaguely aware of hiding behind that structure. This poem allowed me to pretend that the emotions in it were conjured up in order to fill out the rigid structure I'd plotted out, when, in reality, it was the other way around. Writing about something so messy and emotional required me to wrangle it into a specific shape because that proved that I *was* in control of it, after all. Until, of course, it slipped out of my control and ended up in that magazine.

When I look at the poem now, my heart breaks for my 13-year old self, who longed for it to have been written to me, not by me. Maybe that's why, in all the years since I wrote that poem, I have only once willingly shared it with another person, and he was my fiancé.

—Julie Valley
(E-mail communication, April 23, 2005)


*Lesson learned*: Do not submit a student's writing for publication without permission, even if you think it will be good for the student. It's disrespectful and wrong. I never did that again.


## CLOSING THOUGHTS

Reading my own weekly poems aloud ("publishing" them) made it safe for students to create and publish their own. Also, frequent poetry recitations influenced students when they wrote; since they were constantly being exposed to new poetic forms, vocabulary, styles, and parodies when they leafed through anthologies in search of a poem to memorize, they composed more easily. Because students were asked to prepare writing for publication on many occasions during the year, they improved their writing skills. Or, as I once observed in a weekly poem, "their verse / got less worse." And because they had choice of subject matter, students felt comfortable expressing themselves.

So, ask your students to write poems about what they know. And join them by creating poems of your own. Write about your students, your school, your teaching, your life—and publish your poetry. To paraphrase Robert Frost:

> I'm setting out to write a little poem.
> I'll only stop to think, and jot ideas,
> And wait and watch the clouds outside, I may.
> I shall not write long.—You write too.

(From the apocryphal *Poems For All Occasions,* 2005)

# POETIC INTERLUDE NO. 4: POETIC TERMS

When composing poetry, you and your students may find the following terms useful.

*Alliteration*— The intentional repetition of the same consonant sound at the beginning of words in a line or verse. (Night never nears nicely nor neatly in November.)

*Assonance*—The intentional repetition of a vowel sound. (In your youth you used to use the ukulele.)

*Iambic pentameter*—Meter employing five stressed beats to the line. Shakespeare's plays were written in iambic pentameter (see *meter*).

> Two households, both alike in dignity,
> In fair Verona, where we lay our scene,
> From ancient grudge break to new mutiny,
> Where civil blood makes civil hands unclean.

*Image*—A mental picture created through words; what you see in your mind's eye.

*Imagery*—All the images in a poem, which taken together suggest a sense experience.

*Irony*—Saying one thing and meaning the opposite. See "Earth," by John Hall Wheelock—"A planet doesn't explode of itself . . ."

*Metaphor*—An implied comparison between two things that are not alike.

*Meter*—The number of poetic beats in a line (from one to eight).

*Onomatopoeia*—The representation of something by a word that sounds like it; whisper, bang!, hiccup.

*Rhyme*—When two words sound the same, usually at the ends of lines.

*Rhyme scheme*—The pattern of line-end rhymes in a poem. The initial rhyme is indicated by an A, the second rhyme by a B, and so forth. Frost's *Stopping by Woods on a Snowy Evening* uses an AABA, BBCB, CCDC, DDDD pattern.

*Rhythm*—A repetitive beat.

*Simile*—A comparison using *like* or *as*: Her eyes were as big as saucers because he ate like a horse.

*Symbol*—An object or idea that stands for something more than it is; the flag of the United States.

*Symbolism*—Using symbols in verse to convey more than the literal meaning of the words: ". . . and miles to go before I sleep."

# Chapter Five

# Discussing and Interpreting

*This chapter presents a method of examining poetry through observations, questions and, eventually, interpretations. I argue that poetic interpretation is a potential minefield; consequently, in discussions, teachers should allow students their own understandings rather than advancing just one interpretation of a poem.*

When you read a poem, ask, "What does it mean?"
Think for yourself. Imagine the scene.
What's it about? Who says it's so?
Why do they say that? How do they know?
What of the title? What of the sense?
Is the poem simple, complex or dense?
In a discussion, ideas abound,
Some of them basic, some quite profound.
Interpretations vary, so we
Ought to agree that we might not agree.

—RMB

[A] poem is not static—held to one fixed, intellectual meaning for all people and all ages. . . . Instead, the significance of a true poem shifts and adapts itself, or better, is living and flexible, so that it may be shaped by each reader to his own comprehension.

—Donald A. Stauffer
(Stauffer, 1946, p. 111)

## WHY DISCUSS AND INTERPRET POETRY?

How do you teach students to interpret poetry? Why should you? What skills do they develop as they endeavor with poetic interpretation? What classroom strategies allow them access to a poem on their own terms? How should a teacher respond to impulsive interpretations? How much of your own opinion should you inject into the discussion? How does the interpreting of poems advance critical thinking skills? These were among the questions I addressed when considering poetry interpretation.

Inherent in the word "interpretation" is the sense of a specific meaning. Yet poems operate on many levels. Teachers ought to pursue the interpretation of poems in ways that allow students to succeed, not to feel inadequate for failing to come up with the "correct" answer. Consequently, asking students to discuss a poem by raising open-ended questions makes the text more accessible:

- What do you see in the poem?
- What does the poet say to you in this poem?
- Why do you think the poet said that?
- What does the poet do to make the poem more inviting?
- Can you state the main idea of the poem in one sentence?

When they respond to such questions, students are compelled to look to their own experiences and lives for answers. In this way, they are not so much guessing at an author's intent as they are shaping their own, emerging ideas.

## WHAT DOES A POEM MEAN, ANYWAY?

Poets are intentional in their choice of vocabulary, line length, stanza formation, tone, imagery, meter (or lack thereof), title, and form. They clearly have an image, a sensation, a message in mind when they create verse.

But recall the words of Archibald MacLeisch from "Ars Poetica," where he famously said, "A poem should not mean / But be." If he is correct, we tread on thin ice when we focus too much attention on any single interpretation of a poem.

## ASSERTIONS ABOUT INTERPRETING POETRY

My classroom lessons on poetry interpretation were structured around a set of assertions, the theory that informed my actions in class. Consider them, then adopt or adapt them to suit your practice. My contention is that you will be a better teacher if you understand the assertions that underlie your pedagogical decisions in the classroom.

- *Exposing students to poetry enhances their understanding of literature and the world.* If so, what actions should the teacher take in class?
- *All students can "get" poetry at some level.* In a heterogeneous classroom, you encounter varying levels of ability and development. Every student is capable of responding to an image, a rhythm, a pattern, a rhyme, or some combination thereof.
- *A poem often operates on many levels and thus is subject to more than one interpretation.* What does this assertion suggest to a teacher who intends to reveal to students his or her ideas about the meaning of a poem?
- *The skills of memorizing poetry, writing poetry, and interpreting poetry are interrelated.* If students memorize and compose poetry regularly, it follows that they will bring greater interpretive skills to any discussions.
- *Teachers who exhibit a love of poetry communicate that passion to their students.* If enthusiasm is contagious, what attitude should the teacher project in class when discussing poems?

I did not invent these assertions by teaching just one lesson on the poetry of Robert Frost. They evolved though trial and error and unexpected insight as I reflected on a class session or on a comment a student made. Through students' candid reactions to the poems we examined, I eventually realized that they were teaching me how to teach poetry.

I also learned that when I listened carefully, students proposed interpretations that satisfied them. Their desire to have a say about what a particular

poem meant and not have it explicated *ad nauseum* by the teacher is reinforced in a verse from Jean Little's *Hey World, Here I Am!*:

### After English Class

I used to like "Stopping by Woods on a Snowy Evening."
I liked the coming darkness,
The jingle of harness bells, breaking—and adding to
　—the stillness,
The gentle drift of snow. . . .

But today, the teacher told us what everything stood for.
The woods, the horse, the miles to go, the sleep—
They all have "hidden meanings."

It's grown so complicated now that,
Next time I drive by,
I don't think I'll bother to stop.

(Little, 1990, p. 28)

Over time, I learned to trust my students. Their refreshing honesty and
varying levels of understanding when discussing poems helped me to see
that they could learn from one another, particularly when I introduced a
strategy for interpreting poetry called OBQUIN.


## IN THE CLASSROOM, PART ONE

Early January—a light blanket of fresh snow covers the school
grounds. Outside, the custodian shovels sidewalks. Inside, on the
chalkboard I write the word "observation." Class has been underway
for two minutes.

"What is an 'observation'?" I inquire. "What does that word mean?"
Slowly, hands go up as students focus on the question.

"It's what you see when you look at something," Michele responds.

Next to "observation" I write the words, "What you see."

"Is everyone okay with this definition? Does that nail it?" I ask. No response. I press the issue.

"How do *I* know what you are seeing, Michele? How do *I* know that
you have made an observation? What *evidence* do I have?"

"Well, I know what I saw," Michele replies uneasily, not sure of what I am asking.

"Exactly, but does anyone else? What's missing in your definition?" Another student raises his hand. "Yes, Dave?"

"It's like what she said, when something happens and you see it, you observe it, but then you have to say what you saw."

"Okay," I respond, adding the words "say what you saw" to the definition.

"So, in order for something to be an observation," I summarize, "you have to see it and then communicate it to someone else. Keep that thought in mind, because in a moment I'm going to ask you to make some observations."

I look at my plan for the day. The lesson is centered on a poem by Robert Frost.

"Now, take out your English Journal and turn to EJ No. 21. The title for this entry is 'SBWOASE,'" I say, writing seven capital letters on the board next to the definition of "observation."

Automatically students open their journals and enter the appropriate heading, repeating a task they have performed twenty times previously:

| EJ No. 21 | January 5 |
|---|---|
| | "SBWOASE" |

No one questions the title; four months in my classroom have taught them that I use acronyms for almost everything. As they write out the heading, I distribute a poem.

"Who would like to read this poem aloud to the class?" I ask. Five hands begin waving.

"Okay, let's have Cheryl and Kevin as readers. You first, Cheryl," I instruct. "Read the title and the author, also." We are seated in a circle. Twenty-three students and I listen intently as Cheryl begins reading.

"'Stopping by Woods on a Snowy Evening,' and it's by Robert Frost."

Glenn interrupts. "I remember this poem. We read it in sixth grade. I like it," he comments. Several other students nod in assent.

"Great, Glenn," I respond. "Now, see if you notice anything new about the poem and what Robert Frost is saying. Cheryl, please continue."

"'Whose woods these are . . .,'" she continues. I watch the other students as Cheryl reads aloud. Their eyes move from the text on the sheet in front of them to Cheryl, then back to the text. Some look outside absent-mindedly at the snow-lined branches on distant trees. A slight breeze causes occasional flurries of flakes to fall to the ground.

When Cheryl finishes, I nod to Kevin. His reading of one of the best-known poems in America is more animated; his emphasis of "horse" and "downy flake" contrast with Cheryl's sing-song delivery.

When Kevin finishes, I say, "Let's acknowledge both Kevin and Cheryl for their reading." Acknowledging students is something we do regularly. As the applause dies down, I continue.


## FIVE OBSERVATIONS

"Okay, what I want you to do now is to read through 'Stopping by Woods . . .' one more time on your own, then write down five observations about the poem in your journal. Remember, an observation is something you see, something that actually is there."

"Hey, I get it," David suddenly blurts out, grinning. "'SBWOASE' refers to the title of the poem!"

"Great observation, David," I smile back. "Now, please begin."

As they write, one or two students occasionally gaze out the window at the fresh snow. I walk around the outside of the circle of desks and read over their shoulders. When most students are finished, I go to the chalkboard again and, underneath the term "observation," write a second word: "question."


## FIVE QUESTIONS

"What is a 'question'?" I ask.

Silence. They know the answer but cannot immediately find the words.

Jessica raises her hand. "It's like when you ask somebody something," she ventures.

On the chalkboard next to the word "question" I write "when you ask."

"Why would you do that? Why would you ask somebody something?" I inquire.

"I dunno, maybe to find out something you don't know," she replies.

I add the words "to find out something" to the chalkboard.

"So," I summarize, "a question is when you ask somebody something to find out something. Good."

Glancing at my lesson plan again, I issue another set of instructions. "Now, read through your five observations, then read the poem one more time to yourself silently. After that, write down five questions you have about this poem. Some of your questions might be based on your observations. Please continue."

Another five minutes pass as students enter questions in their journals. I then instruct, "Now, reread your five observations and five questions silently." They do.

## FIVE INTERPRETATIONS

I write a third term on the board: "interpretation."

"What does this word mean?" I ask.

Zach raises his hand. "I think it means when you say what something means. But," he adds, smiling broadly, "that's only my interpretation." Several classmates laugh.

"Good point, Zach. Interpretations are personal," I note. On the board I write, "when you say what something means." Fifteen of the class period's forty minutes are behind us.

"Okay, now read through 'Stopping by Woods' a third time, and as you do, create five interpretations about the poem. Your interpretations might be responses to some of your questions, or they might be ideas about the poem that occur to you as you read. Please continue."

Eyes shift from journal entries to printed poem, then back again as students engage in making meaning out of Robert Frost's 16-line classic. I walk around the room again, reading what students are writing in their journals, patting kids on the arm, occasionally asking a question *sotto voce* to an individual student, all the while enjoying their industriousness. They are engaged with poetry. Another five minutes pass.

## STATING OBSERVATIONS

"Thanks for taking these tasks seriously, kids," I compliment them. "You did excellent work. As I walked around I read some really good ideas in your journals. Now, who would like to share an observation or two about 'Stopping by Woods'?"

I pause. Four hands go up—Zach, Jenny, Dani, and Fallon. On numerous prior occasions, students have read aloud from their journal entries, whether composed in class or completed as homework. From the very beginning of the school year, I have asked students to share journal excerpts, both as icebreakers for discussion and as model entries for other students. Our practice of constant sharing makes today's request easy for students to accept.

I ask Zach to state his observations.

"His horse thinks it's queer," he begins. "The horse gives his harness bells a shake. He will not see him stopping. He hears the bells, wind, and snowy flakes. And the woods are lovely."

"Thanks, Zach. Dani, can you share your observations?"

Dani smiles and starts reading from her journal. "The poet was good at making sure the setting was dark and cold. There are four paragraphs. There are four lines in each paragraph. It was written by Robert Frost. And 'Stopping by Woods on a Snowy Evening' is the title."

"Thank you, Dani," I say when she finishes. "Who's next?"

"I'll go," says Jenny. Her observations are similar to Dani's until she comes to her fifth one. "The last word in the first and second line of a paragraph rhyme."

"When you say 'paragraph,' Jenny, what do you mean?" I ask.

"I guess I mean verses, Mr. B.," she replies, "and I observe that there are four of them."

"Great. Next? Fallon?"

Fallon observes, "In the first three verses, the three end words rhyme in sentence one, two and four. Also, the last two lines repeat."

"Thank you, Fallon. Anyone else?" I ask. Katelin raises her hand.

"There is a driver who is riding a horse," she begins. "The horse doesn't understand why he is stopping without a farmhouse near. The driver has promises to keep. He must keep on going without any sleep. It's a snowy and windy night."

"Thanks, Katelin." Then, to the class I request, "Let's acknowledge everyone who shared their observations." Students offer brief, polite applause.

## POSING QUESTIONS

"Okay, we've heard a few observations, and we've learned something about 'Stopping by Woods.' What are some questions that you have about this poem?" Again, hands go up. As students speak, I list their questions on the chalkboard:

- Why are there four lines per paragraph?
- Why do the last lines repeat?
- What does the title mean?
- Who is Robert Frost?
- Why does only part of the poem rhyme and not the whole thing?
- Why did Robert Frost decide to write this poem?
- Why does his horse shake the harness?
- Why are the woods lovely?

"Now," I say, "I know we don't have all of them, but take a look at these questions. One thing I've repeated all year, kids," I emphasize, "is that you will learn more from each other than you will ever learn from me. Look at this list. We could spend an entire class dealing with just the questions you have posed. Good job."

Ten minutes remain in the class. I move ahead.

## OFFERING INTERPRETATIONS

"The last part of this exercise was to write down five interpretations about the poem," I say. "Let's hear some."

Several students raise their hands, anxious to contribute.

"Robert Frost repeated the last two lines because he wanted to make a point," Fallon says, calling attention to one of the most famous poetic endings of all time.

"He won't see them stopping because he lives in the village," Zach offers.

"He's on an important journey somewhere," suggests Jenny.

As more and more students offer interpretations, I listen closely and nod, consciously avoiding the pitfall of reacting to a student's particular understanding of the poet's intent. At the end of class I collect journals and thank students once again for their active participation in the lesson.

## JOURNAL RESPONSE

That evening as I read through 24 journal entries, I encounter more responses to the poem. Dani reveals her uncertainty when she writes, "He keeps his promises because he's good at it?"

Katelin's journal entry includes the following questions and her responses to them:

Why does the driver stop? Maybe to see how beautiful the woods look "filling up with snow." Whose house is "in the village"? The owner of the woods' house is in the village. What promises does he have to keep? He has to get to a relative's house, or go to a job. Why would he want to stop in the cold? He had to see the beauty of the forest in the snow. Why is he in someone else's woods? It's the only way to get there, or [maybe] you're allowed in his woods.

She adds the following note to her entry:

I couldn't think of any good questions. After observing and thinking of questions, I began to really understand the poem, and I never really did, or take time to think about it.

—Katelin Tinley
(Eighth grader in 1992–1993; excerpt from English journal, January 1993)

I am pleased with my students' responses to this initial effort at observing, questioning, and interpreting poetry. I also suspect that as they do more OBQUINs, they will become more insightful about poetry.

## IN THE CLASSROOM, PART TWO

I invented the acronym OBQUIN to represent the interrelated processes of *ob*serving, *qu*estioning, and *in*terpreting a poem. That way, I can use shorthand when assigning students homework, as I do for EJ No. 22 the next day and EJ No. 23 two days later.

But first, we revisit "Stopping by Woods."

"One of the observations that some people made in their journals in class yesterday," I begin, "was that, quote, 'The title has seven words in it,' end quote. Another was that, quote, 'The poet was good at making sure the setting was dark and cold,' end quote. What is your reaction to these two 'observations'? Are they of the same importance or significance?"

After a moment, David raises his hand.

"Nope. I mean, c'mon, so the title has seven words, big deal. It's not that important. But that stuff about a cold and dark setting, that sounds important."

"Maybe it is, and maybe it isn't, Dave," I respond noncommittally. "Let me reword the question. What constitutes a useful observation of a poem? What can you observe that the poet does that might help you to understand the poem?"

It is a rhetorical question; I want them to think about the quality of their observations, questions, and interpretations and raise the bar as we proceed through four more poems during the next four days. And they do.

Students clearly improve when completing their second OBQUIN. Dani, who in her first attempt observed such items as the title of the poem, the author's name, and the number of lines per verse, becomes more insightful in her observations about "Not in the Guidebooks," by Elizabeth Jennings:

1. The author does not tell where or what the place is she's describing.
2. The poem describes a dreary unwelcoming place to visit.
3. The Poem does not just come out and tell what kind of house or shelter it is. Instead large details about the shelter is given to the reader.
4. Elizabeth Jennings tells her piece of writing in a way many ideas could be thought when trying to understand what is really being said.

5. You get a good picture in your mind of the way the shelter is that Elizabeth Jennings is explaining.

—Dani Saviano
(Eighth grader in 1994–1995; excerpt from English journal, January 1995)

Dani's questions and interpretations include the following:

No. 3. QU—Why didn't she explain in a less complicated way the point of
the poem?

IN—She did not want to tell us in a non-complicated way what the poem
was really about or we would be able to discover right away without thinking what it really was telling us.

In EJ No. 23, Meghan raises a question about Theodore Roethke's "My
Papa's Waltz": "Why is [the son] so determined not to let go?" Then she
answers her own question:

Maybe he feels no one else will be there if he stops taking care of his father.

—Meghan Carey
(Eighth grader in 1994–1995; excerpt from English journal, January 1995)

Jenny asks: "Why does the title ['My Papa's Waltz'] sound like a happier poem, when the words in the poem sound so upsetting?" She responds with this interpretation:

The title sounds happier then it really is because the author felt not all things
seem the way they really are. So you have to look deeper. And in this case
you had to read the poem to discover what it really was about.

—Jenny Furano
(Eighth grader in 1994–1995; excerpt from English journal, January 1995)

Katelin asks and answers the following question about Roethke's poem:

Where did they live? They probably live somewhere out by the farms, since
the father's hands were 'caked with dirt" he probably worked on a farm.

—Katelin Tinley
(Eighth grader in 1992–1993; excerpt from English journal, January 1993)

We examine "Mending Wall" by Robert Frost for the fourth OBQUIN, reading it aloud in class and adhering to the now familiar protocol.

For the fifth exercise, students delve into e.e. cummings' "anyone lived in a pretty how town"—a genuine challenge. Ben asks an important question but has no answer to it:

QU—Why is "Women" the only word in the poem with a capital letter (lines 5 & 33)?

IN —Because?

Ben also asks, "Why is [the man's] name 'anyone'?" His response:

Because people thought that he wasn't "anyone" special, like he had no life and he wasn't "someone."

—Ben Kalb
(Eighth grader in 1994–1995; Excerpt from English journal, January 1995)

Jenny asks, "What is meant when the poem keeps referring to sun, moon, stars, rain?" She answers her own question:

It's the seasons. And seasons never stop continuing so the poem is letting us know that life goes on like the seasons and weather or not things are not perfect and people die life will always continue.

—Jenny Furano
(Eighth grader in 1994–1995; excerpt from English journal, January 1995)

As students examine this fifth poem, I add a new instruction: "Tell what the poem means to you." Katelin sums it up this way:

Since Woman is capitalized maybe Women care about men and men don't care about women since they say: She (meaning women) laughed his joy and cried his grief. It is about life and death everyone lives and dies not caring about anything. "no one loved him more by more" "Women and men (both little and small) cared for anyone not at all." I think it is about one caring person in the town who cares about everyone but everyone else doesn't care so they all live and die a fast uncaring life.

—Katelin Tinley
(Eighth grader in 1992–1993; excerpt from English journal, January 1993)

During the week as students share observations, questions, and interpretations about the poems presented to them, they grow in their understanding of poetic intent in general and of certain poems in particular. They also demonstrate a steadily improving ability to make observations about text and context; to raise pertinent questions; to respond to those questions; and to learn by listening to one another. Through this process they become a community of inquirers, examining poetry and sharing ideas.

*Suggestion*: Once you complete four or five OBQUIN exercises with your students, revisit the very first poem you examined. Student responses, now informed by experience and the examples of peers, will be much improved compared to their original observations, questions, and interpretations.

## THE PEDAGOGY OF POETRY

When I began to teach poetry interpretations using the OBQUIN approach, I did not deliver a long-winded explanation of what was about to happen, nor did I even suggest the onset of a new area of study. I simply began class one day by asking students to define three familiar terms, to read a specific poem ("Stopping by Woods . . ."), and to follow three instructions ("Make five observations, pose five questions, offer five interpretations"). Later, when students looked back, they realized what they had accomplished. In language arts classes, middle school students know that they are going to be interacting with the English language in some way. Do they need to know all the details ahead of time? My advice—get to the action. Don't spend time explaining what you are about to do—instead, do it!

The OBQUIN approach is a deliberate design, an attempt to give all students access to poetry. By using a protocol of examination and reflection again and again, students learn how to dig into poems and come up with understandings of their own. As I used this technique in class day after day, more and more students gained confidence with it. And as they shared their written observations, questions, and interpretations, students provided positive models for other classmates to emulate.

Once we had defined all three terms and these definitions were printed on the chalkboard, I underlined the first two letters of each term: OB QU IN. Students saw the acronym created before their eyes.

I used Frost's "Stopping by Woods" for the first OBQUIN exercise because this poem is, in many ways, more accessible and more familiar than most. Over the years it proved to be a good departure point for discussions. Also, the likelihood of snow is greater in January than in, say, April. Some poems lend themselves to certain seasons or holidays, and when I could, I took advantage of these inherent connections.

When Glenn announced, "We read [this poem] in sixth grade," I did not resist his interruption. Earlier in my teaching career I would have been disappointed, feeling that the surprise and delight of "Stopping by Woods" was ruined. But I learned that one can reread a poem many times and still discover new meanings in it. If a student is exposed to a poem as a sixth grader, in most cases he or she will bring new understanding to it as an eighth grader.

Since I introduced journals during the first week of school as a continuing responsibility for all students, they understood exactly what to do when I instructed, "Open your journal to EJ No. 21." The routine of creating a proper heading for a journal entry, something students had done many times previously, was so familiar that they did it automatically, quieting themselves and getting down to work. Familiarity with procedure helped them to focus.

I deliberately did *not* say, "We are going to do an OBQUIN." Rather, I asked students to define three terms, then make observations, then pose questions, and then interpret a poem. Once they had done these tasks, I explained to students that this activity is known as an OBQUIN, giving a name to a protocol with which they now had direct experience.

Having two students read the poem aloud, then asking all students to read the poem silently, twice, familiarized them with words, lines, and stanzas, making the three tasks—observing, questioning, and interpreting—somewhat easier. When students write about a poem before discussing it in class, the ensuing discussion usually goes better because kids have thought through their ideas, raised a few questions in their minds, and formulated preliminary opinions about the poet's intent. And because, through rereading, students were somewhat conversant with the text, they could refer to actual words or lines to support their ideas about meaning.

By walking around the room and reading what students were writing, I communicated my interest in their ideas. I also monitored how well they were responding to the OBQUIN challenge. My attention helped students to stay on task.

When students shared observations, questions, and interpretations, I was careful not to signal that any particular response was better or worse than the others. I wanted kids listening to others and thinking for themselves. My neutral yet reassuring support of their evolving interpretations— "That's interesting, say more"—was well received, and I sensed growing engagement as well as developing levels of interpretive skill when students examined one poem a day for several days.

I felt that Zach's comment, "That's only my interpretation," added to the class's understanding of the term being defined through his joke, and I welcomed his use of humor to make a point.

By asking the question, "Who would like to share an observation or two about 'Stopping by Woods'?" I let students know that I did not expect them to read all five of their observations. This put some pupils at ease because they could then select which observations to contribute to the class discussion.

## CONCRETE, TRANSITIONAL, AND FORMAL THINKERS

Making meaning is the responsibility of every student. When middle school students read and discuss poems, they have to think, compare, contrast, listen, remember, take inductive leaps, offer ideas, and engage with others.

Jack, who in a journal entry in *Love That Dog* (Creech, 2001, p. 20) revealed that he "really really really / did NOT get" Robert Frost's poem "The Pasture," reveals one aspect of the young adolescent mind when confronting the abstractions of poetry. Jack may be a concrete thinker.

Jean Piaget, a Swiss educator and philosopher, suggested that as children grow, their capacity for thinking evolves through three stages: concrete, transitional, and formal. Concrete thinkers are often literal, while formal thinkers move more easily among abstractions.

In Piagetian terms, many middle school students are concrete thinkers, some are in transition between concrete and formal thinking, and very few are formal thinkers. Consequently, a teacher at the middle level is likely to elicit a variety of opinions about the meaning of a particular text when he or she asks students in a heterogeneously grouped classroom what they think.

Ginsburg and Opper (1979), in *Piaget's Theory of Intellectual Development*, wrote:

> In Piaget's theory the final period of intellectual development is that of *formal operations*, which begins at about age 12, and is consolidated during adolescence. . . . [T]he adolescent's thought is flexible and effective. He can deal efficiently with the complex problems of reasoning. . . . [T]he adolescent can imagine the many possibilities inherent in a situation. Unlike the concrete-operational child, whose thought is tied to the concrete, the adolescent can deal with hypothetical propositions. (p. 178)

Knowles and Brown (2000) explained further:

> In the concrete stage, [young adolescents] can classify and order objects, reverse processes, think of more than one thing at a time, and think logically about concrete objects. They still need direct experiences and do better with real as opposed to abstract objects or thought. Middle level students in this concrete stage of cognitive growth are better able to cognitively grasp abstract principles when ideas are taught with the use of hands-on activities and materials rather than presented in a lecture or by reading a textbook. (pp. 17–18)

In an obituary honoring the late Louise Rosenblatt that first appeared on the New York University website in February 2005 and was reprinted in NCTE's *Voices from the Middle* in March 2005, educator James Devitt noted:

> Rosenblatt stressed that every act of reading involved a "transaction" of reader and text in which both were essential. In her view, any text—Toni Morrison's *Beloved*, a car owner's manual, a poem—was lifeless without a reader who is active: active readers create multiple readings of the same text; no reading is uniquely "correct." (p. 2)

Rosenblatt understood that different readers bring differing interpretations to any piece of writing. Her seminal work supported "a community of readers who sought to refine their reading and test their responses against the text" (p. 2).

Consider, then, the implications of having concrete thinkers sitting next to transitional and formal thinkers in the classroom. The concrete thinker may insist that Poe's raven is actually there in the room, just above the door, and that the raven actually says "Nevermore" "because it says so right here in the text, Mr. B." At this stage in their development, concrete thinkers often are literalists with little appreciation for the concept of metaphor. On the other hand, the transitional or formal thinker might see the raven as a darker symbol of Poe's anger at the world, or a harbinger of death, or an alter ego. When classmates share ideas in discussion, each student is forced to think for himself or herself. This was one of my goals.

In her insightful book *Errors and Expectations,* Mina Shaughnessy (1977) suggested that a student's mistakes in writing should not necessarily be seen as negatives but rather as indications that the student is reaching out, breaking boundaries, attempting something new. Basic writing students, she declared:

> write the way they do, not because they are slow or non-verbal, indifferent
> to or incapable of academic excellence, but because they are beginners and
> must, like all beginners, learn by making mistakes. (p. 5)

In the same vein, a teacher has several possible responses when a student suggests an unusual interpretation to a poem:

"You're wrong."

"That's dumb."

"Bad answer."

"Why do you say that?"

Which of these reactions is most likely to elicit a positive response from a young adolescent, I ask rhetorically.

When a student offers an unexpected interpretation, why not ask, "What in the text leads you to that interpretation?" Such a question forces students to examine the text more closely and to suggest ideas that, at least to them, are grounded in the poet's own words.

When we discussed Frost's "Stopping by Woods" (and we did so every year), on more than one occasion a concrete thinker offered something like the following: "I think I know what this poem is about. The guy has a horse and a sleigh, and some bells. It's December, 'cause it's snowing, so it's about Santa Claus going to deliver presents, and he has many miles to go before he delivers all the presents."

Meanwhile, a transitional or formal thinker might focus on the last two lines.

"What's this about 'sleep' at the end of the poem, Mr. B.," one student asked. "Isn't 'sleep' the same as 'death,' like when you put a cat to sleep? Is this poem about life and death?"

In both instances, I refrained from uttering a quick "yes" or "no." Middle-level students are in the middle third of their public schooling, and many will go on to higher education. Over time, the cumulative effects of 12 years in schooling will have an impact, and they will grow in their ability to interpret text. Be patient—they are evolving learners.

Sometimes it is impossible for a young adolescent to explain what his or her mind senses, even when other students offer similar interpretations. Some kids just don't have the words yet, and even if they do, not all will arrive at the same interpretation.

## SUGGESTED POEMS TO READ AND DISCUSS

Good poetry reveals something significant about the human condition and how we spend our time here, and there are countless poems suitable for class discussion. The specific poems that you select for students to discuss and interpret are less important than the fact that you offer a range of poetry from easy to difficult. I recommend that you choose poems you like, and, over the years, add new ones, discarding those that don't engage students. Their reactions will tell you which poems are best suited for an OBQUIN exercise.

A suggestion: get a copy of *The Top 500 Poems*, edited by William Harmon (1992), and begin leafing through it, noting the verses that appeal to you and, because you know your students, that might appeal to them as well. Listed in chronological order from "The Cuckoo's Song" (c. 1250–1350) through Shakespeare and Donne to Wordsworth, from Keats and Shelley to Dickinson and Yeats, and ending with Alan Ginsberg's "A Supermarket in California" and Sylvia Plath's "Daddy," *The Top 500 Poems* is a comprehensive anthology. Harmon offers anecdotal notes on each poet and, in many instances, on the poems. In the introduction, titled "This Is *It!*," he explains:

> [T]his collection of the 500 poems that (according to *The Columbia Granger's ® Index to Poetry*) have been anthologized most often impresses me as exactly the sort of book with which I would want to welcome [my

three-year-old daughter Caroline] to the world of poetry in English. As a
poet, teacher, editor, and father, I am satisfied that these 500 poems, with a
bit of commentary, will serve as a splendid way for somebody to become
acquainted with the best that has been written in the shorter poetic forms for
about 750 years. As I have said to myself repeatedly, this is *it!* (p. 1)

The poem "what if a much of a which of a wind" by e. e. cummings is
wonderful to read aloud. Shelley's "Ozymandius" is great to dig into; kids
find much meaning there. A colleague of mine uses Langston Hughes'
"Mother to Son" with her sixth-grade students, some of whom are already
into gang activity after school. She explained to me that reading the poem
and discussing it with them was like peeling the skin off an onion, one
layer at a time; the more her students discussed the poem, the more insights they shared.

## CLOSING THOUGHTS

My students came to the OBQUIN activity with prior poetic knowledge.
Earlier in the year they recited several poems, bringing to life mere lines
of text on a sheet of paper. They also crafted words and images into coherent verse. Through these activities, they were better able to appreciate
what a particular poet was trying to say. The interrelatedness of these experiences prepared students for the task of interpreting various verses
through open-ended discussions.

# POETIC INTERLUDE NO. 5: IMMERSE / YOURSELF IN VERSE; OR, WRITE A RHYMING POEM

Below are opening lines to three incomplete poems, each followed by a list of rhyming words (you can add others to the list).

**Task:** Write a poem that rhymes.

**Suggestions:**

- Do this activity by yourself and see what rhymes you create. Compose at least eight lines that have end rhyme.
- Ask students to do this exercise, then have them compare poems.
- Share your drafts with students after they have created their own rhyming poems.
- Using a rhyming dictionary, create your own "rhyming poem" introduction and rhyme list.

**The poems:**

> Immerse
> yourself
> in verse.
> It's not a curse . . .

| terse | reverse | disburse |
|-------|---------|----------|
| purse | inverse | universe |
| nurse | adverse | converse |
| worse | diverse | perverse |
| coerce | disperse | obverse |
| hearse | rehearse | traverse |

> Would you agree
> that when you see
> a carefree . . .

| fee | tree | emcee |
|-----|------|-------|
| bee | flea | yippee |
| lea | glee | family |
| tea | plea | urgency |
| key | knee | guarantee |
| free | spree | bumblebee |

I viewed
the breakfast food
as crude . . .

| rude | who'd | attitude |
|------|-------|----------|
| dude | you'd | solitude |
| elude | shrewd | subdued |
| prude | prelude | conclude |
| mood | exclude | fortitude |
| brood | latitude | ingratitude |

*Chapter Six*

# The Process of Student Poetry

*This chapter describes the composition processes of three student poets and suggests what we can learn when we look closely at the writing of individual students.*

> Student voices thinking back,
> reflecting on their poetry,
> offer insights we might track
> as we study fluency.
>
> —RMB

## HOW DO STUDENTS COMPOSE POEMS?

What happens to student writers in a classroom that employs a comprehensive approach to poetry? What can we learn from students when they reflect on their writing process? What skills do they develop as they compose poems and then explain how they created them? How can the information we glean inform classroom practice? These were some of the questions that I had in mind when I asked students to compose journal entries in which they described what happened as they wrote poems.

Three eighth-grade classmates—Andrea, Alyson, and Dawne—knew one another well. Serious students all, they participated in the same learning activities from September to June: memorizing and reciting poetry; drafting, revising, and publishing poems and other pieces of writing; composing journal entries; working with one another in writing groups; participating in class discussions about the meaning of specific poems; assembling booklets of their poetry; listening to my weekly poems; and creating individual magazines at the end of the year. Through these learning activities, Andrea, Alyson, and Dawne experienced growth as writers. And through their writing and reflections, they revealed what students can achieve when they are encouraged to draft, revise, and publish poetry and to reflect in journals on their composing process.


## ANDREA

Well before she arrived in my class, Andrea Dicks felt comfortable writing poetry. Poems that she composed in sixth and seventh grade appeared in *Contemplations*, the school literary magazine. In fact, during eighth grade Andrea served as an editor of that magazine. This untitled poem, published when she was seventh grade, reflects Andrea's style of poetry:

> Tall and mighty are the trees
> Rich green
> > towering the earth
> But they are never too vain
> > to give shade
> To a poor man
> > that may come walking by.
>
> —AD

In a letter of introduction written to me the first week of eighth grade, Andrea said confidently, "I really like writing a whole lot. The thing I like to write the most is poetry. I usually write in a loosely structured version of a haiku. I almost always write about nature."

She continued:

Last year Mr. Katzoff had me write more about my thoughts and feelings. I still don't feel comfortable with that but I'm going to keep trying. He also had me try other forms of poetry besides haiku. The only one I got any good in was sonnets. This year I would like to learn some other forms (I don't like writing without some guidelines).

—AD

Along with her letter of introduction, Andrea loaned me her poetry notebook containing 16 poems she had composed in sixth and seventh grade. These verses revealed Andrea as a strong writer capable of crafting arresting images:

> The mountain smiles
> While a stream
> Trickles down its side.
>
> —AD

My response was a two-page typed letter in which I included some of my own poems and my reactions to several of hers:

Poetry is also my favorite form of expression—as you can see, Andrea. I write both rhymed and free verse—but almost always employ a form or a pattern. Sometimes I write about nature. More often I write about feelings or situations or reflections on life.

". . . the mountain smiles . . ," This is one of my favorites. I picture a huge Fuji-type mountain looming majestically in the distance, sitting serenely and quietly—but all of a sudden the mountain breaks into a grin— the rollicking, bouncing, splashing, darting stream bursting down its side causes the mountain to smile—and the similarity between "trickle" and "tickle" is an extraordinary "coincidence" that pulls it all together; the mind reads one word but thinks, quite appropriately, of the other. A gem of a poem.

—RMB

## September

"This evening as homework," I instructed students early in the second week of school, "compose two free verse poems. Then write a journal entry describing how you wrote each poem." In class that day we had read four free verse poems composed by students from the preceding year. We discussed each poem, then constructed a set of guidelines for composing free verse poetry based on the common features of the four poems.

At that point, most of my students had limited experience reflecting on their own writing. Unsure and tentative, they wondered if they would do it correctly. Andrea, who stunned her classmates and me later that year with an ambitious recitation of Longfellow's "Paul Revere's Ride," was no exception.

Andrea began her free verse poem by writing the word "Autumn." She then listed 11 images, adjectives, and ideas.

**Autumn**

fluttering leaves
temple of trees
radiance
trembling leaves
red sun
scorch
shedding leaves
leaves—beautiful _____
vanishing ~~autumn~~ summer
~~wistfully~~ wistfully
the sadness of it.

Just below this list, Andrea jotted down eight more ideas. The phrase "leaf circling" became the central, connecting image.

ending / beginning
<u>soaring</u>
height greatness −> dying          trying to live again
gusts + gales of wind
leaf circling
free
triumph
leaf - ~~I can do something!~~

Then Andrea turned her two lists into a first draft:

Leaf stuck on tree
gets blown in wind
is free (living)
starts falling (dying)
goes up again (alive again)
falls to ground—*dead*

—AD

In her very first journal entry, Andrea wrote:

September 14—"Poem"
At first I didn't know what to write about. I started writing about autumn
but it wasn't working. I used some of the ideas from that poem to make this
one. There's not much I can write about this piece yet since it's mainly still
just words. I like the main idea of it, and I think it has good possibility of
becoming something I can be proud of. It's still in too much of a rough copy
to have any strong or weak parts to it. All I can say is that I like it—so far.

—AD

Three days later Andrea revealed:

Help! I don't think I'll be able to do this piece, I'm having soooo much
trouble! I had so many ideas for this, but its not working! . . . I thought this
piece was going to be super, but I can't do it! I've been trying for so long.
Forget it, I'm going to pick another piece. I'll do the one about the man
walking through the woods, for that one can still go through alot of revision.
Maybe I'll try to do this one again some other time.

—AD

Andrea then composed the following untitled poem, loosely basing it
on ideas she explored in her first draft:

**Poem**
A man was walking / down a country road
      the air smelled fresh and clean
in the distance / a bird was singing
The trees on both sides of the road
      were huge, and gnarled with age
sunlight was filtering through the spaces
      between the leaves,
making everything appear radiant and glowing
But all this beauty and serenity
      went to waste
for the man walking down the road
      never saw the things around him.

—AD

Next, she added these explanatory words in her journal:

After I was in bed half asleep I got some more ideas to add to the poem.
When that happened it was already 11:00 p.m. I think that the second copy
turned out better.

Finally, Andrea concluded her journal entry with a dismissive statement. Little did she know how far off the mark her comments would prove
to be:

I don't think I'm going to work on this poem anymore. I don't like it enough
to keep improving it.

—AD

Along with her journal entry, Andrea turned in the second draft of the
poem. She thought that her first draft was too messy to submit. I gave Andrea a √+ to acknowledge her work, then responded:

Andrea—
Your journal entry is good—you let me know where the idea came from and
how you developed it. I'd like you to turn in all drafts of poems, even if they
are messy. I like to see the ideas progress. Thanks.

—RMB

## October

In early October after students completed three journal entries, I typed up
25 anonymous excerpts, specifically selecting positive examples as models for students to emulate. Some sample comments:

2. I'm in my room thinking about the poem assignment. I feel this one is
hard because I never wrote a poem before and I don't have the slightest idea
on how to begin. I've been thinking of writing one about fall but the words
just don't seem to fit. . . . I was just fooling around with some words and
poems. I like the ones where the word is spelled out. Oh, I just got an idea
on death. Don't ask me how, it just came to me. . . . I'm looking over my 5
line poem that took me so long to write. I first started off by writing one
line, then I wrote the second, then came the third letter—"A". That one was

hard to find an opening word, so I got out the dictionary and started thumbing through it to find an "A" word, when I decided I didn't like the second line, so I changed it. . . .

16. So I started by trying to rhyme words with words and then thought to myself, should I have every line rhyme with the next, have every other line rhyme, or just have the last word of each paragraph rhyme with each other? I decided on every other line as you'll see when you read it. After I got started it was getting easier except the last four lines I couldn't get. I was trying to fit the "Last Day" in there somehow and I did. By the way, I did this lying on my bed in complete silence. I think my work is a lot better when I do it in complete silence. I don't understand how people can work with the radio playing. Oh well, I have more to write but my hand's getting tired. Maybe I'll add more tomorrow.

23. I don't know what I'm going to write my poem on. I think poems are the worst type of writing because I can't write poems. I don't think it is going to be good but I'm going to try. . . . It came out good! It was not that hard. It took me a while to start.

Andrea found the sample excerpts both informative and instructive:

October 13—"Reaction"
I'm surprised at how similar most of them are. Yet they're also very different. I think giving us excerpts from everybody else's process journal was a good idea. From reading them I learned some new ways to get ideas. Such as from books or TV or dreams etc. I'm going to save that [set of anonymous journal excerpts] because I think it will help me when I'm stuck, and don't know what to write.

I have a question: are the entries suppose to be organized and have everything spelled right, in perfect penmanship, or can it be like this, with ideas all over the page?

—AD

To Andrea's questions I responded, "No, perfect penmanship in a journal entry is not important," "Yes—I prefer them 'messy'!" and "I enjoy reading your ideas all over the page." Armed with new possibilities for her journal, Andrea began submitting longer entries that described in greater detail how she went about drafting and revising.

In October, our team went on a three-day outdoor education field trip to Frost Valley in the Catskill Mountains. In a journal entry titled "Today" that she composed the first evening there, Andrea compiled a list of things she had observed at Frost Valley:

> mountains
> leaves falling, changing colors
> mirror like
> rippling stream
> peace serenity quiet
> soft nose of a deer
> stone walls
> castle
> root cellar
> hunger

Later that evening Andrea used this list as the basis for a poem, one describing her impressions of the first day at Frost Valley:

> The scenery is gorgeous
> The mountains are spotted with different colored trees
> All the water is crystal clear
> I wish we could go swimming
> I love it here
> It's so beautiful
> A deer!
> Another one!
> I love it!
> Fresh smell
> Clean
> Root cellar
> Rocks
> Silence
>
> —AD

## November

On November 7, Andrea turned in drafts of two untitled poems along with explanatory journal entries. The first poem:

?

A gorgeous nightingale
    locked in a golden cage
jealously watched a little daisy
    growing freely
in a meadow nearby.

—AD

In her journal Andrea explained:

For the first poem I got my idea at 2:00 a.m. I had been in my bed half
asleep when I got this image in my head. It was of a beautiful bird in a really fancy cage. I could tell the cage must have been really expensive, but
the bird isn't happy, even though he has a life of luxury, instead he's very
sad. He has been watching a poor little daisy, who even though the daisy had
a hard life, is totally free! And the bird is very jealous of the flower.

I'm thinking about maybe doing a second verse from the flower's point of
view, jealous of the bird's easy life, and how much more freedom the bird has,
being able to move while he is rooted to the ground. I'm going to try that now.
   *Later.*

I don't like how the second verse sounds. It changes the whole tone and
meaning of the poem, and I'm happier with just the 1st verse. Maybe I'll try
a second verse some other time.

—AD

Andrea's second poem:

?

Why must everything I touch
    with tenderness
prickle back
        in return? . . .

—AD

Regarding this poem, Andrea noted: "I wrote this poem over the summer, so I don't remember the process. I just want to get some suggestions
from the writing group about it, OK?"

Andrea's writing group was helpful. On her draft, the question marks
that served as place holders for eventual titles were overwritten in pencil.

The first poem was now titled "Envy," and one word—"jealously"—was circled. Andrea's second poem sported a two-word title: "The Rose."

Two days later Andrea reflected: "I'm really happy with how my poems turned out. I know it's only a first draft but the writing group and I couldn't think of anything to add/subtract. I know they aren't perfect but I like them how they are."

I responded to her journal entry with encouragement:

Each time I read this journal, I admire your ability as a writer to express yourself. You make it very clear what your process is, and I am really pleased with the quality of your writing <u>and</u> your process entries.

I loved the "nightingale" poem—it captured a real emotion of envy for me. It works!

$$-RMB \sqrt{+}$$

In mid-November, Andrea returned to the unfinished draft of the poem that she composed in mid-September, embellishing it somewhat:

**Poem**

A man was walking / down a country road
     the air smelled fresh and clean
in the distance / a bird was singing . . . a beautiful song
The trees on both sides of the road
     were huge, and gnarled with age
sunlight ~~was~~ filter~~ing~~ed through ~~the spaces~~
~~between~~ the leaves,
making everything appear radiant and glowing
But all this beauty and serenity
     went to waste
for the man walking down the road
     never saw the things around him.

$$-AD$$

In the left margin Andrea circled the word "sunlight" (line 6) and, next to it, entered the phrase, "the glow of a sunset." From the word "glowing" (line 8), she drew an arrow to a newly composed fourth stanza below:

A ~~small~~ breeze ~~appeared~~ filtered through the forest
making the grass ~~dance~~ look like
~~it was~~ dancing elves

In Draft 3, Andrea included the three "breeze filtered" lines, but upon re-flection she crossed them out. Draft 4 included two versions of a new stanza:

**#1**
A soft carpet of moss
    covered the ground

**#2**
A deep green carpet
          of moss
  covered the ground
    It was soft
    and looked like green velvet.

The following day, Andrea noted cautiously in her journal:

Poem
I can't think of a title. I'll be interested to see how my writing group reacts to this piece, and what suggestions they can give me. I like it, but it can still use some more work. I'm not going to do anymore with it until I get an idea of what people think of it.

        —AD

Two days later, Andrea declared the poem complete:

**Untitled**
A man was walking
    down a country road,
the air smelled fresh and clean.
In the distance a bird
    was singing a beautiful song.

The trees on both sides of the road
    were huge and gnarled with age.
The glow of a sunset
    filtered through the leaves

making everything appear radiant
and glowing

But,
all this beauty and serenity
went to waste.
For the man walking down the road
never noticed
the things around him.

—AD

In her journal, Andrea commented with relief:

I just finished my "final" copy. It's not one of the best things I've done—
but it's not to bad. My writing group couldn't help me with a title, and I
still couldn't think of one, so I gave up. I'm not using the verse about the
moss, I never really liked it, and the poem didn't flow with it. For the next
thing I write it's going to be funny. I'm really tired of writing about not
funny things. I'm glad I don't have to work on this poem anymore—I'm
sick of it.

—AD

## March

Several months later students submitted writing for a class anthology, and
Andrea chose her still-untitled poem. When the anthology came back
from the central office printing facility, each student drew a classmate's
name from a hat, then wrote a letter of appreciation to that peer author
about his or her piece writing.

Andrea received a letter from Jennifer Kehl, a fellow editor on the staff
of *Contemplations*:

Dear Andrea,
I really like your poem because it has so much meaning in such a small
amount of words. You set a scene, a picture in the reader's mind, and then
follow through, smoothly, which is really nice to read. I can just see everything that is happening.
     The only part I have any question about is at the very end, you say, "He
never noticed the things around him." The word "things" really sticks in my

mind. I was thinking maybe it should be something softer. Besides that, it's great. I really like it.

Jennifer Kehl

Below the body of Jennifer's letter, in pencil, Andrea scribbled the following notation:

things = make it Beauty

Andrea then went back to the very last draft of her poem, crossed out the word "things," penciled in the word "beauty," but then erased "beauty" and wrote in a new word. The last line of the poem now read:

> For the man walking down the road
> never noticed
> the wonders around him.

In mid-March Andrea composed a "smile" poem and wrote the following journal entry:

I wrote this poem on the spur of the moment. I was trying to write the "American Dream—a Shining Vision" essay and I was having a lot of trouble. I was frustrated and angry. I needed to do something that would make me feel better. Cause I was in a really bad mood. I decided what I should write about is smiles. I don't know how that idea came to me. I don't think it had anything to do with your and Dawne's poem about smiles. Maybe it made me realize that I had a lot of ideas about this topic that I could easily write about.

I'm very happy with them. I think they are very good. The only problem is that I still don't have an essay!

—AD

## April

In an early April journal entry, Andrea commented on the recently completed poetry writing activity:

As you already know, I <u>love</u> to write poetry. And I write alot of it, so this activity was no biggie. It's very easy for me to write poetry, but it's not very easy for me to be satisfied and happy with what I've written. I throw out 90% of what I write. But the other 10% is then great. I work very hard on my poetry. I'm not sure why poetry is so much easier for me then stories, it just is.

I always think it's funny how people who know me and have read some of my poems before can <u>always</u> pick out my writing They can read a poem of mine and right away say "This is an Andrea poem all right." Whether they like the poem or not is a different story.

The easiest form of poetry for me is free form. As you know it usually takes a rough form of a Haiku. I like to write about nature and animals and things like that.

The hardest form for me is the sonnet. With the 14 lines, with 10 syllables a line and the ABAB rhyme scheme, it's enough to drive a person to drink! That's why I did one. I had to prove to myself I could do it.

Well I have to do my Math, French, social studies journal, health and then go to a "West Side Story" rehearsal so I have to stop. Good-bye.

—AD

An accomplished violinist, Andrea had been invited to play in the high school pit band for their spring production when the Sharks took on the Jets.

## May

The culminating English activity of the year, the individual magazine project, held Andrea's interest from the start. Once she selected her theme (nature—no surprise there), she forged ahead. Ultimately Andrea composed eight pieces of writing for her magazine, five of them poems. One was a reworking of a poem published in *Contemplations* the previous year. Now titled "Maturity," she used it because it echoed her theme:

> Tall and mighty
> are the trees.
>> Rich green and
> towering the earth.
>
> Yet they are
> never too vain
>> to refuse shade
>> to a poor man

that may come

walking by . . .

—AD


Andrea illustrated her individual magazine with black and white ink drawings, doing her own calligraphy for one of the poems. On the very last page of her magazine, Andrea placed a poem finally titled "Wasted Beauty." The opening line was familiar:

A man was walking
down a country road . . .

So, a poem that Andrea had all but abandoned in September became, after much drafting and revising, the exclamation point for her year of composing poetry. Andrea stayed with the poem, nurtured it, developed it, absorbed critical comments from others, revised the poem, and, ultimately, selected it as the concluding statement of her eighth-grade year.

Andrea's final process journal entry looked back on both the magazine project and eighth grade:

I'm so relived that it's over. No more writing groups or deadlines or anything else. I can't wait till school is over. Don't get me wrong, I like school and English is my favorite subject but I like swimming better!

I enjoyed doing the magazine. I would have liked more time to have done it. The deadlines were reasonable but I felt rushed. I had a hard time finding time to work on it, but that's my own fault.

Maybe next year the magazine should be done on and off. Instead of doing it all in one month spread it out between Authors Week etc. I started to get tired of writing about one subject. Many times I wished I had picked a broader topic, like Dawne for example.

My writing group (Kelly, Michelle and Barbara) was super! Thank-you so much for switching me in to that group. I wish I had that kind of writing group since September. They listened and picked up on every little details. It was such an improvement over my old writing group.

As you know I had a very hard time writing four modes. Before I had finished my magazine I thought that having to write in that many modes was stupid. I got so frustrated. But now I'm glad that was a requirement. It taught me that I can write more than poems. Having three type-written pages was no problem at all.

I think this magazine project is a very worthwhile assignment. I want to hold on to it because I know that it will be very valuable to me when I'm older. My magazine is a reflection of me, and it will probably become (when I'm older) a way for me to remember the person I was in 8th grade.

—AD

Andrea taught me a great deal about drafting and revising. She demonstrated that students can persevere, and that eighth graders are able to play imaginatively with words. From her I learned that time and reflection often help a writer, and that some pieces cannot be rushed. I inferred from Andrea's dedication that other students shared a similar outlook and, if given the appropriate setting, would engage with writing as energetically as Andrea had.

Andrea, now a business consultant to financial planners in Nevada, remembers her eighth-grade experiences with poetry and process:

Looking back on the experience, it was tremendous to have a dialogue with an adult, a teacher and a writer. Interesting also to work with peers who might not normally journal or write had it not been assigned. It would be lovely to have that kind of time again, to work on a book, to revise and craft something without tight deadlines. Having the process woven throughout the school year, instead of isolating it as an intense module in a series of different projects, added richness and depth to the learning.

—Andrea Dicks James
(E-mail communication, March 31, 2005)

## ALYSON

Alyson Montgomery was a classmate of Andrea's. A pleasant, even-tempered individual, Alyson took her assignments seriously, shared her thoughts readily, and composed reflections on her writing process that were models of insight and excellence. A super gymnast and the only bass clarinet player in the school band, Alyson selected "Competition" as the title of her individual magazine. She explored her theme in three areas—music, sports, and friends—and included the following poem:

**Ingredients for Competition**

| | |
|---|---|
| C | ourage |
| O | rganization |
| M | otivation |
| P | erserverance |
| E | ndurance |
| T | enacity |
| I | nstruction |
| T | emperance |
| I | ndependence |
| O | pportunity |
| N | ecessity |

—AM

I was impressed by Alyson's dedication and diligence from the moment she entered my classroom, so I was not surprised when she created an extraordinary cover for her magazine. She layered paper of four different colors (green, pink, orange, and yellow), each sheet a successively smaller photocopied replica of the larger cover, and created a telescoping illusion of the title zooming inward.

Entries from Alyson's journal, and my responses, offer perspectives on the stages of writing that young adolescents experience as they compose.

## September

In her very first journal entry, reporting how she got the idea for her poem "Piece of Paper," Alyson underscored the importance of peer influence, observation, and the pre-writing (rehearsal) stage of the writing process:

*September 14*—Process entry for "piece of paper" [*the title of Alyson's poem*]

How I actually came to writing a poem wasn't my idea I was thinking of writing a story but Pam told me that it was easy to write a poem. I thought about what I should base the poem on and as I looked down I said "That's it" a piece of paper was what I would write about so I started.

I thought about where it came from—[tree] bark and what rhymed—spark. Then I thought of where it's found And I said Pen or Pencil has to

be in it since that's what you write with on it, and so I came up with a
poem.

—AM

I responded:

Alyson—I loved your poem—it is clever, it rhymes, and yet it also tells the
truth! And your process entry above is really super! You explain carefully
how you went about it—thanks!

—RMB √+ 9/17


## October

Alyson also went to Frost Valley in mid-October. On her first evening there,
she completed a process journal entry in which she described how she created a poem. Alyson's entry reads like a roadmap, detailing how she proceeded from Point A to Point B while inventing her poem. The acknowledgment of her friend Pam reflects the unselfish attitude Alyson had about life.

*October 13*—P.E. on Frost Valley
    I'm sitting on my bed. I don't know what to write. Should I write Step by
Step? No he doesn't want that. Should I explain my feelings about the trip,
no everyone's doing that, I know I'll write a poem I better get started it's
9:30 all ready.
    *—10:15—*
    Just finish my poem. The way I did it was I thought of all the activities,
the food, the rain, and how we ran down all of the hills on the hikes. So I
started by trying to ryme words with words and then thought to myself,
should I have every line ryme with the next, every other line ryme, or just
have the last word in each paragraph ryme with each other? I decided on
every other line as you'll see when you read it. After I got started it was getting easier except the last four lines I couldn't get I was trying to fit the
"Last Day" in there somehow and I did.
    *5 minutes later*
    It's not tomorrow but let me write this one thing before I forget to. I never
would have ever tried to write a poem if Pam hadn't convinced me to try it
about a month ago when I wrote about the piece of paper so I think that
credit should be given to Pam for convincing me to try it because I thought

it would be very hard but I actually think that sometimes it can be very easy even easier then writing a story.

A few years ago I used to write poems but they were just poems that were Spring is here, Spring is here All the children jump and cheer School is out School is out All the children run and shout. They were little kid poems but I geusse maby scinse I used to write them it is making it easier for me to write now and one more thing before I stop writting I want you to know that I'm sorry if this is too long and is boring you it's just that some days when I start to write I keep going and can't stop, well this is one of those days. But . . . Then I also have days when I write three or four sentences and that's all I can say.

—AM

Moved by what Alyson wrote, I responded at length:

Thank you! Your journal entry was the most amazing thing I've ever read this early in a school year—it was incredible. I loved it. I write poems, so how people write poems is of great interest to me. I read your poem first, without having glanced at your P.E. [journal entry]. Boy, was I surprised when I turned the page and saw <u>two</u> more pages of notes on just that "short" poem—you wrote about 4 or 5 times as much in your P.E. [journal] as you did in the piece.

I liked the poem—and felt that the images you selected were great—the way you rhymed them was also great—skipping every other line.

Are there activities that ought to be mentioned that aren't? Look at the list I'm giving out in class today—maybe you will want to add a few lines based on those.

Also, thanks for acknowledging Pam, as you did—that was considerate, sensitive, appropriate & plain nice!

I really liked the description you wrote of your early school poems—how good it is that you can see now that they lacked something. And how good that you can laugh at yourself about them—they were good for what they were then, but you have grown since then, as you observed.

Thanks again, Al—your entry really made me feel great.

Where is the first draft to your poem—the copy you turned in is so neat that I can't believe it is the first draft. Were there earlier drafts? If so, remember to staple them all together & turn them in to keep in your writing folder.

—RMB 10/17 √+++

P.S. Notice how such a little piece of writing (your poem) can generate so much writing!!

When students returned from Frost Valley, I asked them to compose pieces of writing about their three-day experience in the woods. A number of pupils, including Alyson, opted for poetry. In her journal she wrote:

*October 19*
I'm sitting in the living room thinking about what to write about, I know that I'm going to write a poem but I'm not sure about what activity, I'm looking at the list let's see maybe I'll do one of these—Mt. Hayden [*a rock climbing wall at Frost Valley*], (on belay, belay on, climing? climb away), underwear on the flag pole, the walk from cabins to meals, Thursday night rain storm, trust fall backwards.

The reason I picked them is because they have alot to talk about and would be a little easier.

When I wrote down "trust fall backwards" I thought "that would be a good interior monologue" so you might find both a poem and I.M. If you do I'll write about how I wrote both.

I'm going to write know hope it comes out good! (just pray)
*10 minutes later*
I just finished my poem, the first draft was so sloppy but I wrote it over. The poem came out different than my others but I think it's still a poem. I wrote about the climbing of Mt. Hayden and what happened when I did it.

— AM

Alyson then composed a piece about a "trust fall" activity she had done at Frost Valley, noting:

The way I wrote about it was I remembered how scared I was to try it and hoping write before I went I would all of a sudden loose 30 pounds so I could be sure I would be caught then I would only weigh 65 pounds (I used to be 100 but I lost 5 pounds at F.V.) then I just started writing.

— AM

She next composed a piece about "underwear on the flagpole" (some playful boys had raised a pair as a satirical salute to one of their classmates):

It's very short, only 2 paragraphs the first one is what I heard 2 people saying and the second one is my reaction to it.

It may be short but you said that if you feel it says everything you want to it's done and that's exactly what mine says.

Alyson then offered two apologies:

I'm sorry about the curse word but that's what I heard.
    I hope you're not mad that I wrote 4 pieces of writing when we were only supposed to write 1. It's just I felt like writing alot tonight.

—AM

My response:

It seems clear to me that writing & planning in the process journal is helpful to you. Feel free to use it to write about when you get stuck, or when things don't work out—I'm interested in all aspects of your writing, not just the successful parts.
    Thanks for the effort & for sharing.

—RMB √+++

## November

In November, Alyson drew on personal experience for a poem:

It's 8:30 P.M. and I'm thinking about what to write a poem on. Then my hands started to hurt because at the high school Gymnastic meet I worked out so that gave me the idea to write about Gymnastics.
    I'm going to start writing now.
    *9:15 p.m.*
    I'm done and I think my point came out clear in the poem what do you think?

—AM

Alyson had spelled out the word "gymnastics" vertically and, for each letter, used an adjective to capture her vision of the sport. I responded in the margins of her journal entry: "I agree—the way you spelled it out is super! Using 'graceful' for the letter G is an excellent word to begin."
    Alyson continued: "I feel like I've done a good job on expressing the point and I think it's a good poem (sorry this is so short I'm tired it's 9:45)."

A week later Alyson's journal entry concluded with this request: "Oh, can you please have the class write more interior monologues and poems? If you can, *thanks!*"

"Later in the year," I wrote back, "we're going to do a poetry writing activity, and also you'll have chances to write in *any* mode you want."

## February

In February when students created Gifts of Writing, most wrote in prose. Alyson decided to compose a poem for her friends. Successive journal entries reveal her writing process:

*2/1*
I don't know what I'm going to write yet. I keep thinking but never come up with an idea. I want to write either about a tradition or if not, a poem maybe both. Maybe I won't even write with my parents in mind as the audience maybe someone else. Does it . . . never mind I forgot. I was going to ask if it had to be for someone related to you in some way but you all ready said yes it does. So forget that question. I think this will be easy if I ever think up a topic. For some reason I can't think of what else to write and that makes me mad because I love to write. Oh well, I wish someone could help me with a topic oh? can it be friends? (I hope) (wish) I got an idea—Frost Valley

—AM

*2/2*
I had no idea how to write my poem so I started writing down just little notes which you'll see if you look at my rough (1st) Draft. It's a mess, but then I saw yours Wednesday night so I realized that it didn't make a difference right now. Then I just started writing. First I'de think of a ryme then I'de write it and re-read it to see if it needed. . .

I just read over the poem, changed a lot more words and then wrote another verse. I think this is going to be an O.K. poem.

—AM

*2/4*
I'm just about to start my second draft on my poem my writing group gave me an idea for my title it's Midnight Walk. Well I'm going to start writing now.

I just finished my poem and it turned out pretty good if I say so myself all I changed was a few words. I know I didn't have to do a journal entry but I felt like it.

Sorry it's short but it's all I have to write.

—AM

Two weeks later Alyson looked back on her Gift of Writing project:

When I gave my poem to the people I wrote it for, they all liked it. It wasn't 'cause it was really good ('cause it wasn't perfect) but it was because it was written for them. I don't really know what to write because they acted how I thought they would so there's not much I can write but that they liked it!

—AM

My response: "I'm glad you have had the experience of bringing joy to others through your writing."

## March

In March, Alyson and her classmates began a poetry-writing activity. Two process entries reveal her thinking and learning:

*3/15*
I'm just about to write my poem and I know what it's about. Here I go.

I circled that sentence and jotted a margin note: "Al—in a future process entry, tell me more about this *before* you write the piece and see if it helps your writing."
Alyson continued:

I'm done I like it. It could use some work though what I like is it came from inside of me this time. Last night I was remembering when I was at Oxbow Lake and I did exactly this! It brought back great memories! I really like my pieces when they come from inside, they are more meaningfull to me. When I wrote it I got the vision of being there again although I haven't been there in 4 years. It's the first piece that really meant something to me!

—AM

When students completed the 10-day poetry-writing activity, I asked them to reflect on the experience in their journals. Alyson wrote:

*3/24*

The poetry unit for me was fun. I like writing poems. I used to think that when you write a poem it had to ryme now I know that it doesn't. The hardest poem for me was the tristina because you had to use the same 3 words 3 times! I like writing scattered and pattern poems, something like this (3 words / 1 word / 3 words).

I don't have any questions! All I have to say is do it every year. Don't stop, and I'm glad you decided to teach another year.

—AM

With students like Alyson, who wouldn't want to continue teaching for as long as they could?

From Alyson I learned about the dedication that a student can bring to an assignment, the ability of young adolescents to reveal their thinking process, and the engaged enthusiasm eighth graders can bring to the task of writing.

Looking back on her composing process two decades earlier, Alyson, now a home-schooling mother of two in Connecticut, reflected:

Reading the process entries was quite fun. I still spell about as good as I did then. As I was reading them I could remember laying on my bed writing. I searched for the writings but found nothing, sorry. I don't remember the "piece of paper" poem. I do remember that I wrote about it, though.

As for my writing today. . . I don't do much. However, all through High school and college I kept journals, I must have gone through 4 or 5 and wrote basic diary entries and poems in there. The process journals started my ability to simply write what I was thinking. I believe that was the best lesson I learned. Being able to put down on paper what I am feeling has always helped me.

I recall the process entries having made the writing easier. When writing in that journal the thoughts would come to me of what I missed or what should be taken out. Even at times simply a better word to use. It made me think about the piece of writing in a different light.

—Alyson Montgomery Perry
(E-mail communication, July 7, 2003)

## DAWNE

Dawne Donohue, a classmate of Alyson and Andrea, was a member of the chorus and the track team. Always ready with a smile, Dawne was diligent about doing her schoolwork, and she added joy to my language arts classes.

An entry from Dawne's journal in late fall offers a glimpse of her sense of purpose and dedication to the task at hand:

*5:25 p.m.*

I don't know what to write. I just got done with my social studies. Missy [*a neighbor and classmate*] is here reading the poem she wrote, rather I wrote. Well, I just helped her with a few words. I am going up a wall trying to figure out what to write . . . . . . . . . . . . . . . . . . . . . . . . . . . . . . . . . . . . I can't think of anything. Help! I will go nuts before the day is through! I am going to set my mind to it . . . . . . . . . . . . . . . . . . . . . . . . . . . . . . . . . . . . O.K., my mind didn't come up with it my radio did. I want to write about someone who is all alone, or rather feels that way. I think I'd better get started or I will forget.

*6:30 p.m.*

Sorry it's been so long. Well it took me till about 10 to six then my mom called me for dinner and I got to talk with her.

Anyway I think my poem came out pretty good. I just can't find a good title for it. I was thinking about lonelyness. I don't know. Wat (oops!) matters is that I got it done and it's pretty good. Well I have to go my hand is killing and I have to go to religion—fun fun.

—DD

The next day in writing group, Dawne's friend Pam, commenting on the poem about loneliness, said, "It sounds like a poem that an adult would write."

Dawne was an accomplished poet when she arrived in my class. *Contemplations*, our school's literary magazine, published four of her eighth-grade poems, including this one:

### Writing

A way to learn . . .
A place to set your

Emotions free . . .
A land
Of imagination and
Reality . . .
It is a talent,
A gift not shared
Often enough . . .

—DD

For her end of the year individual magazine that she titled "Silent Shattered Thoughts," Dawne worked in a writing group with Alyson and two other girls. Over the course of five weeks she composed 35 pieces of writing, 32 of which were poems (the requirements were to compose at least five pieces of writing in at least four different modes). Why did Dawne go so far beyond the minimum requirements? Clearly, something about writing poetry impelled her to produce such a volume of work. And there were other issues involved as well.

Halfway through eighth grade Dawne composed the following:

[Poetry] is the only sensible way to express my feelings. Poetry places no stress upon my back, but frees me from the pain, and I am able to relax. I wish to know more, to really write in this special form. It is a confusing task, and the confusion leads my words to paper, to fill it with warming riddles of words.

—DD

The poems in Dawne's magazine ranged in length from 4 to 76 lines on topics as diverse and complex as Life, Death, Insanity, Wind, and War. The last piece in her magazine provided both a summation and the magazine's title:

## SILENT SHATTERED THOUGHTS

My thoughts are
Silent
Yet Shattered
I feel my
Mind all
Scattered

I do not understand
Does this happen
To everyone
My emotions are
Free yet caged
I am sometimes
Raged
But maybe a sweet
Tender kiss of
Love
Would get rid of this
Yet
This is something
I can not
Explain
My
    Silent
     Shattered
      Thoughts

—DD

Words came easily to Dawne, who noted in her "About the Author":

She enjoys writing very much. Her writing talent only began this year because Mr. Burkhardt helped open up a new world for her in writing. Her
magazine "Silent Shattered Thoughts" has taken a lot of time and effort. She
wrote this with one goal in mind: to have people come out and express their
feelings.

—DD

I appreciated Dawne's compliment, but I knew that I only nurtured
what was already there.

Dawne's foreword explained her theme:

This magazine is about your inner feelings thoughts and how you see and
feel things. I wanted this magazine to be about unheard emotions and
thoughts. I always had a feeling for other people's emotions. So I wrote
about them. It felt good to write them because some of the feelings I never
shared with other people. Now in this magazine I can share it with you.

It took some time to write this and a lot of new feelings came out. I've learned a lot from doing this and I hope when you read this you'll have a whole new perspective of your thoughts. Some of these poems you have to think and reach deep into in [order] to get the feeling. This is the whole point, to reach into your mind and be able to relate to the poem.

I would like to thank my writing group—Alyson, Tanja and Gina—for helping me create better poems and stories. But most of all for helping me understand them. I would like to thank my friends (Tracy, Barbara, Kelly, Jen, Vanessa, Pam, Wendy, Jen, Michelle, Mary, and Missy) for helping me and giving me ideas for this magazine and for standing by me in some hard times.

But most of all I would like to thank Mr. Ross Burkhardt for helping me create this magazine, which I feel proud of only through the help of him.

—DD

Dawne was a committed writer, realistic in her outlook and brimming with the idealism of youth, as were the other members of her writing group: Alyson, who used "Competition" as the theme for her individual magazine; Gina Nordstrom, whose magazine theme was "Friends"; and Tanja Gatz, whose magazine theme was "Thoughts." Dawne, Alyson, Gina, and Tanja created an excellent writing group experience for themselves as they assisted one another in producing quality writing for their magazines.

Dawne opened her magazine with this poem:

### **LIFE**

Life:
>     is a moment which no one
>         seems to take advantage of
>     it is a gift
>             which should be treasured
> you should live it in peace
>         it should be a crisp clean
>             world of your own
>         but you should still
>             be in touch with reality
> it is like the springtime
>         yet like the winter
> Life is a wonderful gift
>         which should not be wasted
> 'cause you only live it once

—DD

In another poem, Dawne recalled sunset walks on the beach near her home in Wading River:

## <u>A SILENT DREAM</u>

The colors from the now
                  setting sun
Seem to warm my soul
    Yet
           it is only for an instant
                for the frosty air silently
Stalks the dusk.
I see the pastelled colors changing
              with the time
    The waves crash against the rocks
      and spray the gulls
  who cry in a very melancholy tone.
        Their soft feathered wings, gently lift
            them up to where the sun's
     colors are brightest.
         I feel a chill, and shudder
for I must go and leave all this beauty,
        the beauty
          that only
             GOD
               could create.

          —DD

Stylistically, all of Dawne's titles were typed in capital letters and underlined; the first line of the poem restated the title, followed by a colon. Twenty-five of her thirty-two poems used this repetitive pattern.

Dawne created a disturbing image in a poem that alluded to the turmoil in her life:

## <u>MY MIND</u>

My mind:
        is shattered
into pieces
        i do not
            know why
              but i
              can feel it

i can feel myself going, growing
                              insane
      god help me,
                i pray to you
                          don't put me
through this dark and lonely place
                of horror and pain
i want
        to be like all the rest
                happy, joyful
i want to live again,
            please
                take me out of this
                        HELL
            please.............

—DD

Dawne also composed sunnier verses, as in "Smiles":

### <u>SMILES</u>

Smiles:
        they touch
        the hearts
        of many,
                    yet are
                    only
                    fleeting
                    wisps of
                    Love

—DD

More than 20 years after creating "Silent Shattered Thoughts," Dawne, now a stay-at-home mother in Texas raising two children with one on the way, reflected at length on her passion for poetry in eighth grade:

I started writing because of what you taught us in 8th grade about poetry, and I remember that it changed my life. I believe I chose to write mostly poetry because I could in a way mask the true stories behind elusive words, where as in stories I needed to be more direct, forthright, truthful.

Once I found poetry had no boundaries, that it was a work of art rather than literature, I felt I could put my entire being into. It was such a huge release for me to write, I felt as if it "flowed" from me. I could put things onto paper that I couldn't easily say or talk about with anyone. I felt like I was actually good at something, and it was something I could do that didn't cost money or need the assistance of anyone. It was a true pouring out of my heart and soul, perhaps a cry for help or hope. It was a way for me to expose my feelings of loneliness, rage, hopelessness and gut wrenching pain without actually identifying myself in them. It was beautiful and depressing all in one. It was a hidden diary or journal entry and I could reread these poems and understand myself a little better, work though my thoughts and then sometimes find the joy in myself and my words. I felt I actually could accomplish something through the writing of poetry. I did not have a whole lot of self esteem, and poetry was something that made me feel I had a better understanding of than most kids my age. I was a young girl yearning for closeness and aching to be heard.

Writing and reciting poetry at such an early age made a great impression. It taught me about inner spirit and strength. It helped me to read between the lines and see the truth in things. I felt like I understood something for a change, something that understood me. I think it was a perfect age to be exposed to poetry. I was yearning for a way to express, and it taught me how to, and that I could, in a very personal way. It also anchored me, kept me going when I could have easily let go.

I went thought so much inner turmoil in my youth, and I believe there were several factors. I didn't have the happiest of home life, my sister, brother and I weren't often praised or encouraged. Our father wasn't very involved with us and generally he didn't have anything nice to say. My mother, who was an active alcoholic until she received help when I was 13, was herself struggling with her own inner demons, and thus not much of a nurturer or parental figure in our young impressionable years. And finally, I was raped at the very young age of 13, by my boyfriend. Being raised by strict Catholic parents made it very difficult for me to deal with my rape. I did not tell anyone until I was a adult, and for many, many years it made me feel less of a person, and guilty. These events were difficult to deal with, sometimes unbearable, and I wasn't given any tools or advice on how to handle them. I turned to self mutilation (at 13) and later to alcohol and promiscuity. So when poetry entered my life, it was like something deep inside me opened up and I took a giant gulp, as though life had been poured into me. It took me many years to come to terms with all of these things, and during those years I continued my poetry, journals full, notebooks full

and now two boxes full. It kept me on the brink of sanity, but still in touch
with my inner most dreadful thoughts.

I do not write poetry today . . . I put it down because I changed . . . I grew.
It helped me to get to where I am today, as I've said before it anchored me.
I've looked back at those boxes and put them away again because I am not
that person anymore, and I am happy to say that. It is almost painful to read
some of those poems, surreal. I associate sadness, depression and suicide
with my poetry, and I am far from that today. I still write, but stories, truthful and whole. I am currently working on a children's story with my daughter and her favorite stuffed animal as my main characters. That is who I am
today.

I am not ashamed of my past, but proud that I have lived through some
very difficult and dark moments and I have turned out on the other end a
motivated, joyful and loving person. Sometimes we need to go thorough the
bad to get to the beautiful. I am very blessed today, and I am very grateful.

—Dawne Donohue Smith
(E-mail communications, May 1, 2003 and April 19, 2005)

It is both painful and reassuring to read Dawne's words today, and I
now understand why she turned to poetry in eighth grade with such intensity. I was unaware of Dawne's troubles then, and while I regret that
I missed her signals, I also am glad that writing helped her to cope. That
Dawne turned to poetry to address the upheavals in her life and rise
above them underscores the importance that this mode of expression
had for her at a transitional time in her life. It becomes clearer and
clearer to me that when students are given real reasons to write, they
often are able to confront their concerns, overcome problems, and re-
solve issues.

How many other students are using poetry to deal with the issues be-
deviling their lives?

## LESSONS LEARNED

What do teachers learn by listening to students, both those we teach and
those we taught? Dawne, Alyson, and Andrea are but three of the hun-
dreds of students who engaged with poetry in my classroom. Their stories
are instructive.

By examining one student closely, teachers gain empathy for all student writers because we understand their struggles better. We achieve a clearer understanding of our own writing process as we study others, as we note the similarities and the differences. There are the unknowns as well— things that we learn but do not value until one day, perhaps two or three years hence, when we find ourselves in a teaching situation where we can apply that knowledge. Looking closely at one student's writing can be beneficial in many ways, not all of them self-evident.

What can you learn from your students?

# POETIC INTERLUDE NO. 6: TIPS FOR WRITING POEMS

- Use consistent meter (the number of beats per line) throughout.
- Have a rhyming dictionary handy.
- Build the poem around a particular word, or phrase, or image that appeals to you.
- To avoid choppiness, end lines appropriately, either at a phrase break or the end of a sentence. Which poem below reads better: A or B? C or D?

**A.**

When writing a
poem at school or at home, end
lines with a rhyme all
of the time.

**C.**

The
author composed a short poem to
demonstrate to readers just
where to break the
lines so
as to
achieve a poetic effect.

**B.**

When writing a poem
at school or at home,
end lines with a rhyme
all of the time.

**D.**

The author
composed a short poem
to demonstrate to readers
just where to break
the lines
so as to achieve
a poetic effect

- A few days after you have completed a poem, revisit it to see if it really says what you want it to say. If not, revise, and then revise again.
- Save all drafts—an idea you discard in draft three may prove significant in draft six.
- Let the poem go where it will. You might begin composing about one topic and end up writing about something else.
- You have poetic license to violate any of the "tips" cited above *if* doing so serves the poem.

*Chapter Seven*

# Back to the Beginning

*This chapter provides an overview of how I began the school year from Day One through Day Fifteen, introducing the teacher as poet, interweaving a host of poetic practices that engaged students in memorizing, composing, and interpreting verse, and establishing poetry as a recurrent aspect of the language arts curriculum.*

> Meet them with poetry. Greet them with verse.
> Day One's the moment when you should immerse
> Students in stanzas and rhythms and rhyme.
> Hit the ground running—you haven't much time.
>
> —RMB

## BEFORE CLASS, DAY ONE

On the very first day of school, a Wednesday, 24 students enter the classroom at varying speeds as a booming rock tune, selected especially for the occasion, fills the air. Some students saunter, others skitter, and a few edge in cautiously. One girl claims a desk by placing her new notebook on top of it, reconsiders, looks around, then moves to an adjacent desk. Her best friend sits down beside her in the circle. Several students dance in their seats to the music.

8:44 A.M.: Class officially begins, but the music continues for another minute. Students gaze intently at a host of posters adorning walls, cabinets, and ceiling—an eclectic collection of athletic heroes, pop stars, historical figures, and famous authors. A few kids wave to friends they have not

185

seen for a while. Soon, all settle in, awaiting the lesson, anticipating the beginning of their eighth-grade year.

## HOW DO YOU BEGIN?

How do you begin teaching poetry to young adolescents? Where do you start? What are the first words you utter on Day One? Which poetic activities do you do first? Which activities logically follow? How do you weave together three aspects of poetry—reciting, composing, interpreting—early in the school year so that they complement and support one another?

Earlier chapters describe what happened once I got the snowball rolling down the hill. This chapter explains how I actually created the snowball in the first place—by consciously addressing and reiterating the poetic practices listed below.

Effective newspaper articles address six questions: "Who, what, when, where, how, and why." Years ago I asked myself the same basic questions about how to begin teaching poetry.

*Why*? Why poetry? What are my beliefs about the significance of poetry and its place in a language arts curriculum?

*Who*? Who are the students, so narcissistically absorbed in their search for self, stability, friendship, and purpose in this fast-paced world? What do I know about them, and how can this knowledge inform my teaching?

*What*? What poems and practices will best engage these young adolescents? And what is the optimum balance among these activities?

*When*? When during the school year do I incorporate poetry into the curriculum? How often should students write poems? Publish them? Memorize and recite them? Discuss and interpret them?

*Where*? Where do I begin? With composition? Memorization? Discussion?

*How*? How do I organize these three aspects of poetry into a coherent pedagogy?

By consistently addressing these questions over the years, I eventually designed a comprehensive approach that worked for me and for my students. My goals were:

- to expose students to the many aspects of poetry;
- to develop academic skills such as reading, writing, and critical thinking;
- to enable students to express themselves poetically in verse;
- to provide opportunities for students to publish their poems;
- to give students an understanding of the tools of poetry, including rhythm, rhyme, meter, rhyme scheme, imagery, alliteration, and metaphor;
- to teach students to recite and interpret poetry;
- to celebrate students and their school life through occasional poems;
- to enable students to appreciate poetry as literature and as art;
- to furnish students with positive poetry experiences throughout the school year.

## HOW I BEGAN: A PINHEAD'S EPIPHANY

As I was growing up, I did not realize that listening to my mother recite poems, or singing songs at camp, or memorizing "Daffy Duck's Rhapsody" were significant events. Everything seemed perfectly normal through my unlettered, preadolescent eyes. Yet when I look back, I see that poetry was all around me, and that I was absorbing rhythms and rhymes, unaware of the lessons about language I had learned until much later. Ultimately, an incident during my junior year at Dartmouth triggered my poetic creativity.

In 1961 I was accepted by The Experiment in International Living to spend a summer with a family in Germany. Six other college fraternity brothers were also headed across the pond, and that prompted Tony Horan, a senior who had toured Europe the preceding summer, to offer for our edification "A Pinhead's Guide To Europe," an information session on youth hostels, cheap restaurants, and the pleasures and perils of touring the continent.

During his presentation, Tony described a sunset visit to a beach near Naples, with the distant Isle of Capri illuminated in reddish hues. The idyllic scene moved him to compose an eight-line poem about the sun, the sea, and the island; he read it to us on an April evening 10 months later as we sat in the basement of Alpha Theta, entranced by his poetry.

I remember thinking, "That's the first serious poem I've ever heard that wasn't written for English class." Tony, a friend and a peer, had composed verse for the sheer pleasure of capturing a moment.

Three weeks after my pinhead epiphany, I was walking back to the fraternity during an April rainstorm, and I noticed slanted gray sheets of rain splashing like white sparks on black macadam edged by green grass. That image led me to my first earnest attempt at poetry. A peer's example had unleashed the poet inside me.

## GENERAL ASSERTIONS ABOUT TEACHING POETRY

Young adolescents need academic challenges, opportunities to share ideas with peers, and exposure to timeless literature. They want to develop competence in public speaking and demonstrate fluency in reading and writing. They enjoy exhibiting their academic skills to others, and to do so they need occasions for public performance. They appreciate teachers who can write poems about them and recite poems with them. Because I subscribed to these ideas, I developed a set of general assertions to guide my teaching of poetry to young adolescents:

- *Students should be able to read, write, understand, and appreciate poetry and be familiar with our poetic heritage.* So, I taught poetry every year, using a comprehensive approach.
- *Poems, which are often short and thus more accessible, are an excellent activity with which to commence a language arts program.* Consequently, begin the school year with poetry.
- *A comprehensive approach to poetry should continue all year long.* Thus, poetry was present in my classroom every week of the year.
- *Eighth graders have had prior exposure to poetry.* Therefore, whatever I do will add to their growing knowledge base.
- *Many students have been asked to compose poems before.* Thus, my request to draft verses will not be "new" to them.
- *I am the educational leader in the classroom.* Thus, I set the agenda.
- *Students will norm up to my classroom expectations.* If I ask them to do something, they will respond positively to the challenge.

- *By giving proportional emphasis to composition, interpretation, and memorization, I provide students with a multifaceted exposure to verse.* Each facet reinforces the other two, and students become better at doing all three by engaging with each of them regularly.
- *When the teacher does tasks such as memorizing or composing verse along with students, he or she projects a powerful example.* Hence, be the model, the teacher as poet.
- *Asking students to revise their initial free verse poems establishes drafting and revising as a classroom practice.* Begin promoting revision as the key to good writing immediately.
- *Developing the norms of trust and support among a community of writers takes time.* Consequently, start building a sense of community from Day One.
- *Engaging students in poetry develops their academic skills, including reading, writing, and critical thinking.* One cannot write or interpret with thinking first.
- *Students appreciate poetry that celebrates them and their school activities.*

Hence, compose poems for and about students.

These assertions, along with those cited earlier describing my beliefs about memorizing, composing, and interpreting poems, constitute the theory that animated my teaching of poetry in the classroom. Use them as a departure point to inform your own teaching of poetry. Add your ideas, and revise mine to fit your teaching style. Having an articulated set of beliefs about how to teach poetry makes the task less ambiguous and more comprehensible — you know what you are attempting to do and where you are headed.

## THE FIRST FIFTEEN DAYS

During the first 15 days of school, my focus was on introducing all aspects of poetry. In these initial three weeks my students:

- heard me recite three poems from the canon and five poems that I composed specifically for the occasion;

- drafted and revised two free verse poems;
- heard peers read aloud their drafts of more than 40 original poems;
- identified several criteria for assessing poetry recitations;
- completed two poetry recitations and began preparing for a third;
- briefly discussed 20 poems and heard each of them recited by class-mates;
- completed three journal entries about composing and memorizing po-ems.

But before engaging in any of these activities, I had to introduce myself each fall to a new group of students, create a positive tone for the year ahead, and establish a safe community of writers.

My aim was to hit the ground running on Day One. And I did, with po-etry.

## POETIC PRACTICES IN PLAY

Why were my students so engaged with poetry? In what ways did I en-courage Dawne, Alyson, Andrea, and so many other pupils to delve deeply into composing, interpreting, and memorizing? How did I set in motion the forces that resulted in students interacting so energetically with poetry? What did it look like in practice? And what can you do in your classroom to construct a similar environment?

My aim was to weave together the three strands of poetry and immerse students in verse right from the beginning. Consequently, from the open-ing moments of the first class of the year, certain poetic practices were omnipresent in my classroom, and I made a conscious effort to introduce and then reinforce these practices each day:

- Exposure to poetry
- The teacher as poet
- Poetry appropriate to the occasion
- Poetry from the past relevant to the present
- Recycling poems introduced earlier
- Free verse poetry
- Rhymed poetry

- Memorizing and reciting poetry
- The importance of choice
- Strategies for memorization
- Public speaking skills
- Recitation assessment criteria
- Drafting and revising poetry
- Sharing drafts as models of the writing process
- The teacher shares first
- Save all drafts
- Publishing poetry
- Discussing and interpreting poetry
- Reflective journal writing
- Poems / Olympics / deadlines

What follows is a set of thumbnail sketches of the activities that I introduced and reinforced during the first three weeks of school. This is not *the* way to teach poetry. Rather, it is the way that I taught poetry to eighth graders on Long Island for many years. I urge you to adapt these ideas to your students, style, and classroom setting.

While this information has been addressed earlier in the book, what is new here is the day-by-day explanation of how I began the school year by mixing the three strands of poetry together each day. Specific references to certain practices and poems are explained in greater detail in chapters 3, 4, and 5.

## IN THE CLASSROOM, DAY ONE

The music ends. As the last note dies out, I close the classroom door.

"It's the first day," I say in a voice purposefully louder than normal to catch their attention. All eyes turn to me.

"In they come," I continue:

> Some pausing hesitantly
> At the door,
> Wondering and waiting;
> Others boldly asserting

> Their presence
> As they stride to seats.

I recite "The First Day" from memory. Composed especially for this occasion, my poem introduces me to students as their teacher and as a poet,
and also welcomes them to the classroom. I recite two other poems,
Robert Frost's "The Road Not Taken" (1914) and Berton Braley's "Opportunity" (1917) (see full text in appendix):

> With doubt and dismay you are smitten?
> You think there's no chance for you, son?
> Why, the best books haven't been written.
> The best race hasn't been run.

These poems introduce the ideas of opportunity and promise for the
school year ahead, as well as demonstrate how poems from the past can
speak to the present.

After introducing myself and talking about my three cats, two children,
twin brother, and passion for poetry, I instruct students to pair up. Since I
had not assigned seats, most students are seated next to their friends; el-
bows touch surreptitiously. I ask students to "interview" one another and
then introduce their partner to me and to the class. Consequently, every
student stands and speaks on Day One. This activity constitutes the beginning of their practice in public speaking, a skill they will develop further when reciting poems later in the year. To conclude the opening day
class, I read Max Ehrmann's salute to every child in the universe,
"Desiderata" (1927), emphasizing its ringing affirmation: "You have a
right to be here."

## DAY TWO

On the second day of school I distribute Recitation No. 1. Students choose
one of six poems to memorize and recite in class the following week.
Three of the poems are recycled from Day One. Three new poems pay
homage to the canon.

To familiarize students with the poems, we read aloud and discuss each
of them briefly. I assign a journal entry—"Memorizing My Poem." As

homework, students write an explanation of how they are going about memorizing the poem they selected for recitation.

## DAY THREE

On Day Three, a Friday, I begin class by asking pupils which poems they have selected for Recitation No. 1. As hands go up, students look around the room and see that they are not alone, that other classmates made the same decision they did, and they feel affirmed. I invite volunteers to read excerpts from their journal entries regarding strategies for memorization. We discuss the six recitation poems again. After collecting journals to read over the weekend, I ask students why reciting a poem is like competing in the Olympics, and I stress the importance of honoring deadlines. I then read and distribute a free verse poem that celebrates the third day of school.

## DAY FOUR

On Monday I return student journals and announce that a sign-up sheet for Recitation No. 1 has been posted. I distribute four free verse poems, all composed by students from years past. After we read and discuss each poem, students identify the components of a free verse poem. Then I assign the first creative writing task of the year—composing two free verse poems. I tell students that the following day I will share drafts of my free verse poems first, and I remind them to save all drafts.

## DAY FIVE

Class begins with a reminder to students to sign up for Recitation No. 1. I read one of my free verse poems and circulate three messy drafts to show students my own struggles with communicating effectively in writing. Students share their initial attempts at free verse. As homework I ask students to revise one of their poems, complete a journal entry titled "Revising My Poem," and, of course, save all new drafts. I recite John Masefield's "Sea

Fever" twice—first properly, then poorly—and invite students to suggest assessment criteria for recitations based on my two distinctly different performances. Their recommendations, including eye contact, accuracy, and projection, become the basis for the recitation assessment form.

## DAY SIX

Students read aloud their revised free verse poems along with excerpts from journal entries describing their revision process. I read one of my revised poems, comment on the changes I made, then distribute a recitation assessment form and ask students to complete the top portion. We review the assessment criteria one more time; students have ownership of the assessment because it incorporates ideas they suggested the previous day.

## DAY SEVEN

To establish a positive yet serious tone for Recitation No. 1, I begin class by reciting "The Road Not Taken." Then, in the order in which they signed up, 24 students recite the first of several poems they will memorize during the year.

## DAY EIGHT

I return the graded assessment forms from Recitation No. 1. We discuss ways to improve at reciting. I then read "C Fever," composed especially for the day after the first poetry recitation. Next, I distribute Recitation No. 2, a set of seven short poems, each eight lines or fewer. Students select two or three to memorize and recite the following week. We read aloud and discuss each poem briefly, then break for the weekend.

## DAY NINE

I remind students to sign up for Recitation No. 2, noting that I have already volunteered to recite first. We again discuss the poems for Recitation No. 2, and I ask students for new insights and understandings that emerged from their efforts to memorize. Students fill out an assessment form as another reminder of the recitation scheduled for the next day. Once again we review the criteria for a good poetic performance.

## DAY TEN

For Recitation No. 2, I recite first, followed by students in the order in which they signed up.

## DAYS ELEVEN, TWELVE, AND THIRTEEN

Our team of 48 students goes to the Pocono Environmental Education Center (PEEC), where students participate in three days of outdoor education. On the second night we hold a Talent Show. To capture highlights of the trip, I compose the PEEC Rap, sung by the trip chaperones.

## DAY FOURTEEN

I collect student journals and return the graded assessment forms from Recitation No. 2. Once again we review the criteria for a quality poetic performance. I compliment several students on their improved performances, then distribute a set of poems for Recitation No. 3 (two longer poems of 16 or more lines, and five shorter poems of 4 to 8 lines each). I hand out copies of the PEEC Rap and another poem about our trip. I assign a reflective piece of writing about PEEC. Many students choose to compose poems and later publish them in our PEEC anthology.

## DAY FIFTEEN

On Day Fifteen I ask pupils which poems they are memorizing for Recitation No. 3. Once again as hands go up, students look around the room and see that they are not alone, that other classmates chose the same poems they did. We read aloud and discuss all of the poems. I announce that the sign-up sheet for Recitation No. 3 has been posted, then assign a journal entry—"Long or Short?"—asking students which they find easier, memorizing one long poem or several short poems.

## THE REST OF THE YEAR

During 40 weeks of school, I spent approximately six weeks on poetry, and the remainder on other aspects of language arts. The first three weeks of school included four days devoted to memorizing (later in the year we did eight more memorizations, for a total of twelve days spent memorizing and reciting) and three days composing free verse poetry. In January my students and I spent five days working through OBQUIN exercises, and in March we devoted ten periods to creating individual poetry booklets. In addition, each Friday during the last five minutes of class, I shared a weekly poem. Students were given opportunities to compose poetry after class trips, when they read *The Miracle Worker*, when they created gifts of writing, and when they produced individual magazines at the end of the year. Students quickly learned that poetry could be part of any class, at any time.

## OBSERVATIONS

My 15-day introduction to poetry did not come together until long after my first year of teaching. Decades passed as I developed and refined this approach. Over time I accumulated a poetic repertoire, poem by poem and lesson by lesson. I wrote seven drafts of "The First Day" to get it right, but then used that poem on opening day for the next 17 years. I memorized "The Road Not Taken" once, but recited it to my students again and again, several times a year, for the rest of my teaching career.

Why did I teach poetry this way? Several reasons. Students responded positively to verse and, concurrently, they developed skills such as public speaking, divergent thinking, and creative writing. Students enjoyed poetry because my passion was contagious. To be sure, enthusiasm is a crucial factor. If you look as though you are enjoying yourself, your students will follow. And remember, be a teacher who composes poetry—students cannot be what they cannot see.

## CLOSING THOUGHTS

Starting the school year with poetry and making it a part of every day for the first three weeks seems as natural to me as breathing. I cannot imagine doing it any other way. The accessibility of free verse, the power of poets like Frost, Dickinson, and Poe to speak to young adolescents, the satisfaction that I enjoyed while drafting and revising occasional poems for students, and the life skills my pupils developed as they composed, interpreted, and recited are among the reasons why I did so. But primarily I used this approach because it worked, because it engaged kids in poetry.

## POETIC INTERLUDE NO. 7: OVERVIEW—POETRY ACTIVITIES FOR THE YEAR

The overview chart (see figure 7.1) allows you to plan ahead and keep track of occasions during the school year when you intend to engage students in poetry. Why not design a comprehensive year of poetic possibilities?

Questions for consideration:

- How many poetry memorizations/recitations will you schedule?
- What poems will you memorize and recite to your students?
- How often will students compose poetry?
- What kinds of poems will students compose? What forms will they explore?
- How often will students publish their poems?
- How often will you share your own poetry with students? Will you share unpolished drafts as well as finished poems?
- How often will you have poetry interpretation discussions? Which poems and poets will you examine?
- How often will students complete journal entries about poetry, whether about recitation, composition, or interpretation?
- What poems will you create about aspects of your language arts curriculum that will provide models and information to students and that you can use year after year?
- What existing poems for special occasions will you share with students? When and why?
- Which poets will you celebrate during the year? How will you celebrate them?
- Will you organize a poster session or a festival to celebrate student poetry later in the year?
- Which organizations, such as newspapers, historical societies, local festivals, and civic groups, will you contact that can publish and promote student poetry?
- Will you post your students' poems on the school website?
- Will you hold a slam poetry contest? Geoff Hewitt's book, *Hewitt's Guide to Slam Poetry and Poetry Slam* (2005), tells you how.

| Activity | September | October | November | December | Jananuary | February | March | April | May | June |
|---|---|---|---|---|---|---|---|---|---|---|
| Memorization | | | | | | | | | | |
| Composition | | | | | | | | | | |
| Publication | | | | | | | | | | |
| Interpretation | | | | | | | | | | |
| Teacher as Poet | | | | | | | | | | |
| Journal Entries | | | | | | | | | | |
| Special Poems | | | | | | | | | | |
| Other Events | | | | | | | | | | |

**Figure 7.1. Poetry Activities for the Year: Planning Guide**

- Will you invite the cast of *Poetry Alive!* into your school to do an assembly and poetry workshops with students? Allan Wolf's *Something Is Going to Happen: Poetry Performance for the Classroom* (1990) offers a wealth of ideas about poetry performance.
- What other aspects of poetry will you bring into the classroom during the school year?

*Part III*

# BEYOND THE CLASSROOM

## Chapter Eight

# Cross-Curricular Poetry

*This chapter describes a variety of ways of infusing poetry into the larger curriculum and further explores the notion of the teacher as poet.*

> "Under the sun
> there's nothing new,"
> Heraclitus remarked,
> and I think he knew
> that ideas resurface
> regularly,
> reaching the world
> through poetry.
>
> —RMB

On Sunday, November 24, 1963, in the midst of a two-year stint in the Peace Corps, I left the small town of Zaghouan, Tunisia, where I worked as a physical education teacher, and went into Tunis to be with other Americans. In her living room, Nancy Graham, the Peace Corps Director's wife, had on display a collage of newspaper headlines reporting the death of the president, John F. Kennedy, in English, French, and Arabic. In the center of her collage was the text of an e. e. cummings poem, *Buffalo Bill's,* with its haunting reference to "Mister Death" in the last line.

I had never seen poetry used in that way before. What has stayed with me all these years was Nancy Graham's use of a specific poem to express her sense of loss at a time of personal grief.

# WHAT ARE SOME USES OF
# POETRY BEYOND ENGLISH CLASS?

We celebrate the human experience through lines of poetry. Familiar phrases serve as shorthand for larger ideas, and snippets of verse speak to us across the ages:

"The proper study of mankind is Man."
—Alexander Pope (1688–1744), *Know Then Thyself*

"The best laid schemes o' mice and men / Gang aft a-gley . . ."
—Robert Burns (1759–1796), *To a Mouse on Turning
Her Up in Her Nest with the Plough, November, 1785*

"Water, water, everywhere, / Nor any drop to drink."
—Samuel T. Coleridge (1772–1834), *The Rime of the Ancient Mariner*

"The time has come," the Walrus said, / "To talk of many things: . . ."
—Lewis Carroll (1832–1898), *The Walrus and the Carpenter*

I memorized Rudyard Kipling's poem "If–" (1910) as a sixth grader. The opening lines—"If you can keep your head when all about you / Are losing theirs and blaming it on you"—have become a common literary frame of reference. Nicholas Kristoff, writing on the opinion page of the *New York Times* in January 2003, cited "If–" when he wrote, "It's also possible that if all your friends say you're making a mistake, they're not mendacious back-stabbers but simply right. As Kipling said: 'Trust yourself when all men doubt you / But make allowance for their doubting too.'"

Kipling also understood that individuals move more quickly than groups. In "The Winners" he wrote:

Down to Gehenna or up to the Throne,
He travels the fastest who travels alone.

Whenever I expressed regret while growing up, my mother would quote lines from John Greenleaf Whittier's "Maud Muller" (1856):

God pity them both! and pity us all,
Who vainly the dreams of youth recall.

> For of all sad words of tongue or pen,
> The saddest are these: "It might have been!"

Later in life I used those couplets to encourage students to say what they needed to say in their "Memory Minutes," closure remarks each student made to the class at the end of the school year.

My early exposure to the musicals of Gilbert & Sullivan brought me in contact with the poetic wisdom they espoused in *The Mikado* (1885), where the title character states his intention "to let the punishment fit the crime."

One year as part of a "Making a Difference" project in which students had to make some kind of a difference in the lives of others, I quoted Henry Wadsworth Longfellow's "A Psalm of Life" (1839):

> Lives of great men all remind us
> We can make our lives sublime,
> And, departing, leave behind us
> Footprints on the sands of time.

Longfellow was an astute observer of the human drama. For example, lines extolling the "big fish, little pond" adage can be found in his celebrated poem, "The Courtship of Miles Standish" (1858):

> Better be first, he said, in a little Iberian village,
> Than be second in Rome, and I think he was right when he said it.

Arguably the most popular nineteenth-century poet in America, Longfellow coined many phrases that we still use today: "ships that pass in the night," "the patter of little feet," "I shot an arrow into the air," "under the spreading chest-nut tree," "into each life some rain must fall," "speak for yourself, John," and "the mills of God grind slowly." Even Robert Frost borrowed from Longfellow for the title of his first collection of poems, *A Boy's Will* (1912), taking a line from Longfellow's "My Lost Youth" (1858).

Such thought-provoking lines can be used as writing prompts to inspire student writing. Poems also provide commentary on current events. Robert Frost's "The Hardship of Accounting," composed in the 1930s, presages Enron, WorldCom, and other twenty-first century corporate scandals. In social studies and science, in sports and theater, and as a means of reaching out to individual students, poetry becomes a way to capture students' attention. As you consider these possibilities, ask yourself, "How can I use poetry in my teaching?"


## POETRY IN SCIENCE AND SOCIAL STUDIES

The sciences, both hard and "soft," have provided poets with fascinating topics. Walt Whitman's "When I Heard the Learn'd Astronomer" underscores the notion that sometimes scientific explanations are trumped by actual experience. In Whitman's poem, the observer who wearied of listening to "the learn'd astronomer" ultimately found the heavens far more satisfying when he "Look'd up in perfect silence at the stars."

*Question*: Which is more descriptive—science or art?

Chemistry teachers introducing the Periodic Table may find that students will appreciate singer-musician Tom Leher's "The Elements," a listing of all known elements in the 1950s, an amusing and educational song set to the tune of "I am the Very Model of a Modern Major-General" from Gilbert & Sullivan's *The Pirates of Penzance* (1880).

*Question*: What poems about scientific principles or processes could your students create using the song, "I Am the Very Model of a Modern Major-General," as a model?

In science class, students read the magazine *Science World*, then did creative writing in English class. Several pupils selected poetry to convey what they learned, and their writings were published in a class anthology, *E.S.P.* (*English-Science Project*). One student, Scott Rom, who was avid about aviation, read a *Science World* article describing a new jet plane being developed by the military, and he used information gleaned from the article to compose the following:

**Spy Jet**
look at that plane
flying high in the sky
it's the military's new invention
they use it to spy,
how fast can it go
Mach 3 to be exact,

how fast can it fly
22 miles
how about that
it is specially painted
to withstand heat,
because it expands
and contracts which is quite a feat,
the SR-71 is a magnificent machine
from the pointed nose to the V-shaped wing,
the only problem with this machine
is that every hour it burns 8000 gallons of gasoline.

—Scott Rom
(Eighth grader in 1987–1988)

*Question*: What scientific understandings does Scott reveal in his poem?

Often, a succinct poem summarizes a complex problem. Sarah Norcliffe Cleghorn's "The Golf Links" (1915), a brief but devastating indictment of child labor, raises issues of social inequality and economic injustice. A modern version of her masterpiece might read:

The sneaker sweatshop's near the beach
so almost every day,
exploited children can look out
and watch the tourists play.

—RMB

Candace Thurber Stevenson composed "Signatures," a 16-line, cross-generational poem tracing the rise of technology from "ax and plowshare" to "splintered atom." In four verses, Stevenson raised numerous issues about the impact of the Industrial Revolution and subsequent inventions on our lives.

*Suggested activities:*
- Invite students to write a fifth verse about the latest "signatures" in modern technology.
- Ask students the following open-ended questions:
  - How much technology is too much technology?

- Has technology helped or hurt mankind?
- What technological inventions are most needed today?

International conflict is older than the Bible. Handel's *Messiah,* composed in 1742, quotes poetry from the Old Testament (Psalms 2:1–2) and poses the question: "Why do the nations so furiously rage together?" My students and I used this passage in 1972 in *imagine:peace,* a multimedia production set against the fury of the Vietnam War. Today, more than three decades after that production, two and a half centuries since Handel composed *Messiah*, and more than two millennia since the Psalms, how much has actually changed?

*Questions*:
- Why do nations continue to "furiously rage together"?
- Can we ever expect a world without violence?
- What should we do in the face of continued international conflict?

## "WE DIDN'T START THE FIRE"

In 1989 when he turned 40, singer-songwriter Billy Joel composed "We Didn't Start the Fire" to reflect on the history of his own life. From Harry Truman to Tienamen Square, four decades of American and world history are catalogued in a laundry list of important people, places, and events. Students in my social studies classes memorized all 19 verses as a device for remembering the chronology of events during the Cold War era.

In succeeding years, my students created their own verses to the tune of "We Didn't Start the Fire," using Joel's lyrics as a model. One year I posed the question, "What song would Billy Joel have written had he lived from 1865 to 1948?" Their response began with an echo of the original: "Appomattox, John Wilkes Booth, Lincoln shot, Sojourner Truth . . ."

The following year I asked, "What if Billy Joel had been born in 1979?" Again, basing their work on the original, the students began: "Jimmy Carter, Rockefeller, Three Mile Island, Margaret Thatcher . . ."

In 1994 I asked students to create a one-year version of "We Didn't Start the Fire." They obliged, once again echoing the original opening: "Bill Clinton, Hillary . . ."

*Question*: What chronology would your students write about the twenty-first century using Billy Joel's "We Didn't Start the Fire" as a model?

## COURAGE AND CONTROVERSY

Many poems laud the courage of specific individuals. Thomas Babington Macaulay's "Horatius" (1842), an epic portrayal of bravery in ancient Rome, celebrates heroism and loyalty to one's country:

> Then out spake brave Horatius,
>> The Captain of the Gate:
> "To every man upon this earth
>> Death cometh soon or late.
> And how can man die better
>> Than facing fearful odds
> For the ashes of his fathers,
>> And the temples of his Gods?"

Other poems take a more sanguine view of life in the military. Alfred, Lord Tennyson's "The Charge of the Light Brigade" (1854) raises important questions about blind obedience to orders:

> "Forward, the Light Brigade!"
> Was there a man dismayed?
> Not though the soldier knew
>> Someone had blundered.
> Theirs not to make reply,
> Theirs not to reason why,
> Theirs but to do and die.
> Into the valley of Death
>> Rode the six hundred.

Of the more than 600 Light Brigade cavalrymen who charged headlong into the battle of Balaclava in October 1854, 113 were killed, 134 were wounded, and 231 were missing or captured.

*Question:* Should a soldier speak up in the face of ill-conceived orders from on high?

Wilfred Owen, who died at the youthful age of 25 near the end of World War I, composed "Dulce et Decorum Est," a sobering poem about that war to end all wars, while serving in it as a soldier.

*Compare and contrast:* Ask students to compare and contrast the central message of Owen's poem, asserted in the Latin phrase referenced in the title ("Dulce et decorum est pro patria mori"—roughly translated, "It is sweet and proper to die for one's country"), with the ideas and ideals expressed in Macaulay's "Horatius."

In 1966, "The Ballad of the Green Berets" celebrated American's military elite. A few years later, a hit from the mid-seventies, "Billy, Don't Be A Hero," released as the war in Vietnam was winding down, urged young men not to risk their lives unnecessarily in times of war.

*Compare and contrast:* Have students compare and contrast the sentiments expressed in "The Ballad of the Green Berets" and "Billy, Don't Be A Hero."

"To An Athlete Dying Young," A. E. Houseman's 1896 elegy to the transient glory of sports (where "the name died before the man"), resonates today in a culture rocked by steroid-abusing athletes.

*Suggested activity*: Have students compose poems about controversial issues in sports—graduation rates of student athletes; age limits for entry into professional sports; drug abuse; overly intense fans.

Edward Arlington Robinson's "Richard Cory" describes a man who, in the eyes of his public, appeared to have everything—he was "richer than a king." In the last line, however, Richard Cory puts a gun to his head.

*Question*: What does being "rich" mean?

Lyrics from Broadway musicals, often pure poetry, provide possibilities for classroom discussion. "America," an energetic tune from *West Side Story,* raises issues about newcomers and their idealized vision of the United States. "You've Got to be Carefully Taught" from *South Pacific* deals with the nature of prejudice. "Is a Puzzlement" from *The King and I* poses a dilemma about leadership in a complex world. "What I Did for Love" from *A Chorus Line* goes to the heart of what is really important in life.

*Suggested activity*: Read and discuss several Broadway musical tunes as commentary on American life.

# THE CONTINENTAL CONGRESS

Each year my social studies classes examined the events leading up to the American Revolution, then participated in Radicals and Tories, a simulation game that culminated in a reenactment of the Second Continental Congress of 1776.

Following the simulation game, I composed a seven-verse poem reporting the outcome, written from the loser's perspective:

### The Tory Story

We met in the Continental Congress yesterday
and went on to the stage with a great deal to say.
Our costumes were super, our signs were great,
but little did we know what would be our fate:
. . . *war*

Kurt Thorn took the podium and spoke right out loud;
he presented our case to the Moderate crowd.
Then Suki spoke up and she made it clear
that Loyalty was something for which we should cheer, not
. . . *war*

—RMB

To prepare students for the inevitable test, I crafted a 58-line poem called "Radical and Tory Review." The verses referenced King George III, economic issues in the colonies, and Candace Thurber Stevenson's "Signatures":

Once upon a time, before King George sat on the throne,
(that's George the Third), England wanted colonies of her own
for purposes of trade—raw material to finished good
on British ships across the ocean—cotton, tobacco, wood.
And so explorers traveled west and established colonies
from Massachusetts to Virginia, but 'twas no life of ease.
Nay, hardships were the norm for these transplanted Englishmen;
each ax and plowshare, hard to get, spelled out a promise . . . but then . . .

—RMB

Pupils studying the American Revolution can memorize Henry Wadsworth Longfellow's "Paul Revere's Ride" or Ralph Waldo Emerson's "Concord Hymn," with its famous line in the first verse:

> By the rude bridge that arched the flood,
> Their flag to April's breeze unfurled,
> Here once the embattled farmers stood
> And fired the shot heard round the world.

When students studied quota laws and immigration policy issues, they memorized Emma Lazarus's "The New Colossus." Lazarus, the daughter of an immigrant, saw her 1883 sonnet become part of the American credo. Her words are inscribed on the base of the Statue of Liberty (*see full text in appendix*):

> Give me your tired, your poor,
> Your huddled masses yearning to breathe free,
> The wretched refuse of your teeming shore.
> Send these, the homeless, tempest-tost to me,
> I lift my lamp beside the golden door!

*Questions for discussion*:
- Is the "golden door" still open?
- How open should it be?
- What value does this nation of immigrants place on its "melting pot" heritage?
- How do we balance immigration policies and national security?

The following passages and poems ought to be familiar to every American. Have students memorize and recite them:

- The Preamble to the Constitution of the United States ("We, the People . . .")
- The opening of the Declaration of Independence ("When in the course of human events . . .")
- Lincoln's Gettysburg Address ("Fourscore and seven years ago . . .")

## COMPOSING AMERICAN HISTORY POEMS

One year I asked students to compose American history poems based on a famous person or event since 1865. We published their poems in a class anthology, whose introduction explained:

> This year in social studies, students on Team 8-I created American history poems. They studied several well-known poems including *The New Colossus, The Golf Links*, and *Signatures*. Each student then selected a topic and wrote several drafts. Poems had to include an introductory "fact sentence," be at least sixteen lines in length, and highlight some aspect of American history 1865 to the present.
>
> In their poetry, students celebrated many famous American individuals and events. Most students chose to focus on a single topic, and a few addressed the sweep of history. The results are at once lighthearted, serious, patriotic, personal, and compelling.

Rae Mannino chose a major event from her mother's past—the assassination of President John F. Kennedy:

### JFK

*November 22nd John F. Kennedy was shot down by Lee Harvey Oswald
who was then shot by Jack Ruby. Many Americans were scared.*

In Dallas, Texas, 1963
at 12:30 p.m. stood a man named Lee.
John F. Kennedy had arrived by plane,
then shot by a man who they called insane,
with jealousy, maybe. A loud bang was the sound,
while people stood staring all around.
Why, oh why, did this man pass
while students sat silently praying in class?
For no apparent reason he was shot.
We know his family still loves him a lot.
Especially his son
whose birthday was on the day
of his father's funeral, where his father lay.

—Rae Mannino

Six years later, Rae, studying abroad in Spain, recalled:

I definitely remember asking my mother about her experience with JFK. That's where I got the image of kids kneeling and praying beside their desks in the classroom. My mother was young at the time, and attended a Catholic school. She told me that an announcement came over the loudspeaker requesting that all students say a prayer.

I recall wanting the [poem] to rhyme, and after you helped switch some wording, it was easier for me to do. Although, it may very well have been the confidence you gave me. Students can sense when a teacher isn't encouraging or confident about their writing. It helps when the instructor lets the students know he truly enjoys the piece or knows there is definitely potential for improvement.

—Rae Mannino
(E-mail communication, August 29, 2003)

In her poem, Jessica Hodess, who is white, imagined being a slave at the time of the Civil War:

### To be a Negro in a White Man's World

I lay here
in my cold damp corner
he calls a bed,
my eyes full of tears,
my heart full of sorrow,
my body full of pain,
from the deep slashes
of the burning whip.

I think of how cruel,
how inhumane
it is that we are treated
as animals and why,
because of the color of our skin?

My Lord had a reason
for giving me my skin color.
He must have had a good reason,
and I am proud, proud
to be a Negro
in a White man's world.

I will be diminished
to nothing, body and soul,
but as long as I am alive
I will stand by my God,
my God's choice,
and my color.

They say this war
is for us.
That the South is against,
and the North is for.
They are not fighting for us.
They are fighting for themselves,
and for their own dignity.

I have been waiting
since I was four
to fight for my country,
and to be proud of America.
If America has come down to war,
and bigotry, why should I be proud?
I am proud, and only proud
to be a Negro in a White man's world.

—Jessica Hodess

Six years later, Jessica, a college student in Maryland, reflected on why and how she wrote her poem:

I remember sitting in the Library of our Middle School and just writing. It was as if I had subconsciously known what I needed to say and how I was going to say it. I remember sitting at a table with some classmates of mine and them questioning how I was able to write something without taking a lot of time to plan it out in my head before hand.

It was just something that interested me. I remember some classmates wrote poetry about specific battles fought during the Civil War, but that wasn't my concern. I wanted to touch on the emotional, the sympathetic, and not on the physical.

It was easy to put myself in a position of a male slave during the civil war, because I believe that at some point in all of our lives we feel as though we do not have control over the course we are taking. I took that feeling and multiplied it by a hundred, no maybe a thousand, and I thought about how awful it must have been for slaves at that time. I wanted to express that feeling the best I knew how.

When I first reread this, I felt a bit nostalgic. I think I was a very innocent girl who didn't really know what was ahead of her. I think that for an eighth grader it's a decent poem; could I do better today, of course; but I look back at this piece and in a sense, I am very proud of it.

I gave the man in the poem strong religious conviction because I believe that I possess the same quality. I also believe that in times of great crisis, God is there when some other people are not or cannot be.

Eighth grade was a personal introduction to poetry. I had previously learned the technicalities of writing prose, but I had never really opened myself up to its possibilities. I appreciated the opportunity to do that at such a young age and I think this poem is an excellent reflection of that.

—Jessica Hodess
(E-mail communication, October 29, 2003)

My contribution to the American history poems anthology was a memorial to some of the fallen heroes of the sixties:

**Leadership and Loss**
*During the 1960's, several political and civil rights leaders*
*were assassinated, at great cost to the future of the United States.*

Names, and numbness . . .
Kennedy, King, Kennedy
A litany of leaders . . .
Medgar, Malcolm, Martin
A loss of leadership . . .
John Fitzgerald Kennedy
Thwarted possibilities . . .
Medgar Evers
Sudden silence . . .
Malcolm X
Diminished dreams . . .
Martin Luther King, Jr.
Abruptly absent . . .
Robert F. Kennedy
Murdered memories . . .
Medgar, Malcolm, Martin
Heroes and history . . .

Kennedy, King, Kennedy
Futures forever foreclosed . . .

—RMB

*Writing activity*: Have your students compose poems about historical figures and events, recite them in class, and publish them in a class anthology.

## POEMS FOR SPECIAL OCCASIONS

Predictable annual events present opportunities for using certain poems to their best advantage. A sixth-grade teacher at Shoreham-Wading River Middle School, who was also a diehard Yankees fan, read Ernest Lawrence Thayer's "Casey at the Bat" (1888) to his students on the opening day of the baseball season. When the first snowfall of the year occurred, I played a cassette tape of Robert Frost reciting "Stopping by Woods on a Snowy Evening." James Russell Lowell's "The Vision of Sir Launfal" (1848) poses the question, "[W]hat is so rare as a day in June?" Edgar Allan Poe's "The Raven" (1845) is a perennial Halloween favorite in many schools. And on October 12, Joaquin Miller's "Columbus" adds to the occasion:

> Behind him lay the gray Azores,
>   Behind the Gates of Hercules;
> Before him not the ghost of shores,
>   Before him only shoreless seas.

As you read more and more poems in more and more anthologies, you eventually discover verses that seem just right for specific occasions.

If you feel the urge to compose a poem that comments on some aspect of an academic subject, here are some titles that might inspire your muse. What lines of poetry would you or would your students compose, inspired by these titles?

- After Math (after/math)
- Since Science . . . (Science Since . . .)
- The Art of Language—The Language of Art

- Math Bath
- Fraction Frazzle
- re:Verse
- Gym and Him
- French Fête
- Spanish Speech
- Social Studies Story
- English Anguish
- Algebra Attack
- Tech Wreck
- Grammar Grumbles
- Punctuation Poem
- Awesome Adjectives & Alluring Adverbs

## THE TEACHER AS POET REVISITED: CELEBRATING INDIVIDUAL STUDENTS

One way I reached students was through original poetry, penning verses that celebrated their exploits. In most cases, I shared these poems with all of my students. Occasionally, I composed poems for just one or two students and did not publicize them.

Scott Kramer, a short, bright student whose dark-rimmed glasses and slight physique set him apart from the crowd, was buttoned-down, dutiful, and not at all versed in the ways of the woods. One spring we went hiking at a Hudson Valley locale called Mineral Springs, a lovely glen replete with rocky cliffs, towering pines, jutting ledges, and splashing waterfalls. When I saw Scott climbing near the top of a waterfall some 40 feet above me, I did something very foolish which I regret to this day. In a moment that goes beyond sheer stupidity, I yelled up to him, "I bet you five dollars that you won't jump off." I was joking, and Scott, literally a babe in the woods, knew it. However, he did not fully grasp the frictionless properties of wet moss.

When Scott tried to win the bet by jumping down two feet to a small ledge beneath him, he slipped, tripped, and tumbled 40 feet to the bottom, looking not unlike a fish flopping down a staircase as his body bounced off rock ledge after rock ledge. Fortunately, Scott immediately went unconscious and, in spite of his fall, had not a scratch on him. This incident inspired the immortal "Kramer on the Rocks":

### Kramer on the Rocks, or "Slide, Scott, Slide!"

Acknowledged by his peers as the freefall champ,
Scott (in doing so) got just a little damp
At Mineral Springs where he won a fiver
For his death-defying feat—would he survive or
Meet his Maker while breaking many bones,
And become a convulsive heap of fractures and groans?
Like a flailing mackerel flopping down the stairs,
Scott bounced on the rocks to horrified stares.
He landed, grinned, and waved to the crowd.
Spontaneously they cheered and shouted out loud:
"Do it again!" But Scott calmly replied,
"No thanks, you guys, I almost died!"

—RMB
(From the apocryphal *Poems For All Occasions,* 1981)

I gave Scott a copy of the poem along with the five dollars, and I apologized profusely to him and to his parents. It could have been much more expensive.

Years later, Scott, now a software developer for an options trading firm in Chicago, recalled:

I have absolutely no recollection of the fall itself. I do remember the "ledge" I was going for, though it was more of a dimple. And there was a girl near the takeoff point, her name was Doreen. I remember her looking at me in shock as I fell.

After landing, I remember seeing you running towards me, and I simply stood up, unscratched, wearing my American Voices Tee-Shirt. (I still have the shirt BTW.) I've often reflected on the fall and thought about how amazing it is that even the Tee-Shirt didn't rip. On the bus ride home, Billy Joel's "Big Shot" was playing, and I think a couple of kids sang to to me. We then went as a group to see the first Indiana Jones movie (an appropriately stunt-oriented film.)

I have a theory that the fall, and the surrounding hype, made me a lot braver. After all, if I could survive a 40-ft flopping tumble down a rockface, I should be able to conquer any sketchy situation. I know most people figure that these kinds of incidents make you timid, but maybe it's different when you're really young. Whenever I am reminded of the infamous fall, the word Invulnerable comes to mind . . . I don't really go through life as carefully as I probably should.

—Scott Kramer
(Eighth grader in 1980–1981; e-mail communication, May 2, 2005)

## "THE OPEN DICTIONARY"

One day after school I discovered a classroom dictionary open on a desk; a student had been looking up a word. Seizing the moment, I quickly penned a poem and shared it in class the next day, in hopes that the anonymous word sleuth would know that I appreciated his or her inquisitiveness:

**The Open Dictionary**

The
open dictionary
on the table
after class
cheered
my teacher soul.

Who sought
what word
independently?

Godspeed,
curious student.

—RMB
(From the apocryphal *Poems For All Occasions*, 1984)

## "PATIENT"

When Craig Misener, a student in my advisory, ended up in the hospital with pneumonia the week before his big percussion solo in the spring concert, I was moved to compose "Patient," a 102-line tribute to his plight. Some excerpts (*see full text in appendix*):

> On Wednesday evening, June 1st, 6:10 p.m.,
> oversized green visitor's pass in hand,
> I slowly edged open the door to Room 208
> and peered inside . . .

> This percussion soloist,
> bedridden ten days before his final
> Middle School Advanced Band performance,
> looked at me, then away.
> In his now hunted, now handsome eyes
> I saw his incomplete completeness . . .

> And I reflected on:
> his fourth place finish among all eighth graders
> in this year's American Legion Essay Contest
> for his paper: "Advice To Our As Yet Un-elected President" . . .

> This young man now lay in a strange room
> on the second floor of St. Charles Hospital . . .
> while his father and I conversed.
> Craig continued to cuddle
> a comfortable, floppy-eared doll. . . .
> As I drove from the hospital parking lot,
> . . . what stayed with me
> was the steadfast inconsistency of
> a worn-out teddy bear
> protecting the man-to-be.

—RMB
(From the apocryphal *Poems For All Occasions,* 1988)

## STUDENT MULTIMEDIA PRODUCTIONS

Each year my students and I created multimedia productions, and poetry was always part of the show. Because students recited their poems into a microphone, they were comfortable doing so during the shows; an amplifier eliminated my concerns about voice projection.

For a production titled *We, The People*, students performed a choral reading of Robert Frost's "The Gift Outright." When we created *American Voices*, we drew on the poetry of Carl Sandburg. In productions such as *Child of the Universe, Hands on Hunger,* and *Nuclear Nightmare*, students used their poetry recitation skills as members of the speaking cast.

One year my students and I created *School Is . . .*, a half-hour production that explored education through the ages. The original script incorporated poems and passages from Mark Twain, Carl Sandburg, H. L. Mencken, and others describing their troublesome academic experiences. When we presented *School Is . . .* at a reading conference in New Jersey, the author Avi, in the audience that day as an invited speaker, congratulated us on our production and then asked an important question: "Where are the voices of the students?"

Motivated by Avi's perceptive query, we rewrote the entire script. I asked students to reflect on their experiences sitting behind desks in grades K–7, then compose two or three school memories in the form of poems, interior monologues, and personal essays. Soon we had more than 100 pieces of writing for the new script, about a third of them poems. A small group of students and I had a Saturday morning editing session (which one witty student dubbed "scrap the crap") to identify representative student writing for the show.

Allyson Adams's poem captured a familiar sense of student despair:

**Test Time**

My stomach grinds
My brain unwinds
My fingernails get bitten

My neck is tense
I fear no sense
Can be made of what I've written

I've studied hard
My thoughts are jarred
While others write, I'm sittin'

I'm scared to death
To take this test
That I don't mind admittin'

The time goes by
Yet here sits I
As helpless as a kitten

A mental block
Is what I got
And an F is what I'm gettin'

—Allyson Adams
(Eighth grader in 1980–1981)

Allyson had a real reason to compose her poem: she knew in advance that her words would be considered for the script of a multimedia show. When you give students real reasons to write, they become more invested in the task.

My own contribution to *School Is . . .* was a poem that explored the unspoken similarities and shared perspectives among and between students and teachers. In the show, a student and I performed it, each of us facing the audience at separate microphones:

### Echoality

It's tough being a teacher sometimes.
　*(It's tough being a student sometimes.)*
Meeting all the responsibilities of classes, lessons,
　grades, report cards, conferences.
　*(Meeting all the responsibilities of classes, homework,*
　　*reports, tests, projects.)*
Planning many activities when I know only some will work.
　*(Doing activities I'm not interested in.)*
Living up to the expectations of my students,
　administrators, and colleagues, as well as my own.
　*(Living up to the expectations of my teachers,*
　　*parents and classmates, as well as my own.)*
Trying to be so many things to so many people:
　teacher, guide, friend, disciplinarian, confidant, leader.
　*(Trying to be a complete person in class when I am fragmented*
　　*into subjects, and the things I can do well don't seem to count.)*
Having students see only one side of me
　as I check my personality at the door.
　*(Having teachers see me from only one side*
　　*when I know I have several sides.)*

Choosing the right music for the dance
   when I'm not really sure which steps they know.
   *(Dancing to his music when my melodies make more sense.)*
Doing all the things it takes to be a teacher.
   *(Doing all the things it takes to be a student.)*
Yeah, it's tough being a teacher sometimes.
   *(Yeah, it's tough being a student sometimes.)*

          —RMB
  (From the apocryphal *Poems For All Occasions,* 1981)

*Suggestions:*

- Think of today's troubadours—Neil Diamond, Paul McCartney, Sara McLachlan, Simon and Garfunkel, Joni Mitchell, Tupac, 50 Cent, Bruce Springsteen, and other balladeers. Use their songs as hooks to interest students in lyrics, then move on to the poets you like best.
- Mix in appropriate lines of poetry with all you do. In the classroom, make allusions to poetry and literature weekly, if not daily.
- Looking for resources to enhance your poetry collection? There are endless possibilities, including many that cost little or no money. Go to *www.nortonpoets.com* where you can find essays by and interviews with many contemporary poets.
- Subscribe to Garrison Keillor's online version of "The Writer's Almanac." Every day Keillor sends out an e-mail with a pithy poem and information about writers, noting whose birthday it is and when certain books were published. E-mail *newsletter@americanpublicmedia.org* to subscribe to Keillor's free newsletter.

## THE LAST CLASS

To begin the last class of the school year, I composed an inverse echo of "The First Day" (see full text in appendix):

### The Last Day

It's the last day.
In they come—
Some pausing hesitantly

At the door,
Reflecting and reminiscing . . .

—RMB

My teaching partner and I also created "An Academic Alphabet," a list poem of people, places, and events from the school year. Once we designed the poem's basic format, we were able to use the template year after year, changing specific references as needed but retaining the opening and closing verses. This poem put a positive spin on our all but complete "simultaneously shared journey":

An academic alphabet
Of people, places and things
To recall the year
From September to June
From 1995 to 1996
From English to social studies
From math to science
From Shoreham to Wading River
From us to you . . .

The sum is the total of its parts;
The community, of its individuals.
These alphabetic items,
A necessarily incomplete listing,
Summarize our year together . . .
From Adams to Algebra to Apollo 13 to Acknowledgment
From Burkhardt to Billy Joel to bridges to Boston
From Computer Lab to calculators to chamber orchestra to *Contemplations*
From Distinctions to "Desiderata" to Dartmouth
From Ecology to Erica to Eighth Grade Night
From first draft to *The First Day* to Frost, Robert
From Gift of Writing to Geometry to Great Adventure to Grattan to Good
From Helen Keller to Halloween to Holden
From interior monologue to Inquiry Project to Ingrid
From journals to Jeopardy to jazz band
From Katie to "Keep all drafts!" to Kaplan
From Lukoski to Letters to Self to labs to *The Last Class*
From *Miracle Worker* to Memory Minutes to Maine to Middle School
From Nacirema to newspaper to New York City to NMSA

From "Opportunity" to OBQUIN
From PEEC to portfolio to poetry recitations to Providence
From Quartertones to questions
From Rhode Island to *River Kwai* to recycling
From Special Olympics to *Superman* to solar homes
From Team 8-I to Théo to Timeline to *Twelve Angry Men* to Traina
From "unfair" (what life is) to United States
From Variety Show to visitors
From writing group to "Whose woods these are . . ."
From Xerox copies to solving for X
From zip codes 11786 & 11792 to zero degrees!
From your first class to your last lesson

June is upon us,
September a distant memory.
As we experience this Last Lesson,
We recall what we have shared
And realize that the past is prologue.
Now, the sum of our experiences is total
And we must part.

—RMB
(From the apocryphal *Poems For All Occasions,* 1996)

A colleague and I took a cue from Tom Leher's "The Elements" (based on Gilbert & Sullivan's "I Am the Very Model of a Modern Major-General" from *The Pirates of Penzance*) and inserted every eighth grader's name into the text. Each year on Eighth Grade Night, the "Eighth Grade Song," a 17-verse opus performed by the eighth grade advisors and accompanied by a three-screen slide show that included a picture of every eighth grader, received a standing ovation:

Goodbye, goodbye you Eighth Grade kids, remember all the work and fun
Remember Beach Day, Great Adventure, Perkins, PEEC and Washington
Remember soccer, softball, football, concerts, Quartertones, Madrid
Remember solar houses, finals, and the science labs you did

Remember playing on the team and all the games you won and lost
Remember Jazz Band, Orchestra and Chamber, *Space Pandas* and *Early Frost*
Social Studies, English, Chorus, Gym, French, Health, and Spanish, too
Remember dances in the gym, but most of all remember you

Remember Kevin "Walrus" Jackson, Rae Manino, Mark Nagy
Alana Deegan, Mike Fallacaro, Jessie Frost, Eric Lipinsky
Justin Sindone, Ashley Ferrell, that "Space Panda" Marisa Finn
Courtney Gilmore, Marcy Holloway, and remember Seth Kaplan

—RMB and Jerry Silverstein

*Lesson learned*: You can use any occasion as a reason to compose poems. Before long you'll have a repertoire of verses to share with students each year, and your students will come to know you as the teacher as poet.

## POETIC INTERLUDE NO. 8:
## DRAFTING AND REVISING A COUPLET

Consider the following variations of a couplet:

1. Many travel on the Road in sorrow,
   But the pavement ends before tomorrow.
2. People travel on the road in sorrow,
   But the pavement ends before tomorrow.
3. Many journey on the road in sorrow,
   But the pavement ends before tomorrow.
4. Since the pavement ends before tomorrow,
   Do not travel on the Road in sorrow.
5. Do not travel on the Road in sorrow,
   Since the pavement ends before tomorrow.
6. Many travel on the road in sorrow;
   The pavement ends, however, e'er tomorrow.
7. People travel on the Road in sorrow,
   But the pavement stops before tomorrow.
8. You may travel on the road in sorrow,
   But the pavement ends before tomorrow.
9. Why travel on the Road in sorrow,
   Since the pavement ends before tomorrow?
10. If the pavement ends before tomorrow,
    Should you travel on the road in sorrow?

Word choice, line sequence, capitalization, punctuation—all add nuances to meaning. Here are three activities:

a. Ask students to read these ten versions of the same couplet, then select the one they like best and explain why.
b. Ask students to rewrite the couplet anew.
c. Ask students to compose a couplet, then rewrite it differently five times.

# Chapter Nine

# Poetry Teachers at Work

*This chapter describes poetry classrooms from Hawaii to Delaware. What can we learn from the best practices of our colleagues?*

> Here's a random classroom sample:
> Poetry teachers at work in schools.
> We can learn from their example.
> Just adapt these teaching tools.
>
> —RMB

## WHAT DO OTHER TEACHERS OF POETRY DO?

Earlier chapters described specific poetry activities in my classroom. Yet poetry is taught in schools all across America, in a variety of ways, and at all grade levels. During the course of writing this book, I visited a number of poetry classrooms, conducted interviews, and corresponded with educators and students in an attempt to understand how different teachers approach the many dimensions of poetry. Their stories and strategies offer models of excellence for us all. But where does one begin? At what age can youngsters begin to compose poetry?

## SECOND-GRADE POETS, LA CAÑADA, CALIFORNIA

Just north of Los Angeles in La Cañada, off the 210 freeway and three miles northwest of the Rose Bowl, an elementary teacher, Katie Budde, works in a windowless portable classroom at Paradise Canyon Elementary School. In the spring of 2003, she taught a science unit on butterflies to her second graders. Each student was given a chrysalis and instructed to observe its transformation in a glass jar set in the corner of the classroom. Extending the unit into other areas, Ms. Budde taught her youngsters to make paper butterflies by daubing paint drops inside one half of a penciled outline of a butterfly drawn on a sheet of construction paper, then folding it to create a pair of matching, spotted wings. Students cut out their colorful artwork and decorated the room with butterflies.

While waiting for the larvae to hatch, 18 second graders also composed cinquains about caterpillars. First, Ms. Budde explained to her pupils the basic form of a cinquain, in which each of the five lines serves a specific purpose:

*Definition*: Cinquain—a poem in five lines with no repeated words.
*First line*: Title—a noun
*Second line*: Two adjectives that describe the title
*Third line*: Three verbs describing an action for the title
*Fourth line*: Four adjectives that describe your feelings about the title
*Fifth line*: An adjective that describes the title, or a synonym for the first
    line

Ms. Budde reviewed several scientific terms with her pupils, then posted lists of related nouns, verbs, and adjectives (such as larva, chrysalis, molting, and changing). She encouraged students to search through the lists to find just the right words for their poems.

As students began this exercise, Ms. Budde gave them two choices for their poems: show a change (e.g., caterpillar to butterfly) or show no change (e.g., staying a caterpillar or butterfly). If a poem showed the change in stages, the student had to choose appropriate words. Otherwise, students only had to describe one stage. Aubri's cinquain shows the change, while Zach's does not.

Students also had choices regarding line four of their poem. They could choose four adjectives that described the caterpillar/butterfly, or they could write a four-word phrase instead. Sammi, Zach, and Johnny used four adjectives, while Aubri and Madeleine wrote four-word phrases.

After the second graders completed their cinquains, they typed and printed them out using classroom computers, then posted their poems on the classroom walls. Some examples:

Larva
Tiny, fat
Crawling, hanging, changing
Droopy, pretty, brown, gold
Butterfly

—Johnny Louk

Larva
Fuzzy, spiky
Molting, spinning, changing
Cute, amazing, weird, cool
Pupa

—Zach Speed

Caterpillar
Fragile, small
Eating, changing, flying
Graceful, calm, unique, shy
Butterfly

—Sammi Keys

Caterpillar
Fragile, furry
Eating, molting, changing
A chrysalis is hanging
Butterfly

—Madeleine Fisher

Caterpillar
Spiky, sticky
Eating, crawling, molting
Changing more each day
Butterfly

—Aubri Thompson

Using this poetic form, Ms. Budde taught her second graders to play with words inside a set of strict parameters, to learn some natural science, and to generate poetry based on observable or predicted behavior. The cinquain structure and the posted vocabulary lists enabled seven-year-olds to explore the meanings of words and to communicate their knowledge.

When do you begin teaching children to write poetry? As early as possible.

## FOURTH-GRADE POET, MAUI, HAWAII

Along the Kula Highway in upcountry Maui, Kula Elementary School rests on the slope of the 10,000-foot-high Haleakala volcano. In the valley below the school, looking to the west, extensive sugar cane fields form a patchwork of greens and browns; the cloud-obscured islands of Lanai, Molokai, and Kahoolawe loom in the distance to the west and south.

Fourth grader Kendall Umetsu and her classmates were encouraged to compose poetry at Kula Elementary after the teacher, Ms. Diane Peters, shared her own poems with the class.

On one occasion Ms. Peters played "color" music ("Greensleeves," "The Blue Danube," "Flight of the Bumblebee"), then had students do choral readings of color poems from Mary O'Neill's 1961 classic, *Hailstones and Halibut Bones*. Next, students brainstormed color words on big pieces of paper, and finally created color poems, illustrating them with watercolors.

Kendall told me that she most enjoyed writing poetry in a unique form introduced by Ms. Peters called "four stars and a wish." Using this form, Kendall and each of her classmates selected a friend, then complimented that individual through a five-line poem. The first four lines were "stars," that is, laudatory descriptors of the individual for whom the poem was intended; the fifth line expressed a wish for that particular person.

In order to complete this task, Kendall had to consider audience, draw on personal experience, and make meaning using a poetic template. She had a real reason to compose her poem, a real audience in mind, and she now considers herself a poet.

# SIXTH-GRADE RECITERS, LAS CRUCES, NEW MEXICO

In southern New Mexico, the small city of Las Cruces, situated along the Rio Grande in the Mesilla Valley, lies 45 miles north of the border cities of El Paso, Texas and Juarez, Mexico. Hispanic culture and traditions remain strong in the valley, and the school-age population reflects this diversity. Cotton, pecans, onions, and chile are major crops; the city and surrounding valley communities are crisscrossed by ditches that bring river water to fertile fields.

Sixth graders at Sierra Middle School in Las Cruces began their 2003–2004 school year with poetry recitations, something most of them had never experienced before. Their teacher, Flora Tyler, was eager for the pupils to develop recitation and public speaking skills. However, she had never done such an activity with students.

The second week of school, Ms. Tyler gave her pupils the following instructions:

- Select at least seven lines of poetry.
- Memorize your poem.
- Be prepared to recite your poem five days from today.

Then Ms. Tyler read a poem aloud to her students, modeling appropriate elocution, expression, and eye contact. She and her students discussed the demands of reciting in front of a live audience.

On the first poetry recitation day, student after student walked to the front of the room and delivered their lines. Ms. Tyler was delighted with the initial results. Every one of her 87 students (in three separate classes) successfully completed the task, and several students voluntarily chose poems of 25 lines or more, significantly beyond the required minimum.

By the third recitation of the year, most sixth graders had internalized the routine. The day before the recitation, students selected time slots for reciting by signing their names on a piece of construction paper posted on the chalkboard at the front of the room.

As soon as her sixth graders entered the classroom on the third Recitation Day, Ms. Tyler said, "You have five minutes to take out your poems and practice." Students immediately set to work in their coed clusters of desks.

Holding up an assessment form, Ms. Tyler announced, "Turn this in with a copy of your poem before you recite. Please fill out the top by writing your first and last names." Twenty-seven students began completing forms.

"As other students recite," she continued, "I will be watching how you behave as an audience. No whistling, just snap or clap. We'll begin in this order—Sara, Chris, Gage, Fernando, Cody, Maria, Bonnie . . ." She read the sign-up list aloud as a reminder to all.

The first reciter, Sara, walked up to Ms. Tyler's desk, handed her a copy of the poem and an assessment form with her name on it, then proceeded to the front of the classroom, raised her right arm for silence, and waited as other students shushed those around them. When the room was quiet, Sara pushed the "Record" button on the cassette tape recorder, turned to the class, and began reciting.

When Sara completed her poem, Chris, the next reciter, stood up and, echoing Sara's actions, walked to the front of the room, raised his hand for silence, and said his poem. Before long, all 27 students had recited poems from memory. Selections ranged from Shel Silverstein to Edgar Allan Poe.

Citing language acquisition, public speaking, memorization, writing fluency, and listening as some of the academic skills her students addressed through this activity, Ms. Tyler watched her students have fun with language as they played with poetry. She told me that she was pleasantly surprised by the variety of poems her students brought to the recitations when they were allowed to select their own poems.

## SEVENTH-GRADE POETS, SEAFORD, DELAWARE

In southern Delaware on the flat coastal plain that borders the Atlantic coast, the Nanticoke River runs past the town of Seaford and drains into Chesapeake Bay. Seaford Middle School, an imposing two-story brick edifice originally constructed as a high school in 1928, sits on the northeast side of historic Seaford, half a mile from the river. Annie Darden, a seventh-grade language arts teacher, works on the second floor in Room 207. Ms. Darden, who also works with the National Writing Project in Delaware and is an accomplished educator, incorporates poetry in her curriculum throughout the year.

On a snowy afternoon in late January 2003, Ms. Darden asked her pupils to take out their poems. Twenty-one seventh graders sifted through notebooks and extracted drafts of three poems each had composed as part of a unit related to the Nanticoke River Festival.

Once students had their poems on their desktops, Ms. Darden played an excerpt from a National Writing Project CD recording titled *Rural Voices Radio II*.

"In your poems you are trying to capture an aspect of life here along the Nanticoke," Ms. Darden said. "How well have you expressed your ideas?" She then held up the compact disk.

"Listen to this young boy read about his life on Hawaii, and notice the details he gives us."

Ms. Darden played an excerpt from "I Remember Hilo Rain: A Downpour of Voices from the Big Island" for her students, who listened intently as a young Hawaiian's voice filled the classroom:

> I am what I am.
> A child of color blind people,
> The blood of many races, belonging to none . . .
> A son of immigrant and native flesh,
> Whose names are the heavy ocean mists.

> —Chad Ahia, Hawai'i
> (National Writing Project, 2001)

"What I want you to do next is called a 'walkabout,'" Ms. Darden instructed. "Leave your poems on your desk, then walk around the room and read everyone else's. Take your time, don't rush."

An audible flutter swept through the room.

"Also, keep track of which poems you like, and why," Ms. Darden continued. "We'll talk about them after you're done. You have ten minutes. Please begin." Ms. Darden knew that the ten minutes would stretch into fifteen, but she didn't tell her students that, all the better to keep them on task.

The seventh graders stood and proceeded randomly into the aisles between desks, slowly circulating around the room, pausing at desk after desk to pick up poems and read them silently. Laughter, murmurs of praise, friends exchanging whispered comments and an occasional "Whoa!" could be heard above the shuffling of sneakers.

"This is really good, Kristi," one girl said to another.

Kristi, slightly embarrassed, smiled and looked out the window at the falling flakes.

Most of the poems were substantive, advanced drafts, and they reflected significant work by seventh-grade authors. Evidence of drafting and revising was abundant.

Ms. Darden then invited students to read their poems aloud; several students volunteered. Afterwards, Ms. Darden asked the class for comments. Classmates praised titles, suggested word changes, offered reactions, and posed questions as the authors took notes. Then, another student offered to read her friend Alicia's poem, saying that it was very good.

When one student suggested turning his poem into a series of rhyming couplets, Ms. Darden observed, "The struggle to rhyme can confine, early on. I just don't want to restrict you by having you try to find rhyming words." She explained to students that the flow of ideas was the most important ingredient of their poems.

Another student suggested writing out the ideas for the poem as prose first, then transforming the text into lines and verses.

Finally, Ms. Darden read aloud her own Nanticoke River Festival poem, a melange of food images, tastes, and smells. She read with enthusiasm, first explaining to students that her poem was a work in progress. She asked them to help her with revision strategies and, as students offered suggestions, she listed several on the chalkboard.

For homework that evening, Ms. Darden announced that one poem was due the next day in final form. "And I want to see your process," she added. "Save all drafts."

The bell rang. The seventh graders put away their poems and headed off to other classes. Outside the window, light snowflakes continued to drift onto the street below and into the nearby Nanticoke.

## SEVENTH-GRADE "FOUND" POETRY, CLOVIS, CALIFORNIA

Clovis, California, an agricultural, middle-class community boasting the oldest professional rodeo in California, lies in the San Joaquin Valley 12 miles northeast of Fresno. Reyburn Intermediate School, situated on a large campus, sits next to an elementary school and a high school. In a seventh-grade classroom at Reyburn, reading teacher Janice Smith's students approach the writing of poetry through a technique she calls poetry pairs. They create "found" poems, that is, verses that use lines taken from, or influenced by, specific poems they have read in class.

In October 2003, Mrs. Smith, a peppy classroom veteran, distributed two poems to her students—"For the Love of the Game: Michael Jordan and Me," an 81-line tribute to the former NBA All-Star by Eloise Greenfield, and "Hoops," a 67-line free verse poem by Robert Burleigh that captures the excitement of playground basketball.

After students read both poems aloud in class, Mrs. Smith explained the initial task. "Read through 'For the Love of the Game' again by yourself," she directed, "and underline your favorite lines, five or six, perhaps. Choose lines that you like, for whatever reason."

Next she instructed students to repeat the task, this time using "Hoops" as their text. Before long, students had identified several favorite lines from both poems.

Mrs. Smith then shared her own "found poem" about one of her habitual urges. Two of her "found" lines were "I make my move" and "like a fox on the lurk":

### The Mall

I see the mall.
I make my move.
In my car I travel at reckless speed
To make the sale.

I hear the voices of naysayers,
"Don't spend any money,"
"No checks!"
"We're broke!"

I feel the rhythm of my heart—
As I stand below
The up escalator, the next level

The way the lights of each store flicker throughout
I see through a moment of narrow space.
I choose the path that I will take—
The watching and the waiting,
The decisions.

Like a fox on the lurk,
I take my stance
I make my move,

I go to . . .
Gottchalks!

—Janice Smith


"What I want you to do now," Mrs. Smith announced, "is to create a new poem using some of the lines you selected, or revisions of those lines. Notice that my poem about 'The Mall' includes lines from both poems. Pick whatever topic you like, but in your new poem, try to include some of the lines you found and liked in both 'Hoops' and 'For the Love of the Game.'"

Students set about the task willingly, and before the period ended, most had completed at least one "found poem." Andrew stayed with the original topic:

### Basketball

For the love of
The game and the
Feathery fingertip roll
I step onto the court
And make my move
To the hoop
In the air
The lay up
I am there
At the circle of my life
I feel the spirit of the players
Around me standing like
Swollen trees
In the pale light
I see my path
To success and
Land like a rock falling
To the bottom
Of the ocean
But if I fall I will rise

Again and again and again
And again. . . .

—Andrew Myatt

Katie composed a "found poem" about the major sport in her life:

### Softball

The game.
Feel it!
You bend your legs
Tensing
As you feel your throat on fire.

The bat,
Like a piece of the thin long reach of your body.
The ball zooming like a speeding lightning.
Smack!
The ball glides through the air
Sinking closer and closer to the ground.
Yes.
Like the fox on the lurk
With his smooth skaterly glide and sudden swerve.
Homerun!

The sun has risen but barely in the pale light,
Turning, I smile at the memory of wind in my face.

I see the crowd
roaring for me with happiness on their faces.

For the love of the game
I live.

—Katie Parker

Brandon, a skateboarder, wrote about his sport of choice:

### Blading

I rise from my bed
For the love of the game of blading.
Some day . . .
I will choose the path to go to the X-Games.

I hear the voices of doomsayers
Danger! All is danger!

I take my stand
If I fall I will rise again
I breathe their words
I feel the strength of my spirit.

The sport.
The smooth.
The cool.
The hunger.

The grind of the blade against the sidewalk,
The skittery cat-footed dance
The twirl, the spin.
Blading.
Yes,
Feel it!

—Brandon Salisbury

The passion in these "found poems" is evident. Using lines from existing verses as inspiration, seventh-grade poets in Clovis celebrated their own interests, hobbies, and love of sports.

## EIGHTH-GRADE POETS, NEWCASTLE, WYOMING

Susan Jones, an eighth-grade language arts teacher in Newcastle, Wyoming, has many favorite poetry activities for students, including allowing them to stand on tops of their desks and recite Robert Frost's "The Road Not Taken" in their best *Dead Poets' Society* imitation. But what she especially enjoys doing is the "For my mom who in the ____" project, when each student composes a list poem specifically for a family member.

Newcastle, a town of just over 3,000 people on the plains of northeast Wyoming next to the Thunder Basin National Grasslands, is the "Western Gateway to the Black Hills of South Dakota." Ms. Jones, who has taught at Newcastle Middle School for 27 years, spends several weeks each year on this project, inspiring her students to craft verses for important audiences.

Ms. Jones begins by asking students to think of an important audience, a family member who has helped them in some way. In journals, students recount in detail what they learned from this person. Next, Ms. Jones describes a poem that she is about to share with them as "an expression of gratitude for an older sister's help." She then reads "For My Sister Molly Who in the Fifties," a 50-line Alice Walker poem from *Revolutionary Petunias & Other Poems*, first published in 1973.

After students hear the Walker poem, they discuss how some poems are patterned on lists, and in this case, a list of the poet's memories of her sister. Next, students brainstorm a list of character traits, physical and behavioral characteristics, and actions that they appreciate about their selected audience. They also discuss and create a vivid verb chart. Finally, Ms. Jones asks students to connect the items on their lists in the same manner that the poet Alice Walker does, and to use vivid verbs to introduce each line.

Students spend several weeks on this poetry writing assignment. They are given sufficient time to create lists, draft poems, conference, revise, edit, and, finally, "publish" their poems in PowerPoint presentations. The culminating activity for this project occurs when students invite their important audience to school to see the PowerPoint presentations. Ultimately, students are assessed through rubrics, both in English and computer class.

Eighth grader Patrick Baldwin used rhymed couplets to describe his relationship with his father:

### For My Dad . . .

For my dad who in the Eighties
Was the dude who loved the ladies
Was getting' killed at a card game
When I started the story of my fame
Showed me how to fly a kite
Told me always to sit up right
Baby-sat me many days
Took naps with me in our P.J.s
Went to college and earned some dough
Tolerated the fits I'd throw

Patrick's poem continues for 50 more lines through the nineties and the "two-thousands," where he appreciates it when his dad:

> Treats me like I'm a man
> Always offers a helping hand . . .
> Bought me a nice, new go-kart
> Prays for me when we're apart

> —Patrick Baldwin

Kayla Scheck wrote "My Dad," a seven-page, 41-line poem about her father. She scanned and then electronically inserted fourteen photographs into her booklet, including one of her dad cradling her in his arm while they sat in a recliner, another photo of him gripping her around the waist as they sat astride a horse in a corral, and a third photo of two silhouetted figures, one large and one small, pushing snow shovels down a driveway. Kayla literally grows up in her poem. Ms. Jones described Kayla's project as an "awesome tribute to your dad."

### My Dad

For my dad who in the eighties . . .

Brought me home from the hospital.
Rapidly changed my diapers.
Loved me for who I was.
Rocked me to sleep.
Spanked me when I was bad.
Took me on my first horse ride.

For my dad who in the eighties . . .

Helped me take my first steps.
Told me I was his little girl.
Gave me endless kisses.
Took me to grandma's house.
Ate yogurt with me.
Shoveled the sidewalks with me.

For my dad who in the nineties . . .

Taught me how to ride my bike.
Bought me my first horse, but not my last either.

Told me the difference between right and wrong.
Taught me how to fish and drive a boat.
Took me camping during the summer.
Bought me my first horse trailer.
Tickled me till I cried.
Tried to keep me from spending his money.
Took me to my very first day of school.
Taught me how to ride my bike without training wheels.

For my dad who in the nineties . . .

Helped us dye Easter eggs every year.
Carved the perfect pumpkins on Halloween.
Taught me how to roof a house.
Showed me how to make a fire in the fireplace.
Taught me how to play catch.
Told me I could do anything I put my mind to.
Took me to my first horse show and rodeo.
Told me all boys were bad, but I didn't listen.
Showed me how to shoot a gun.
Left me for a better place.

For my dad who in the two-thousandths . . .

Left me with only memories.
Didn't get to see me finish growing up.
Watches over me as the years pass by.
Remains with me in my heart.

—Kayla Scheck

One of the last photographs in Kayla's PowerPoint presentation shows her talking on a white telephone while her father reclines on a hospital bed next to her.

Three years after composing this poem, Kayla reminisced:

Being daddy's little girl has always been the highlight of my life. Even after three years it feels like just yesterday I wrote this poem for my dad, Paul Scheck Sr. Losing him seven years ago was the hardest thing I have had to go through in my life. This poem helped me and let me express my dad in everything he has done and the great times we have shared together! Losing my dad has made me a stronger individual and realize how important life really is. Today I live on with cherishing memories and knowing that one day I will be with him again in the holy land, walking hand in hand.

In loving memory of my father,

—Kayla Scheck
(E-mail communication, May 3, 2005)

Susan Jones has also used this composition strategy in her Holocaust unit ("For Anne Frank who in the 1940's . . ." or "For Jews who in the 1930's . . ."). Her students have come up with many different applications over the years, including gifts of poetry for Mother's Day, Father's Day, and birthdays.

## "MONTH OF THE YOUNG ADOLESCENT" POEMS, RIVER VALE, NEW JERSEY

"It's good to be a teenager because . . ." was the writing prompt that Debbie Cooke, an eighth-grade language arts teacher at Holdrum Middle School (440 students in grades 6–8), in River Vale, New Jersey, gave to her students in October 2003. A month earlier, Ms. Cooke had attended her first language arts department meeting of the year when. Holdrum's principal, Jaynellen Behre-Jenkins, just four weeks on the job, spoke about Month of the Young Adolescent, an initiative sponsored by National Middle School Association (NMSA) each October to promote awareness and understanding of middle school kids.

"How are you going to integrate writing into our Month of the Young Adolescent celebration?" the principal asked her teachers. She then distributed promotional materials provided by NMSA and encouraged her teachers to visit NMSA's website (*www.nmsa.org*) for further information.

Back in the classroom, Ms. Cooke suggested to students that they respond to the prompt, "It's good to be a teenager . . ." in whichever genre they preferred: essay, list, poem, or narrative.

Christina Rotolo, an avid reader, used the word "Teenager" to structure her poem:

*T*otal freedom is what we'll get soon
*E*veryone values our opinions

*E*nergy is a thing we lack
*N*obody is the same
*A*dults are what we're treated like
*G*radually we prepare to be adults
*E*nabled to make our own decisions
*R*esponsibility is what we get more of

—Christina Rotolo

Annie Marshall, who aspires to be a best-selling author one day, wrote about the pros and cons of being a teen:

You're young enough to go trick-or-treating
You're old enough to go alone
You're young enough to dress up
You're old enough to stay out late

You're young enough so your parents worry
You're old enough for them to trust your judgment
You're young enough to cry
You're old enough to be the shoulder for someone else to cry

You're young enough to hold your dad's hand
You're old enough to hold your boyfriend's hand
You're young enough to act goofy
You're old enough to act mature

You're young enough to daydream
You're old enough to speak your mind
You're young enough to fight with your siblings
You're old enough to agree with your siblings

And as you see, with all of these great things
It's good to be a teenager

—Annie Marshall

*Note: Every year National Middle School Association invites teachers across the country to submit writings by young adolescents as part of the Month of the Young Adolescent celebration. From 2003 to 2005 they received more than 4,500 entries. Contact www.nmsa.org for more information.*

# HIGH SCHOOL SONNETEERS, ESTES PARK, COLORADO

On a cloudless Colorado morning in a mountain meadow 8,000 feet above sea level, eight high school students, one teacher, one teaching intern, and two observers sit on logs in a casual circle, sharing sonnets. Morning sunlight streams through the towering ponderosa pines edging their outdoor classroom. The students, all former high school dropouts, can be generously described as "at risk." None were ever expected to graduate from high school, all were from the bottom half of the economic spectrum, and most had been through traumatic life experiences, yet all are back in high school voluntarily at Eagle Rock School in Estes Park because they had been, as one of them put it, "messing up big time" in high school. Each, however, has decided to turn his or her life around; at Eagle Rock, every student makes that essential commitment.

On this July morning, the teacher, Robert (students call teachers by their first names at Eagle Rock), asks the students to take out their homework. Drafts of sonnets, both Shakespearean and Petrarchian, appear from backpacks, binders, and the inner pages of poetry books. As students unfold poems and read them silently, Robert nods approvingly. Then, after reading his own recently composed sonnet, he invites others in the circle to do likewise. Several students share sonnets about nature, life, and growing up, while others listen attentively.

Robert then conducts an exercise. "Relax and close your eyes," he says. "Take in the warmth of midmorning sunlight, and see if you can generate an idea for yet another sonnet, this time based on your actual experience of nature this morning."

Their eyes shut, students absorb the warmth of the sun's rays shimmering through overhead boughs as they consider Robert's request. In the distance, a dog barks. The raucous cry of a Steller's jay echoes from a nearby pine. Faint voices of students heading to the gymnasium drift across the mountain meadow.

After a few minutes Robert asks, "What is a sonnet?"

A student wearing a gray ERS T-shirt responds that a sonnet is a 14-line poem in iambic pentameter that follows a specific rhyme scheme.

Robert smiles, thanks him, then asks, "What is the difference between the Shakespearean and Petrarchian forms of sonnets?"

A 15 year-old girl responds that the Shakespearean sonnet, sometimes known as the English sonnet, has three quatrains and a couplet at the end in an ABAB CDCD EFEF GG rhyme scheme, while the Petrarchian, sometimes called the Italian sonnet, employs an ABBAABBA octave followed by a sestet using a CDCDCD or CDCCDC pattern, but most definitely no couplet. Robert smiles even more broadly, pleased with his students' command of the subject matter.

"You have the next fifteen minutes to compose a sonnet using either form, Shakespearean or Petrarchian," Robert announces. He suggests that students draw upon their earlier sunlit meditation, and he intentionally challenges them to write with abandon. And they do, as do the teacher, the teaching intern, and the observers.

Most students remain seated on log sections, bodies hunched over notebooks, scribbling, crossing out, looking off into the distance for inspiration, counting out iambic beats on their fingers, and silently reading and rereading a line or two to discover how it might proceed. Two students move to the ground, one bracing his back against a ponderosa pine, the other sitting with her legs crossed. Oblivious to those around them, Robert, the intern, and each of the students seemed equally engrossed in the task at hand—composing a sonnet.

Inspired by their industriousness, I set to work and quickly compose a sonnet in the allotted time period. When Robert calls an end to the writing period, he asks for volunteers to read aloud. After others share, I read my Shakespearean sonnet to the group:

> In a circle sheltered from the sun
> 'neath ponderosa, writers seek a word
> that will communicate, when they are done,
> the message of the sonnet to be heard.
> On rugged tree trunk slices, there they sit
> engaged in poetry and making sense
> of life and living—will the quatrain fit
> and offer meaning stripped of all pretense?
> Struggling with iambic form and rule
> (no AB scheme if AB will suffice)
> they pattern sonnets in this outdoor school
> and slowly grasp what's great or merely nice.
> Pentameter's bounds are truly large,
> yet when I craft a poem, I am in charge!

—RMB

Reflecting on the class afterwards, I am amazed that this unlikely group of poets (or so one might assume about 15- and 16-year-old "at-risk" students) can become absorbed in writing sonnets, a somewhat archaic and highly disciplined form of poetry. The small size of the class, the passion of the teacher, the mountain meadow—these elements certainly contribute to student engagement. But there is something else going on as well—an appreciation of poetry.

Looking through a brochure about the school, I read that Eagle Rock is committed to, among other things, having each student "develop the artist within." Clearly that includes composing sonnets *alfresco* at 8,000 feet.

## LESSONS FROM TEACHERS

When I reflect on the eight teachers and their students described in this chapter, I notice several common elements. Each teacher provided a model to stimulate and engage students in the task at hand. Clear instructions were issued, reviewed, revisited, reinforced, and, where applicable, revised. Expectations were made clear to students in advance. In most cases, students had to make their poems public, that is, share their writing with a larger audience. Students had choice in the matter; they could select the topic and/or form. Teachers went about their work in an unhurried manner, and allowing students sufficient time to complete the task. Throughout, students had to make many decisions. And in half the cases, teachers modeled appropriately by sharing their writing with students.

The point is, there are many teachers all across America who have designed challenging and engaging poetry lessons. All of them include reading, writing, reciting, or memorizing. Steal one of these ideas, make it your own, and engage your students in poetry.

## POETIC INTERLUDE NO. 9: "MIDLEVEL MINDS"

Ron Murray, a middle school teacher in Albuquerque and president of New Mexico Middle Level Educators, Inc., described the youngsters in his school in a poem he composed in 2002:

**Midlevel Minds**

Sixth Graders

Whirling, twirling in a squirrelly world,
Young adolescents, *los perdidos*, pearls . . .
Malleable, morphing, miniature boys and girls,
Midlevel munchkins—in an upward swirl,
Prancing precipitously to new heights unfurled.

Seventh Graders
[*Parents: This, too, whacked-out-alien rite-of-passage, shall pass.*]

Amidst the middle muddle, they, evolving in the social morass,
Teddy bear solace simultasked with peer partner pairing,
Seeking self, safety, bunch-belonging-hold-fast, independence-at-last,
Path-probing procrastinators, meandering, cocky mocking, boundary-bashers.

Eighth Graders

With hubristic omniscience at high school's verge, at ladder's apex
Our looming charges emerge tentativeless, tenacious, verily voracious
Consumers, facebraced, of fast food and fastpace, stimuli over ennui,
Fourteen-turn burn energy, challenge it all in experimental synergy,
Ridge-tossing bridge-crossing promotion passing, *exeunt omnes . . . finis?*

—Ron Murray

A question—how do we teach any subject, not to mention poetry, to "squirrelly," "meandering," "hubristic" young adolescents? Another question—how would you describe *your* students in a poem? And a third—how would they describe *themselves* in verse?

## Chapter Ten

# Reflections from the Classroom

*This chapter offers reflections on teaching poetry. The voices of former students add a compelling counterpoint.*

> Poetry in the classroom—a perfect place for verse
> Have your students draft, revise, edit. Keep it terse.
> Memorize, then recite. Learn a poem by heart.
> Add discussion and interpretation. That's a start.
> Next, compose your own lines; doggerel will do.
> Poetry in the classroom—that's all you have to do.
>
> —RMB

Read the poems you like reading. Don't bother whether they're important, or if they'll live. What does it matter what poetry *is*, after all? If you want a definition of poetry, say: "Poetry is what makes me laugh or cry or yawn, what makes my toenails twinkle, what makes me want to do this or that or nothing," and let it go at that. All that matters about poetry is the enjoyment of it, however tragic it may be. All that matters is the eternal movement behind it, the vast undercurrent of human grief, folly, pretension, exaltation, or ignorance, however unlofty the intention of the poem.

> —Dylan Thomas (Scully, 1965, p. 191)

One summer while serving as a Peace Corps Volunteer in Tunisia, I worked as a lifeguard in a youth camp on the Mediterranean Sea. While walking on a beach near Hammamet with my visiting sister, we saw a path leading into a garden. The owner, an expatriate American, invited us to join him. As we sipped mint tea under shady palms on a hot July afternoon and admired the courtyard of his beautiful home, our host said something that has stayed with me ever since: "Every man should be a poet and an architect." His words still resonate. Each of us has the capability to create, to construct, and to leave behind a legacy.


## GRADUATION MEMORY

Jeannie Waltz came running up to me outside the high school auditorium immediately after her graduation.

"Did you hear him, Mr. B?" she asked excitedly.

"Him" was the graduation speaker, who, when he recited "The Road Not Taken" in his remarks to the graduating class, transported Jeannie and her classmates back to eighth grade. She wanted me to know that she remembered Frost's poem and that she was able to recite it to herself silently along with the speaker.

What was it about that poem, and about Jeannie's experiences with poetry four years earlier, that stayed with her? Why do we remember the things we remember?

The first question raised in this book was, "Why poetry?" Perhaps the real question is, "Why not poetry?"


## SUMMARY POEM

Toward the end of their eighth-grade year, I asked my students to reflect on the writing they had done and to compose a piece that represented their best efforts. In response, Katie Joos submitted this poem:

### Eighth Grade

So much has
been accomplished.
Most everything was shared.
Without hesitation
everyone stepped
forward,
to venture forward
on a journey together.

New friendships were founded.
Memories were made.
Happiness was never
hard to find.
So much has happened since our
first meeting.
Burt now it is time
to move forth in
our lives.
Although we are
saying goodbye,
we will always have
our treasured thoughts.
So as we once greeted each other,
we now bid farewell,
for now.

—Katie Joos
(Eighth grader in 1995–1996)

In her accompanying reflection, Katie said:

There are several reasons why I chose a poem to represent my writing over the past year, and my improvements. Poetry lets me share my personal feelings, even if I don't say so directly. I feel that poetry lets me express myself in many ways.

Another reason why I chose a poem was because I enjoy writing poetry very much. Poetry gives me a chance to share a different aspect of my personality with other people.

["Eighth Grade"] came into being when I was told that I needed to create a fifth piece for my writing magazine that was different then any of the other pieces that I had already included. I decided not to include any of my other poems so that I could create a new one to represent my best writing. This piece was just written one or two days ago, so it is the most recent piece out of everything.

I got the idea for this piece because I wanted to share my thoughts and feelings about eighth grade with other people. My original idea for the poem was completely different then the final product. The first and final drafts were so tremendously different. If you read the first draft you would not believe that it was related in any way to the final product. This piece of writing went through immense drafting and revising.

I feel that this piece reveals that I have the capability to write poetry. Also it proves my improvement in the drafting and revising process.

I would not change anything about this piece upon reflection. I am very pleased with how it turned out. I feel that it gets my emotions across clearly and powerfully. If someone else read it they would understand how I feel.

I enjoy writing poetry very much, and I enjoyed writing this piece. Poetry lets me express myself in any way that I desire to.

—Katie Joos, June 1996

Katie added that she enjoyed writing poetry because it "gave me a chance to be serious or humorous, depending on my mood." I was pleased that she had found a way to express herself. Katie noted that my advice about revision—"Nothing is ever completed in just one draft"—had made a difference:

Before I was told this I would feel that once I wrote something on paper that it was final. . . . I now go back after the first draft I wrote and look for things that I can improve upon. I may not always find grammatical errors until the second or third draft, but I will expand upon my original ideas to make my writing more personal and more explanatory.

—Katie Joos, June 1996

Today, Katie is an elementary teacher on Long Island, and she teaches poetry to her third graders.

## IMPLEMENTATION IN CONCERT

In *This We Believe: Successful Schools for Young Adolescents*, National Middle School Association (2003) identifies 14 characteristics of a successful middle school and underscores this point:

Schools should not choose among characteristics, implementing only those that appear to be more achievable or seem more appropriate for a school or a particular situation. Rather, successful middle level schools recognize that the 14 characteristics described in *This We Believe: Successful Schools for Young Adolescents* are interdependent and must be implemented in concert. (p. 2)

Memorizing and reciting poems is a worthwhile activity. Composing and publishing verse is time well spent. Reading poems and discussing them for meaning is a valid instructional practice. However, none of these approaches to poetry has as powerful an impact on students individually as all of them working together, in concert with one another. The interrelatedness of these activities enhances a student's ability to do each of them better. Students are more likely to achieve success with poetry when all three strands operate consistently, month after month, as part of the normal ebb and flow of the classroom.

What was the impact on students of doing regular poetry recitations, listening to my weekly *Poems For All Occasions*, composing free verse poetry during the first week of school, editing verses for publication in class anthologies, authoring individual poetry booklets, reflecting on writing in journal entries, and participating in a celebration of writing from Day One to Day One Hundred Eighty? It's difficult to know, exactly. But clearly, something positive happened to my students—they learned to enjoy poetry and writing poems, and not just occasionally.

Katie Joos is a prime example. During her eighth-grade year, Katie, who recited "The Unicorn" so well, also did nine other poetry recitations; drafted numerous free verse poems; created a poetry booklet of ten poems drawn from twenty-two that she composed during a two-week span; assembled an individual magazine containing poetry and other writings; analyzed five poems through observing, questioning, and interpreting; listened attentively as classmates recited more than 200 poems; and heard me deliver more than 40 poems created "for all occasions."

Katie also engaged in other language arts. During the year she wrote an article for the school newspaper; composed interior monologues and personal essays; wrote editorials on a variety of topics; penned letters and reflective journal entries; read and discussed short stories, novels, and plays; and did a host of other activities, some of which are described in my book *Writing for Real: Strategies for Engaging Adolescent Writers* (2003).

Participation in all of these activities made a difference with Katie; no one poetic event had as much impact as the cumulative effect of all of them. And Katie's poetic encounters during her eighth-grade year were similar to those of every other student I taught. What she experienced was the rule, not the exception.

## OTHER STUDENT REFLECTIONS

I believe that one of our jobs as teachers is to give students positive experiences from which they extract lifetime lessons. In the process of writing this book, I contacted former students to learn what poetry memories stay with them.

Jeanne Vallely, now the mother of two small children, recently graduated from nursing school in New York State. An eighth grader in 1979–1980, Jeanne remembered a particular classmate and his moment of triumph:

> I was pretty shy and uncomfortable being the center of attention at that time, and being thirteen it was my worst nightmare to have to speak in front of the class, but in Mr. Burkhardt's class, you had no choice. He had this crazy idea that kids our age had something to offer, radical even for SWR. The way I remember it was, we were assigned or maybe chose a poem to memorize on Monday, then we fiddled with it throughout the week, and on Friday you had to stand in front of the class and recite it from memory. ("Two roads diverged in a yellow wood, and I took the one less traveled by . . .") It was hell for me, but then, I was always a good student, I didn't struggle much in school, so a challenge was in order.
>
> But Brian Hawkins wasn't a good student—he was a good guy—the Hawk, everyone called him, and he had brothers who were older than all of us. He knew about sex, drugs, and the music that was popular at the time. Brian was an awfully nice kid, and he must have had some learning disabilities—I recall he often had trouble reading out loud in class, and to watch him on those [recitation] Fridays was torture. He stammered and turned red, and his physical presence was so awkward. He was very thin and didn't ever look healthy, and his body was set at odd angles. Reciting poetry from memory was just not his thing. I'm not even sure he could read . . .
>
> I remember Brian complaining bitterly about these recitation assignments— he probably had some choice words to say—but then one day near the end of the year, Brian hauled his crooked body up to the front of the class, and, determined to not let this [challenge] get the best of him, he pulled himself up and recited his poem. He spoke forcefully and with great emotion, and his eyes were almost wild with the force of the words—he understood the words, he understood the emotions, he understood the assignment! The whole class applauded for him, noisily and loudly.

Brian Hawkins was killed in a car accident during high school—he was crossing the divider line and was struck by an oncoming car.

Maybe this isn't exactly the way it happened, maybe he wasn't as good up there as I remember him being, but it doesn't really matter. What is important is that Brian had a sense of himself that day, a sense of possibility, and that is the gift that you gave each and every one of your students, and I thank you from the bottom of my heart.

—Jeanne Vallely
(E-mail communication, April 24, 2005)

Danny Smith, also an eighth grader in 1979–1980, now lives on Long Island with his wife Betty Anne and his two children, Liam Daniel and Abigail Grace. Danny recalled how his late father coached him years ago, helping him to gain confidence through reciting poems:

Memorizing the [poem] was a frustrating experience for me because in 8th grade I believe the two most important things in my life were hockey and girls. If anything took away from those activities, I was not happy. My father recognized the importance [of recitation] and made me stick with the work. He also was firm about me practicing in front of him, and that was always fun. I'd stumble over a particular verse, and my dad would mimic my mistake and ask me if I had marbles in my mouth. We'd laugh and make fun of each other, but it was always positive. My dad had a strong belief in the value of public speaking, so he was tough . . . [but] never unkind. I felt, after practicing, that I could make a mistake and no matter how ridiculous it sounded, I'd be able to get through it.

—Danny Smith
(E-mail communication, March 20, 2003)

Glenn Valentine, a classmate of Danny and Jeanne and now a respiratory therapist practicing on Long Island, reflected:

Writing poems actually helped me become more confident with my writing. I was never good with grammar and punctuation, and I therefore felt I was not a good writer. With the poetry format I was able to put my ideas and thoughts into my work without having to worry about grammar. I was able to excel, and gain confidence in my writing.

—Glenn Valentine
(E-mail communication, March 11, 2003)

Barbara Duffrin, an eighth-grade classmate of Andrea, Alyson, and Dawne in 1982–1983 and now a middle school principal in Minnesota, mentioned a particular poem that she recited:

> I remember my recitation of "Sick" by Shel Silverstein. It was my second recitation. For my first one I picked a poem that did not lend itself well to young adolescent melodramatic interpretation (my specialty), and I did not get an A. Alyson Montgomery got an A. I remember that, too. But "Sick," now there's a poem I could work with. I don't remember much aside from switching between Peggy Ann McKay's voice and that of the narrator, and hamming it up shamelessly. I suppose Middle Schoolers are going to be dramatic, might as well channel the drama into something productive.
>
> —Barbara Duffrin
> (E-mail communication, April 28, 2003)

Jennifer Chan, an eighth grader in 1984–1985 and now a family doctor in Pennsylvania, turned to poetry during her first year of medical school:

### Face to Face

Behind the yellowed woven fibers saturated with a chemical liquid
your face rests unseen
Time has changed the texture of your skin
the feel of the muscle underneath
Something so easy to palpate in a breathing supple body
is so difficult in you
I'm afraid

. . .

Our dissection is not superficial
Ribs and vertebrae don't stop us
We follow vessels to their ends
and probe our fingers into sliced-open gut
It's hard to remember you are a human being
when we mutilate you like so
Perhaps this is why I'm afraid to see you
face to face

—Jennifer Chan

I asked Jennifer why she wrote a poem in the midst of the intense pressures of medical school. She responded:

It was my way of trying to sort out the feelings I had . . . a release from the methodical daily grind of classes and studying. That particular class was intense in smells, in experiences I never imagined. I think I wanted to picture the body as an object that we were exploring, but I couldn't ignore feelings that this was a human being that deserved respect.

—Jennifer Chan
(E-mail communication, April 30, 2005)

Jay Urgese, an eighth grader in 1984–1985 and now a JAG attorney living in Germany, cited his efforts at composing poetry:

You presented poetry, most memorably from Mr. Robert Frost. It was not just beautiful, but real and inspiring. We memorized poetry and recited it to our classmates. We wrote our own poems and drew images to help express what we had written.

When I . . . attempted to write poetry of my own, it was very difficult. Now, the standards were high. I could not write something mediocre in my mind because I had too much pride and wanted it to mean something. I wanted it to sound as meaningful as the poems we read in class . . .

[Y]our class was the first time I was forced to present myself in front of a group of people, with all of the attendant pressure. It was not simply a church play or an [elementary school] performance. It was very real, very stressful and incredibly important. I look back on that and know that the reason I still know at least three of Robert Frost's poems by memory is because of that experience in your class. It is not just because I used that to court girls in college, which I absolutely did and can laugh about it, but I also learned how to present ideas in front of people at an early age.

—Jay Urgese
(E-mail communication, February 22, 2003)

Aurelie Shapiro, an eighth grader in 1990–1991 and now an oceanographer working for the federal government in our nation's capital, reflected on composing poems:

I always had this notion that writing poems wasn't something you could learn, that you were born with it. But I couldn't have been more wrong . . . It was a continual process, an ongoing project and it wasn't over when the class ended. I recall the results of the continual draft process quite well, where I would start with something so-so and surprise myself after many revisions that I actually had a poem. Once I got rolling, I started looking at everything in order to make a poem out of it. I really surprised myself that I could come up with a pretty set of words—indeed, a poem.

—Aurelie Shapiro
(E-mail communication, March 27, 2003)

In 1992 when she was an eighth grader, Bonnie Snyder wrote a deceptive free verse poem with a provocative title that immediately caught the attention of the class—most eighth graders dare not speak of such passions publicly:

### My First Love

We dance at my own rhythmic beat.
He's very gentle as he carries me along.
And the feelings I have
When I'm with him are hard to put into words.

His dark hair against his light skin
Bounces up and down,
But always lands in just the right spot,
Over his left eye,
Even after every leap.

Suddenly he carries me faster,
Too fast.
And I must take charge again.
I give him a friendly tug and
Once again we're at my pace,
And we're dancing.

—Bonnie Snyder
(Eighth grader in 1991–1992)

Thirteen years later, Bonnie, now an accountant in Washington, D.C., spoke of the poem, which drew upon her equestrian experiences, and her motivation for writing it:

I remember writing this poem. I remember thinking that I wanted to write about something in a sort of riddle, so people would actually have to think when they read it. I remember thinking that so many poems (and we wrote a lot—that's a good thing) were very explicit. I wanted something that would grab attention and make them sit up, pay attention, and wonder what I was actually talking about. I suppose it was kind of a joke I was playing. Just to see who was actually listening. I know that sounds like such a trouble maker, but it seemed like a good idea at age 13!

—Bonnie Snyder Rouse
(E-mail communication, April 27, 2005)

Jean Schantz wrote volumes of poetry independently throughout her eighth-grade year (1992–1993). Ten years later I inquired why:

Mainly, I wrote as catharsis; I was going through my "teen angst" period, and writing aided my passage. Eighth grade was a pivotal time for me: I was realizing who I was and who I wanted to be; realizing that a lot of my so-called friends really weren't friends at all; and trying to cope with transitioning into high school in the next year. So, my writing was a means of communicating all of my fears and frustrations about my life. Sort of cheap therapy for the teenage me.

—Jean Schantz
(E-mail communication, March 11, 2003)

I asked Jean, now a freelance journalist, poet, and photographer, how she now views the poems she wrote in eighth grade:

Some of them make me cringe, which I assume is normal. Largely speaking, I find a lot of the material painful to read. It's a reminder of a very tough time in my life; a time when I wasn't even sure I wanted to go on. So, I do go back and read the material, but it's more a reminder of how far I've come since then. Thankfully.

—Jean Schantz
(E-mail communication, March 11, 2003)

Cheryl Harrow, an eighth grader in 1995–1996 and now a teachers' assistant in a classroom for children with autism on Long Island, remembered Katie Joos reciting "The Unicorn":

Katie did her poem and it was outstanding. I . . . remember her doing it at one of the [teacher] conferences we went to . . . You wanted Katie to do her poem for the teachers that were there that day. She stood up on the table and went at it. To this day I still remember part of the poem, pretty much "the humpy bumpy camels and the chimpanzees." . . . To see her put so much thought into her poem and make it so entertaining to watch has got to be the reason why I still remember it . . . It wasn't until a couple of years ago that I finally realized why you made us do all that stuff.

—Cheryl Harrow
(E-mail communication, December 1, 2003)

I asked Cheryl to explain why she thought I made her "do all that stuff" and what she "finally realized." She replied:

You made us culturally more aware of what was going on, even if some of the poets were dead. Now that I work with children I realize that you should open them up to new ideas, even if they really aren't too excited about them. . . . I mean jeez, I still remember the whole "We Didn't Start the Fire" song . . . and what the terms mean. I guess I just look at the world in a different way now. I'm forced to use my creativity and memorization skills for other things, and you gave us a chance to try them out when we were still vulnerable to learn . . . I don't think I would have ever looked at poetry at all unless I was forced to, and now I'm actually kind of glad that I was.

—Cheryl Harrow
(E-mail communication, December 2, 2003)

John O'Brien, a classmate of Cheryl Harrow and Katie Joos, reflected on his poetry experiences as an eighth grader in 1995–1996:

You provided the first serious treatment of the subject which I ever encountered. . . . The cornerstone of this treatment was the presentation of the masterworks. By needing to not only read and study classics, we the students accumulated excellent models to inspire our own attempts. To this day, I can still recite verbatim Robert Frost's "The Road Not Taken" and I sincerely doubt that I am the sole alumnus with that facility.

Moreover, you were exemplary not only as a teacher but as a poet in your own right. Your own prolific pieces displayed an energy & enthusiasm often lacking in education. Also, your playful engagements in creativity drew a clear connection between the classroom and the real world. *Ars poetic non est pro scholae; sed pro vitae.*

Helpful too was the immortalization of every student verse—poetry or otherwise—in spiral bound volumes. Instead of merely handing back drafts w/grades in red ink, you compiled each item into an anthology to be shared w/the class. This sense of permanence and publicness does not exist when old poems are shoved into binders to be sacrificed to the god of end-of-the-year locker cleanouts.

—John O'Brien
(E-mail communication, May 3, 2003)

Rae Mannino, who wrote an American History poem about JFK the last year that I taught (1996–1997), mentioned the "poems for all occasions" that I shared regularly with the class:

[I] remember enjoying how you incorporated many of us, as students. At that age, we just wanted to laugh about ourselves and our friends. I admired how you dedicated the time to write something we could relate to . . . rather than something uninteresting or difficult to understand. It would have been real easy to lose our attention.

—Rae Mannino
(E-mail communication, August 29, 2003)

What do I learn from Rae's reflections, and those of John, Cheryl, Jean, Bonnie, Aurelie, Jay, Jennifer, Barbara, Glenn, Danny, and Jeanne? Several things. Students benefit from exposure to the canon, the "masterworks," as John called them. Students acquire lifelong public speaking skills when they recite poetry frequently. Publishing student poems raises them to a new level of significance, giving them "permanence and publicness." Students develop critical thinking skills as they engage with poetry. And students remember the poetic triumphs of their peers.

## INGREDIENTS FOR SUCCESS

What conditions allowed my students to immerse themselves in poetry year after year with such success? First, I invited them to write poems regularly. Doing so, and modeling that request by sharing my own verse, enabled students to cross a threshold into the realm of poetry. I treated poetry seriously, and my students took that message to heart, inspired by my own examples of drafting and revising. I suggested to pupils that they compose verse based on actual experiences such as field trips, school events, and family traditions. I asked students to publish their poems, which led them to care more about grammar and mechanics because they knew that their writing would appear in print. Recitations exposed students to a wide variety of poets and poetic styles, which, in turn, influenced them when they composed verse.

Our classroom became a trusting community of writers—I made it safe for kids to give voice to their thoughts. By always sharing first, I established a positive tone and constantly demonstrated new approaches to the problem of crafting or redrafting a poem.

Leafing through poetry anthologies year after year, I discovered verses that I wanted to read to my students, selecting those that tickled my muse. Over time I assembled an eclectic set of poems, adding new ones and dropping those that did not engage students.

Students improved steadily at poetry recitations by observing peers recite, and by heeding my modeling and coaching. As they recited poem after poem, month after month, students developed the skills of public speaking, memorizing, and maintaining eye contact and poise in front of an audience.

Ultimately, the interconnectedness of many factors—delivering memorizations, listening to poems being recited aloud, looking for a new poem to recite every three or four weeks, composing verse in various forms, discussing and interpreting poems selected by the teacher for that purpose, and seeing the teacher share his poems constantly—grounded my students in poetry and advanced their development as poets.

The larger lesson here is that this comprehensive approach to poetry reflects a philosophy of education based on engagement, excitement, and the notion that subject matter should be relevant to the lives of the student.

## ADVICE FOR TEACHERS

Teaching poetry to young adolescents takes sustained commitment throughout the year. With that in mind, I offer the following advice:

- Find a poet you like and read his or her poems regularly. Learn about that poet's life, and share what you learn with your students.

- Have students memorize, compose, and interpret poems throughout the year. Do not restrict yourself to a two-week poetry unit.
- Subscribe to a poetry magazine or journal.
- Ask your friends who their favorite poets are, and why. Ask them what their favorite poems are, and why. You might learn something that you can share with students.
- Read poetry books, and note the poems you like. Don't worry about why you like them—just start collecting favorites for future use. Later on you will discover how and when to use them.
- Write occasional poems that celebrate school events and curriculum activities. Share these poems with students and colleagues.
- Purchase two rhyming dictionaries, one for home and one for the classroom.
- Date, number, and save all drafts. Obtain a loose-leaf notebook for your completed (polished) poems, and file them in chronological order.
- Revisit and revise your earlier poems (Robert Frost did this all the time).
- Feel free to use any of the poems in this book—mine as well as those of the students—as models for you and for your students. Soon you will have your own set of verses that you can use as examples for students to emulate.
- Remember that first impressions are important. Introduce yourself as a poet on Day One. Write a poem about some aspect of school, and share it with your students as soon as they walk through the door.
- Adapt any and all of these poetry ideas to your own students, teaching style, and school setting.
- Start somewhere. Start small. Do something. Do it now.

## AND IN CONCLUSION . . .

You can do it—you can write poetry that speaks to your students. Just begin. Throw some mud at the wall and see what sticks. What are you waiting for? And remember . . .

- Memorize one poem this month, and another one next month. Before you know it you'll have a few poems under your belt that you can recite to students.

- Use poems that mean something to you, be they from the canon or from a magazine you read recently.
- You don't have to know all the answers. When a student asks, "What does this poem mean?" it's okay to respond, "Good question—what do you think?"
- Students cannot be what they cannot see. You have to set the example and become the teacher as poet.
- Life is short—have fun!


## FAREWELL

In June of my last year of teaching, eighth grader Jason Jendrewski, who knew that I admired John, Paul, George, and Ringo, gave me a parting gift—Michael J. Hockinson's *The Ultimate Beatles Quiz Book*, some 442 pages of Fab Four trivia (e.g., "What were the occupations of each of the Beatles' fathers at the time their respective sons were born?"). I appreciated Jason's thoughtfulness, but what impressed me more was the poem he inscribed inside the cover.

As I considered Jason's words, I was struck by several thoughts. His verses were an attempt to emulate some of my poems "for all occasions." His twelve-line, XAXA XBXB XCXC rhymed verse spoke to the occasion and was heartfelt. And that an eighth-grade boy felt comfortable writing a farewell poem to his teacher speaks volumes.

Jason, who later became president of his class at Cornell, clearly experienced poetry in the classroom.

**For Mr. B.**

When I compare you to the Beatles
You're both way above the rest
Both your impacts are tremendous
Every thing you do is the best!

It doesn't take a genius
To discover what is true
That being one of your students
Leaves me proud to have known you.

Our year was like a "Magical Mystery Tour"
You would never just "Let It Be"
So thank you Mr. Burkhardt
You are an inspiration to me!

—Jason Jendrewski
June 25, 1997

## An Afterthought

Now that you have read this book,
Consider how, in school,
You can use poetic verse
As a teaching tool.

You may find that Frost and others
Serve your higher aim.
Integrate some poetry
Throughout your teaching game.

—RMB

# Appendix: Full Text of Classroom Poems by Braley, Burkhardt, and Lazarus

### Opportunity ·

With doubt and dismay you are smitten?
You think there's no chance for you, son?
Why, the best books haven't been written.
The best race hasn't been run.
The best score hasn't been made yet.
The best song hasn't been sung.
The best tune hasn't been played yet.
Cheer up, for the world is young.

No chance? Why, the world is just eager
For things that you ought to create.
Its store of true wealth is still meager.
Its needs are incessant and great.
It yearns for more power and beauty,
More laughter and love and romance,
More loyalty, labor, and duty.
No chance—why, there's nothing but chance.

For the best verse hasn't been rhymed yet.
The best house hasn't been planned.
The highest peak hasn't been climbed yet.
The mightiest rivers aren't spanned.
Don't worry and fret, faint hearted,
The chances have just begun.
For the best jobs haven't been started.
The best work hasn't been done.

—Berton Braley (1917)

**The New Colossus**

Not like the brazen giant of Greek fame
With conquering limbs astride from land to land,
Here at our sea-washed, sunset gates shall stand
A mighty woman with a torch, whose flame
Is the imprisoned lightning, and her name
Mother of Exiles. From her beacon hand
Glows world wide welcome. Her mild eyes command
The air-bridged harbor that twin cities frame.
"Keep, ancient lands, your storied pomp," cries she
With silent lips. "Give me your tired, your poor,
Your huddled masses yearning to breathe free,
The wretched refuse of your teeming shore.
Send these, the homeless, tempest-tost to me,
I lift my lamp beside the golden door."

—Emma Lazarus (1883)


**Patient**

On Wednesday evening June 1st, 6:10 p.m.,
oversized visitor's pass in hand,
I slowly edged open the door to Room 208
and peered inside.
"Three's Company" babbled
from a wall-mounted TV.
His father sat in a vinyl chair
alongside the cumbersome bed.
Both drew my attention,
then my eyes found Craig, smaller,
propped up by white pillows
under the white sheet,
recent brush cut accentuating
a gaunt, pained face,
left arm curled reassuringly
around a stuffed animal.

"Last night was really scary.
I was concerned when we first brought him in,"
his father confided, clearly relieved
that the worst had passed.

"They had to do some rough things to him.
He had a touch of the old pneumonia."

Craig's left forearm bore a splint
wrapped with wide white cloth
to secure in place lifelines:
an array of blue nozzles and valves,
I-V and antibiotic tubes,
clear plastic capillaries filled with clear liquids
dripping gently down,
flowing into his arm,
nourishing his body, attacking lung infections.

"The doctor says
he'll be in here until Monday at least,"
Craig's father related calmly.
"We're shooting for the concert."

This percussion soloist,
bedridden ten days before his final
Middle School Advanced Band performance,
looked at me, then away.
In his now hunted, now handsome eyes
I saw his incomplete completeness.

"It's boring. I want to get up
and walk around," he offered.
The brown and beige animal
nestled in his arm by the liquid tubes
prompted my tentative question.
"What's the monkey's name."
"Chip," Craig replied.
"Chip Monkey. I get it," I responded.

And I recalled:
Day-Glo orange sneakers
on the first day of eighth grade
and many days thereafter;
a uniformed "Ollie North"
repeating only whispered words from his lawyer
in our advisory's "Tonight Show With Johnny Carson" skit
at the annual fall Variety Show.

And I remembered:
numerous notes from the Spanish teacher—
"Craig is missing five homeworks,"
an asthma attack during lunch in February;
Craig wearing his clean blue and gold soccer uniform,
his squinting countenance captured in Kodachrome;
and the advisory pizza when we bid farewell
to Suzanne's Madrid exchange student
and Craig couldn't stop laughing.

And I reflected on:
his fourth place finish among all eighth graders
in this year's American Legion Essay Contest
for his paper: "Advice To Our As Yet Un-elected President,"
and how in a Team IV discussion about tolerance
after one student was unkind to another,
Craig insisted revenge was appropriate
if you were wronged by another.

This young man now lay in a strange room
on the second floor of St. Charles Hospital,
eyes darting occasionally
to the antics of John Ritter on the TV screen
while his father and I conversed.
Craig continued to cuddle
the comfortable, floppy-earred doll.
Against the wall behind his father's chair
stood the roll-away bed awaiting his mother
(she would later spend the night
after Craig's brother's elementary school concert).

As I drove from the hospital parking lot,
a swirl of memories filled me:
from my year as his advisor and English teacher,
and fractured poetry recitations, and incomplete journal entries,
and wrestling in January, and jazz band on Thursday nights,
and Craig leaping wildly from the roof of the minibus onto the lawn,
and me forgetting his birthday, and me enjoying him in class,
and his rhythmic sound effects, popping and hissing
and leading the advisory in the "You Be 'Illin' " rap

(". . . took his order / and a quarter / small fries / BIG MAC!"),
and photographing his drum set for the Team IV slide show,
and cheering him last week at a track meet,
and watching him sing in chorus . . .

and what stayed with me
was the steadfast inconsistency of
a worn-out teddy bear
protecting the man-to-be.

—RMB

(From the apocryphal *Poems For All Occasions*, May 1988)

### The Last Day

It's the last day.
In they come—
Some pausing hesitantly
At the door,
Reflecting and reminiscing,
Others familiarly announcing
Their presence
As they stride to seats.

Heads turn,
Eyes contact the now-barren classroom:
Posters and pictures
(Relics of yesterday)
Gone . . . .
Saving seats for friends,
Listening to the music,
Awaiting the lesson,
They sit, comfortably,
Facing the finale.

For some,
The boredom of school
All but over.
For some,
The restraints of structure
Almost undone.
For most,

An explored world
Now transformed to memory.

The student asks:
"What did I gain from this experience?"
"What did I give to it?"
"What happens next year?"
The teacher asks:
"What did I gain from this experience?"
"What did I give to it?"
"What happens next year?"

A simultaneously shared journey
Through days and months past
Has ended. And now,
All is quiet and still
Because
It's the last day.

—RMB

(From the apocryphal *Poems For All Occasions*, 1983)

# References

Burkhardt, R. M. (2003). *Writing for real: Strategies for engaging adolescent writers*. Portland, ME: Stenhouse.

Creech, S. (2001). *Love that dog*. New York: HarperCollins.

Devitt, J. (March, 2005). Louise Rosenblatt, pioneer in reading theory and the teaching of literature, dies at 100. *Voices from the Middle 12(3)*, 1–2.

Drew, E. & Connor, G. (1961). *Discovering modern poetry*. New York: Holt, Rinehart and Winston.

Ginsburg, H. & Opper, S. (1979). *Piaget's theory of intellectual development* (2nd ed.). Englewood Cliffs, NJ: Prentice-Hall.

Harmon, W. (Ed.). (1992). *The top 500 poems*. New York: Columbia University Press.

Henn, T. R. (1966). *The apple and the spectroscope: Lectures on poetry designed (in the main) for science students*. New York: W. W. Norton.

Hewitt, G. (2005). *Hewitt's guide to slam poetry and poetry slam*. Shoreham, VT: Discover Writing Press.

Knowles, T. & Brown, D. F. (2000). *What every middle school teacher should know*. Portsmouth, NH: Heinemann.

Kristoff, N. D. (2003, January 31). Flogging the French. *New York Times*, Op-Ed, A29.

Lamott, A. (1995). *Bird by bird: Some instructions on writing and life*. New York: Anchor Books.

Little, J. (1990). *Hey world, here I am!* New York: HarperTrophy.

Merriam, E. (1962). *What can a poem do?* New York: Atheneum.

Muske-Dukes, C. (2002, December 29). A lost eloquence. *New York Times,* Op-Ed, Sec. 4, p. 9.

National Middle School Association. (2003). *This we believe: Successful schools for young adolescents*. Westerville, OH: National Middle School Association.

National Writing Project. (2001). Ahia, C. *I remember Hilo rain: A downpour of voices from the Big Island.* On *Rural voices radio, vol. II* [CD, 2 disks].

National Writing Project & Nagin, C. (2003). *Because writing matters: Improving student writing in our schools.* San Francisco: Jossey-Bass.

O'Neill, M. (1961). *Hailstones and halibut bones.* Garden City, NY: Doubleday.

Rothermel, D. (1996). *Starting points: How to set up and run a writing workshop—and much more.* Columbus, OH: National Middle School Association.

Scully, J. (1965). *Modern poetics.* New York: McGraw Hill.

Shaughnessy, M. P. (1977). *Errors and expectations: A guide for the teacher of basic writing.* New York: Oxford University Press.

Sloan, G. (2003). *Give them poetry! A guide to sharing poetry with children K–8.* New York: Teachers College Press.

Stauffer, D. A. (1946). *The nature of poetry.* New York: W. W. Norton.

Tucker, S. (1992). *Writing poetry.* Parsippany, NJ: Good Year Books.

Walker, A. (1973). *Revolutionary petunias & other poems.* New York: Harcourt Brace Jovanovich.

Wexler, B. (2003, May 5). Poetry is dead. Does anybody really care? *Newsweek,* (My Turn), p. 18.

Wolf, A. (1990). *Something is going to happen: Poetry performance for the classroom.* Canada: Poetry Alive! Publications.

# Index

Adoff, Arnold, 19, 108
adolescents. *See* young adolescents
"After English Class" (Little), 132
Ahia, Chad, 235
Alfred, Lord Tennyson, 209
"Alone" (Poe), 38–40
"anyone lived in a pretty how town"
    (cummings), 141
assertions: composing and publishing
    poetry, 72–73; discussing and
    interpreting poetry, 131;
    memorizing and reciting poetry,
    40–41; teaching poetry, 188–89
"at risk" students, 246–48
Author's Week, 19
Avi, 19, 222

Bennett, Henry Holcomb, 16
*A Boy's Will* (Frost), 205
Braley, Berton, 43, 192
Brooks, Gwendolyn, 43
"Buffalo Bill's" (cummings), 203
Burkhardt, Ross: composing process,
    25–26; error in judgment, 123–25;
    poetry training, early development,
    ix–x, 187–88
Burkhardt, Ross, poems by: "An
    Academic Alphabet," 225–26;

"The Atmosphere in the Room,"
    31–32; "C Fever," 51–52, 62, 194;
    "Echoality," 223–24; "Eighth
    Grade Song," 226–27; "The First
    Day," v–vi, 19–21, 65, 191–92;
    "The Gift of Writing," 95; "Kramer
    on the Rocks," 219; "The Last
    Day," 224–25; "Leadership and
    Loss," 216–17; "The New
    Reciters," 62; "Passing Days," 94;
    "Patient," 221; "A PEEC
    Experience," 84; "Resonance,"
    92–93; "Thoughts on Helen and
    Annie," 87–88
Burleigh, Robert, 237
Burns, Robert, 204

Carroll, Lewis, 204
"The Charge of the Light Brigade"
    (Tennyson), 209
Cleghorn, Sarah Norcliffe, 52, 207
Coleridge, Samuel Taylor, 4, 204
community of writers, 29, 264; safe
    environment for, 190
composing and publishing poetry:
    about *The Miracle Worker*
    (Gibson), 85–88; assertions about,
    72–73; computer use, 21, 112–13,

277

# About the Author

**Ross M. Burkhardt**, a 1962 graduate of Dartmouth College, earned a master of science in education from the University of Pennsylvania after serving as a Peace Corps Volunteer in Tunisia. He taught English and social studies in New York State from 1965 to 1997 and participated in a National Writing Project Summer Institute in 1980. A founder of the New York State Middle School Association and its second president, Ross is also a past president of National Middle School Association. He was a member of the Early Adolescent/Generalist Committee for the National Board for Professional Teaching Standards for seven years, and he was inducted into the National Teachers Hall of Fame in 1998. Burkhardt serves on the board of directors of New Mexico Middle Level Educators, Inc. A national consultant in writing and middle-level education, Burkhardt frequently presents workshops and keynotes at middle-level conferences and institutes. Burkhardt lives in Las Cruces, New Mexico, with his wife, Jeanne. He is the author of *Writing for Real: Strategies for Engaging Adolescent Writers* (Stenhouse, 2003).